COLLINS
COMPLETE BOOK OF
~SOFT~
*f*URNISHINGS

COLLINS
COMPLETE BOOK OF

....

~SOFT~
fURNISHINGS

....

WITH A TEXT BY HILARY MORE
AND HELEN BARNETT

....

CONSULTANT: JANE CHURCHILL

....

HarperCollins*Publishers*

First published in 1993 by
HarperCollins Publishers
Reprinted 1994 (twice), 1995

Created exclusively for HarperCollins by Amazon Publishing Ltd
Design by Axis Design
Editor: Jennifer Jones
Illustrator: Kate Simunek
Special photography: Paul Forrester
Text and Illustrations © HarperCollins 1993

For HarperCollins Publishers
Commissioning Editor: Polly Powell
Project Editor: Barbara Dixon

A catalogue record for this book is available from the British Library

ISBN 0 00 412800-1

Colour reproduction in Singapore, by Colourscan
Printed and bound in Italy

Hilary More
Hilary More is a well-known freelance journalist in the home-making/furnishings field. She is a regular contributor to *Living, Women's Weekly* and *Prima* and writes the Homecraft page for *Best* magazine. She is soft furnishings editor on the partwork *Show-Me-How*. Her books include *Soft Furnishings* with Sarah Campbell and *Chairs, Cushions and Coverings*.

Helen Barnett
Helen Barnett worked at *Homes and Gardens* before joining *Ideal Home*, where she became assistant editor. She is now a freelance journalist working for a number of home interest magazines. Her books include *The Art of Stencilling* and *Stencilling* with Susy Smith.

Note on Illustrations
For simplicity and clarity, the right side of the fabric is always shown as a darker blue and the wrong side of the fabric as a lighter blue on the illustrations. If an item is lined, the right side of the lining fabric is also shown as a darker blue and the wrong side as a lighter blue.

Contents

Introduction 7

Fabric File 9

Period Style 41

Contemporary Style 49

Curtains 73

Blinds 117

Covers and Cushions 137

Beds 169

Tables 189

Sewing Guide 200

Index 206

Acknowledgements 208

introduction

Fabrics and interior design are in my blood. My great aunt Nancy Lancaster was the inspiration behind the internationally recognized fabric house Colefax & Fowler, and worked with John Fowler. It is thanks to her and to my grandmother and aunt on my mother's side that I absorbed most of what I know about interior design. They decorated their houses and flats with flair and style, and always with a wonderful, homely feeling. These were early and valuable lessons for me in how to put things together, which didn't necessarily mean using expensive materials or furniture.

Simplicity is definitely the key to successful decorating. If you are decorating on a budget, stick to simple but effective ideas. Instead of curtains use a Roman blind, which takes up much less fabric, and bind the edges with a braid or binding. An old sofa can be transformed with a new loose cover in an upholstery-weight canvas or ticking. Add inexpensive scatter cushions to co-ordinate with the rest of the room and the finished result will look stylish.

Why this book?
As an interior designer, I like to share my knowledge, experience and ideas. I hope that what this book offers, in terms of both inspiration and practical information, will give people the confidence and skills to create the looks they want. But certainly as far as ideas are concerned please venture beyond these pages! Always be on the look-out for unusual or ingenious ways of doing things and if you see something you like, think about how you can adapt it for your own house – perhaps using a different kind of material or adding another trim.

We have placed a special emphasis on fabrics throughout the book because they can do so much to transform a scheme. The important thing to remember here is that it is not so much the quality of a fabric that is important as how it is used. Going back to the example of the Roman blind, left plain it will probably disappear into the background, and this may be the effect you want. On the other hand, add a simple trim – say a stripe cut on the cross or a small check – and it will stand out more. It is the way that things are finished off that make all the difference.

Finally, I would like to make a special plea to be aware of proportion, particularly when making curtains or valances. Proportion costs nothing and yet it always makes or breaks the finished look.

What do I mean by proportion? It's really a question of knowing when something 'looks' right – not always the easiest thing to convey, I agree. One of my basic rules is always to go for full-length curtains. And if there isn't room for full-length curtains, go for a blind instead. You can learn about proportion by looking closely at those interior schemes you find most appealing. Make a note of things like the length of the curtains in relation to the height of the window. Or if it's a bedcover, look at how it balances with the valance. Train your eye for such things and you'll be amazed at the difference such apparently tiny details can make to the look of a room.

Jane Churchill

Fabric file

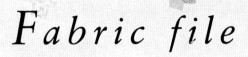

Fabrics are available in more colours, patterns and textures than ever before, providing tremendous scope for creativity when it comes to making things for the home. Although choosing fabric is often instinctive and largely influenced by colour and pattern, it is important to consider its suitability for a particular piece of furnishing. A lightweight sheer material may well be an ideal choice for a bedroom curtain, but it would be totally unsuitable for upholstering a chair. For curtains, look at the way a fabric handles, drapes and folds before making any firm decisions – does it crease and crumple when ruched up, for example, or does it hang in soft billowing folds? And if you want a fabric suitable for upholstery, check whether the weave and texture is strong enough for everyday seating. Over the next pages we explain the characteristics of some of the most popular furnishing fabrics available and offer suggestions as to how they can be used in the home.

Satin weave *Brocatelle* *Jacquard*

𝒲*eaves and textures*

···

Woven textiles are divided up into different weaves. The standard weaves are plain, basket, twill, rib, satin and gauze weaves. A pile weave uses an extra warp thread which is drawn up into loops, while a Jacquard fabric is woven on a special loom which manipulates the threads according to a complex pattern.

SATIN WEAVE
Smooth silk fabric woven with long warp floats. A hard-wearing material for curtains and upholstery.

HESSIAN
Rough, plain-weave fabric made from a mixture of hemp and jute. It is hard-wearing but frays easily and may sag when draped.

Hessian *Twill weave* *Velour*

Damask

Dobby weave

Toile de Jouy

BROCATELLE
Heavy, cross-ribbed Jacquard-woven fabric with raised design. Can be used for upholstery or decorative coverings.

TWILL WEAVE
Firm-weave fabric characterized by a diagonal rib running upwards from left to right. Can be applied to a variety of tough fabrics. Adds slightly to the thickness.

JACQUARD
Fabric woven on a complex Jacquard loom to create elaborate patterns on one side of the fabric.

VELOUR
Soft, closely woven fabric with a thick, short pile. Can be made of cotton, cotton/linen mix, wool or synthetic fibres.

DAMASK
Reversible, soft, glossy fabric woven on a Jacquard loom into self patterns. Originally of silk but now made in several fibres and blends such as linen, which is often used for tablecloths.

CHENILLE
A heavily textured fabric pattern created with design areas of tufted velvety pile. Can be made from cotton or man-made fibres.

DOBBY WEAVE
Fabric woven on a specialist loom which weaves small geometric patterns.

HEAVY-DUTY COTTON WEAVE
Heavy reversible blanket cloth woven on a Jacquard loom. Good for making loose covers to disguise flaws in old furniture.

TOILE DE JOUY
Glazed cotton printed with traditional scenic or floral designs. The resin coating is permanent and repels dirt and dust.

FINE RIB
A straight, raised cord runs diagonally in a regular pattern across the fabric. Useful for introducing textural interest in plain schemes.

Chenille

Heavy-duty cotton weave

Fine rib

Miniprint

Gingham

Colours and patterns

·······································

Animal print

Fabrics come in every conceivable colour and pattern, from the neutrals to vibrant hues, from understated stripes to zingy abstracts. Although various designs and colours go in and out of fashion, the classics such as floral chintzes, paisleys, checks and stripes never seem to date.

MINIPRINT
Any small all-over motif, geometric or floral. A design closely associated with the country cottage look, first made fashionable in the 1970s. Suitable for small rooms as wallcoverings and curtains.

ANIMAL PRINT
Any all-over animal print design. Best used in small quantities as an accent, such as on a stool or chair seat cover, used for covering scatter cushions.

TOILE DE JOUY
White or neutral-coloured glazed cotton printed with an elaborate scenic design in one colour. First made popular in France in the eighteenth century.

BAUHAUS
Bold, geometrically printed fabric, inspired by the 1920s German Bauhaus school of architects and artists. Takes a strong, modern theme.

Toile de Jouy

Bauhaus

Regency stripe

Paisley

Chintz

Check

GINGHAM
White and coloured yarns woven into checks, usually in lightweight cotton. A perennial favourite of rural areas, gingham epitomizes the homely country look. Use it for curtains, tablecloths and bed linen.

REGENCY STRIPE
Regular striped fabric with moiré markings. A popular design of eighteenth-century Europe, and perfectly at home in spacious, elegant interiors with a period air.

PAISLEY
Cloth printed with an intricate all-over design, and associated with Paisley in Scotland. Of Indian origin, a popular textile design in Europe since the seventeenth century.

GEOMETRIC
Reversible fabric woven into geometric design. A close relation to ethnic weaves, both are classics of the twentieth century. Ideal for all modern interiors.

CHINTZ
Large floral patterns printed on glazed cotton. Another design that has remained popular since the eighteenth century. Suitable for curtains and cushion covers.

TARTAN
Woven worsted plaid giving a chequered appearance. The design is associated with the clans of Scotland. A wide range of modern interpretations is available for soft furnishings.

Abstract

CHECK
Small pattern of woven squares. A basic design that is very adaptable and versatile in many different schemes.

ABSTRACT
Any non-representational design, which includes geometrics. Closely associated with abstract painting, abstract fabric designs range from bold and colourful to restrained and subtle. Ideal for modern interiors.

Geometric

Tartan

Ticking

Double cotton piqué

ℕatural fibres

. . . .

Natural vegetable fibres include cotton and linen. They are strong,
hard-wearing and, particularly in the case of cotton, versatile. To make
it drape better, linen is usually mixed with other yarns such as cotton or
synthetic fibres or a mixture of both. Cotton is also combined with
synthetic fibres to bring easy-care properties to the fabric, particularly
for items such as sheeting.

Calico

Canvas

Hopsack

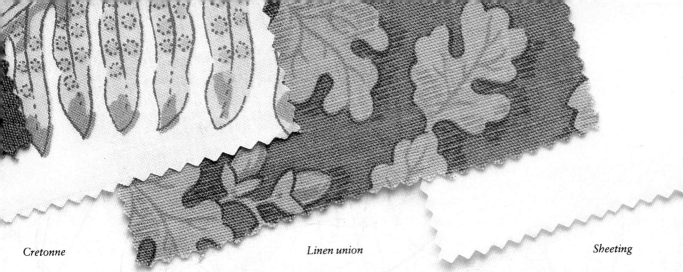

Cretonne

Linen union

Sheeting

TICKING
Strong twill-weave cotton traditionally in two-colour combination. Suitable for curtains, curtain lining, and as contrast fabric for decorative binding.

CALICO
Plain-weave cotton that can be bleached or unbleached. Useful as inexpensive curtaining and cushions. Dress up with trimmings such as striped fabric binding cut on the cross.

DOUBLE COTTON PIQUÉ
Fabric woven on a dobby loom creating small geometric patterns. Quilting effect makes it ideal for bedspreads and headboards. Use as a tablecloth, preferably with a plain cloth underneath.

CANVAS
Strong, heavyweight cotton fabric with a soft or sized finish. Available undyed or in plain colours, or with printed designs, including smart stripes. Hard-wearing and durable, used for upholstery and for wallcoverings. Suitable for roller blinds.

CRETONNE
Unglazed medium-weight cotton fabric. Usually printed with naturalistic designs, such as flowers and foliage. A useful alternative to chintz fabrics, where a matt surface is desired. Suitable for curtains, scatter cushions and bedcovers.

HOPSACK
Rough, plain double-woven cotton. A loose weave suitable for upholstery.

LINEN UNION
Linen mixed with other fibres such as cotton and man-made fibres. A softer texture than pure linen, it is easier to manipulate and drape for curtaining. Also suitable for cushions and upholstery.

HEAVY-DUTY COTTON
Unevenly woven cotton with hand-printed design. Used for upholstery and curtaining. Mixes well with other natural fabrics such as linen, calico, hopsack and canvas.

SHEETING
Printed cotton/polyester mix fabric. Woven in extra wide widths to match bed sizes. Mainly available plain, self patterned or with a small design.

HESSIAN
Loosely woven plain hemp and jute mix fabric. Used for wallcoverings and for curtains, if pre-shrunk.

Heavy-duty cotton

Hessian

Satin cotton

Denim

Tapestry

Cottons

· ·

Cotton is the traditional soft furnishing fabric. It is cheap and plentiful, and it can be woven and treated to achieve a wide range of textures and finishes. These range from pile fabrics such as velvet to finely woven glazed chintzes.

SATIN COTTON
Cotton with a slight sheen on the right side. Used for lining curtains. Printed satin cotton makes inexpensive curtains.

VELVET
Rich-looking cotton fabric with an even pile. Cotton velvet is the cheapest of the velvets available and comes in a good range of colours. Suitable for upholstery and curtains.

DRILL
Strong, twill-weave cotton. Plain and printed versions are produced. Used for upholstery and curtains.

SEERSUCKER
Crinkly effect is made by pulling warp threads tighter during weaving. Makes economical curtains and tablecloths.

Velvet

Drill

Seersucker

Broderie Anglaise

Chintz

Damask

TAPESTRY
Decorative woven pattern formed by the coloured weft threads. An upholstery fabric particularly associated with traditional interiors. Useful for covering small items of furniture. Makes sumptuous covers for cushions.

CHINTZ
Glazed cotton with print design. The glaze coating repels dirt and dust, although it is not a permanent finish and will wear off with washing. Chintz is usually associated with finely executed floral designs in clear, bright colours. A classic curtain fabric.

DAMASK
Jacquard-weave cotton in which the pattern is in reverse on the wrong side. A traditional fabric for covers and curtains.

DENIM
Hard-wearing twill-weave cotton with white and blue yarns. Can be used for upholstery and cushions.

BRODERIE ANGLAISE
Crisp white cotton fabric with embroidered eyelet pattern in a wide range of designs. Use like sheers or for curtains in bathrooms and pretty, feminine bedrooms.

LAWN
Very fine almost translucent plain-weave cotton fabric. Use like muslin for sheers and unlined drapes on a four-poster bed or coronet arrangement.

CORDUROY
Plain-weave fabric with cut pile in regular ribs. Good for upholstery and cushions. Works well with linen or chintz in traditional schemes.

PLAIN COTTON
A smooth-weave cotton which is unglazed. Comes in a wide range of plain colours and printed designs. Used for curtains, blinds, cushions, table linen and bedcovers.

Plain cotton

Lawn

Corduroy

Dobby weave   *Jacquard weave*   *Dobby weave*

f a b r i c s :   c o v e r s   a n d   c u s h i o n s

∙∙

Only fabrics with a strong, firm weave are suitable for upholstery. Covers come in for a great deal of wear and tear and only fabrics with a tightly woven yarn will be durable enough. Suitable weaves include Jacquard and dobby weaves. Always check whether or not the fabric is fire retardant. If it has not been treated, you will need to use a flame-resistant interlining. Cushion covers, on the other hand, can be made from almost any fabric, provided it has some body. Traditional fabrics include chintz and plain and printed cottons.

DOBBY WEAVE
Fabric woven on a special dobby loom. Designs are often small geometrics or dots, which work well in most schemes. A hard-wearing fabric, it is particularly suitable for upholstery.

JACQUARD WEAVE
Fabric with raised pattern woven on a Jacquard loom. The designs can be self-coloured or contain two or more colours. Used for upholstery and scatter cushions.

Indian cotton   *Twill weave*   *Jacquard tapestry*

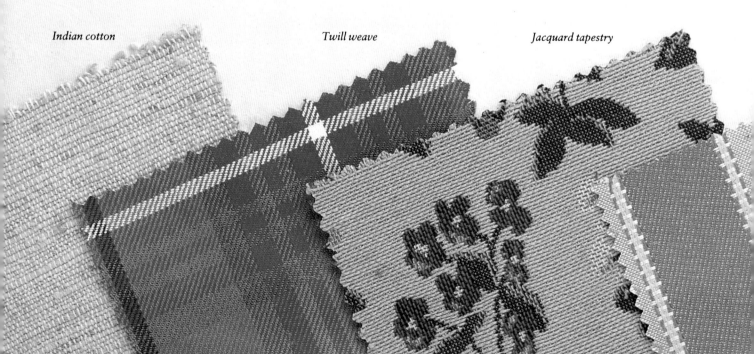

Chintz

Moiré

Jacquard weave

TWILL WEAVE
Strong durable fabric with woven striped design. Use finer yarn twills for scatter cushions; heavier weights are suitable for upholstery.

INDIAN COTTON
Woven cotton with uneven threads that creates a slub appearance. An inexpensive fabric for scatter cushions.

JACQUARD TAPESTRY
Woven on a Jacquard loom, the design resembles hand-stitched embroidery. The fine detail and rich colours suit small upholstery jobs such as chair seat cushions, stool covers and scatter cushions.

CHINTZ
Brightly coloured glazed cotton with floral design. Suitable for scatter cushions. Trim with chintz piping or rope.

STRIPE
A classic design for upholstery and cushions. A wide stripe in two or more colours works well on upholstery.

MOIRÉ
Fabric treated with a watermarked finish. This distinctive fabric works well for scatter cushions.

PRINTED COTTON
Plain woven cotton with printed design. Used for cushions and upholstery.

PLAIN WEAVE
Plain weave fabric with graded warp colours woven with a single weft colour. This weave introduces subtle variations of colour while still remaining basically 'plain'. Suitable for upholstery, particularly as a foil to patterned furnishings elsewhere in the room.

Stripe

Printed cotton

Plain weave

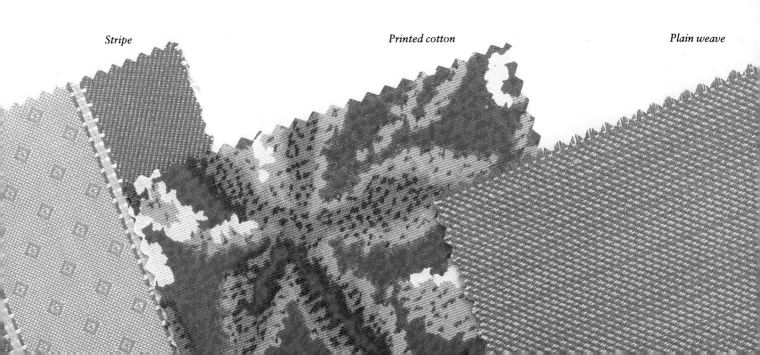

Tartan

Felt

Rep

*W*ools

Worsted

· ·

Wool is a strong, durable and soft fabric. It provides good insulation,
and is naturally flame-resistant. Wool is often mixed with other natural
fibres such as cotton, silk or linen to improve its strength and to prevent
it from shrinking.

REP
Woven fabric with
distinctive rib effect.
Suitable for curtains and
upholstery. Finish with
heavyweight trimmings
such as a wool bullion
fringe.

DAMASK
Suitable for upholstery.
Very adaptable and works
well with other patterns.

MOHAIR
Soft, glossy, plain-weave
fabrics with goat's-hair
nap. Used for heavyweight
curtains and upholstery.

WORSTED
Smooth, strong wool with
woven plaid design. A
hard-wearing fabric
suitable for upholstery.

Damask

Mohair

Jacquard tapestry

Tweed

FELT
Bonded, non-woven fabric that can be cut in any direction without fraying. Useful as a decorative edging for curtains, such as scalloped frills.

TARTAN
Distinctive woven checked fabric, originating from Scotland. Works well in traditional interiors as wallcoverings, and for curtains and upholstery. Gives a strong, masculine look to studies, dining rooms and bedrooms.

JACQUARD TAPESTRY
Woven on a Jacquard loom, this fabric imitates hand-woven tapestry. Used for upholstery.

FLANNEL
Soft, plain-weave wool with flat surface. Suitable for wallcoverings and curtains.

TWEED
Rough wool fabric woven in two or more colours to create a mottled effect. Used for upholstery and tailored curtains. Could also work as wallcoverings.

SATIN WOOL
Satin-weave wool suitable for upholstery. Can also be used for curtains, as it drapes well, and for pelmets and valances.

PLAIN-WEAVE UNION
A plain-weave wool mixed with other fibres such as cotton and man-made fibres. A hard-wearing fabric, suitable for upholstery.

Flannel

Plain-weave union

Satin wool

Damask

Silk rep

Organza

Silks

Silk plaid

• •

Silk is a strong natural fibre spun in long continuous threads from the cocoons of silkworms. It is an expensive and luxurious fabric which drapes well and is hard-wearing.

ORGANZA
Stiff transparent silk, plain or printed. A luxurious fabric for bedrooms and bathrooms. Used like net for drapes round a four-poster bed, and as a skirt for a dressing-table.

IKAT
A traditional woven design from Indonesia. Comes in a wide range of patterns and colours. Suitable for curtains and covers for cushions.

SILK PLAID
Reversible fabric woven in a pattern of coloured stripes. Used for tailored curtains and blinds.

BROCADE
Very distinctive fabric with raised pattern against a woven background. Used for upholstery and curtains.

Ikat

Brocade

Honan

DAMASK
A traditional woven design
which is particularly
suitable for period-style
interiors. Go for curtains
with very tailored
headings, such as goblet
pleats, and add trimmings.

DUPION
Slub silk with uneven,
irregular weave. Has more
texture and body than
some other silks, giving it a
natural, informal quality.
Used for tailored curtains
and pelmets, and for swags
and tails.

Dupion

SILK REP
Silk with well-defined weft
woven in crosswise rib
effect. Silk rep drapes well
and is suitable for tailored
curtains and pelmets, and
for swags and tails.

FAILLE
One of the grosgrain
family of cross-rib fabrics.
Faille is a soft and glossy
silk and is used for
upholstery and curtains.

PEKING
Fine, plain-woven silk with
a slight sheen. Comes in an
excellent range of colours.
It is particularly effective as
a lining for elaborate swags
and tails.

Taffeta

HONAN
Chinese wild silk. A fine
silk, good for bedroom
curtains, bed drapes, and
dressing tables.

TAFFETA
Plain woven silk with a
smooth, lustrous finish.
Best used for generously
draped curtains.

Faille

Peking

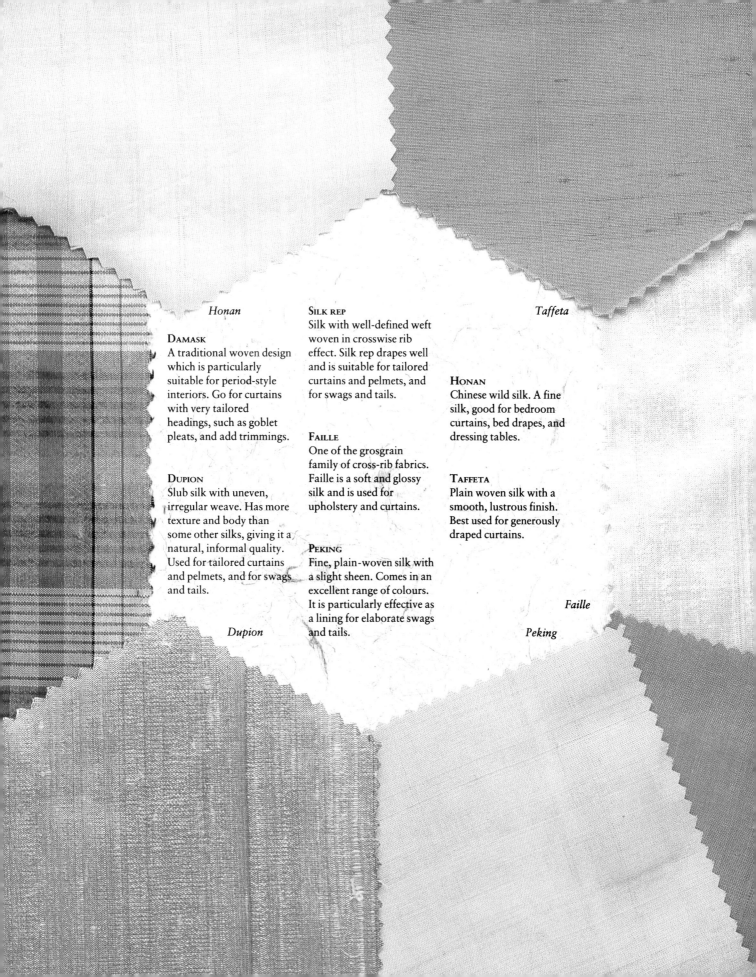

Man-mades

....

Soft furnishing fabrics made from man-made fibres are inexpensive and durable. They are generally easy to care for, although you should always check the manufacturer's instructions before cleaning.

VISCOSE DAMASK
Viscose woven on a Jacquard loom to produce a raised pattern against a woven background. Man-made fibres are now used for traditional weaves and finishes.

VISCOSE RAYON
Fabric made from treated wood pulp and cotton linters. Often combined with other man-made fibres to make it more hard-wearing. This viscose moiré is suitable for curtains and cushions.

PVC-COATED FABRIC
Fabric coated with polyvinyl chloride to provide a tough, waterproof surface. Ideal for tablecloths.

POLYESTER SHOWER CURTAINING
A washable, drip-dry fabric, ideal for shower curtains.

POLYESTER
Fabric made from synthetic polymer fibres. Polyester is strong, easy to care for and wrinkle-free. It is not affected by sunlight, making it suitable for curtains.

VISCOSE/ACETATE
Acetate fibres, made from treated cotton linters, mixed with viscose. This soft, silky fabric drapes well and is suitable for making curtains.

Viscose damask

Viscose rayon

PVC-coated fabric

Polyester shower curtaining

Polyester

Viscose/acetate

trimmings and accessories

....

Furnishing trimmings and accessories add the finishing details to curtains, blinds and covers. They can be made in cotton, linen, wool and silk and vary in price accordingly.

CURTAIN TIEBACK
Ready-made curtain tiebacks come in a range of designs and sizes.

CHAIR TIEBACK
Roped tieback with tasselled ends. Used for holding cushions in place on chair seats.

BRAID
Use braid to trim round upholstery, cushions and blinds.

PIPING CORD
Available ready-made in a variety of finishes. Used for trimming upholstery and cushions.

BULLION FRINGE
A heavyweight fringe for trimming upholstery and curtains.

CORD
Ready-made silky cord for trimming upholstery and curtains.

RUCHE
A fringed skirt used for trimming scatter cushions and curtains.

TASSELLED FRINGE
Suitable for trimming curtains and upholstery.

Voile

Geometric net

Sheers

· ·

Sheers are transparent open-weave fabrics primarily used as window screens to provide privacy. They can also be used as curtains and bed drapes. Laces are used in the same way and as decorative cloths over plain tablecloths. Sheers will last well provided they are handled with care and washed gently.

Cotton lace

Muslin

COTTON LACE
Openwork cotton with delicate pattern. Used as a screen at windows, for delicate curtains and as a tablecloth.

MUSLIN
Fine plain-weave cotton, sometimes mixed with synthetic yarns. Used as a sheer at windows, or for bed drapes around a four-poster bed.

EMBROIDERED SHEER
Slub sheer with embroidered and cut-out detailing. Used as an alternative to the polyester linen sheer. Could be used as curtains in a bedroom or bathroom.

VOILE
Translucent lightweight fabric made from a variety of natural and man-made yarns. Used as sheers.

Embroidered sheer

Cotton/polyester lace

Flocked voile

Polyester linen sheer

Polyester lace

Net

GEOMETRIC NET
Net made from Indian cotton woven into a geometric design. Useful for modern, informal settings.

POLYESTER LINEN SHEER
Slub open-mesh fabric with uneven, irregular weave. Used as a window screen.

POLYESTER LACE
Man-made openwork fabric with lacy design. Polyester is not affected by sunlight, and it is easy to wash and dry. Used as sheers, pretty curtains, or as a decorative cloth over a plain tablecloth.

NET
An open-mesh fabric of cotton or synthetic fibres. Ideal as a window screen.

COTTON-POLYESTER LACE
Lace produced from a mixture of natural and man-made yarns. The polyester strengthens the cotton fibres, making it a hard-wearing lace.

MADRAS LACE
Classic cotton lace with intricate naturalistic motifs. Used as window sheers or for tablecloths over a plain cloth.

BRODERIE ANGLAISE
Cotton embroidery edge trimming with cut-out detail. Suitable for trimming bed linen, such as pillowcases and duvet covers, and as pretty tiebacks for sheers.

COTTON/POLYESTER VOILE
Alternative to voile made with natural fibres. The addition of man-made yarns makes it stronger and more resistant to sunlight.

FLOCKED VOILE
Lightweight sheer with raised self pattern. A decorative alternative to plain voile which introduces subtle texture.

Broderie Anglaise

Madras lace

Cotton-polyester voile

Waxed cambric

Buckram

Cotton sateen

WAXED CAMBRIC
Plain-woven fabric treated with a glaze. Used like calico for cushions.

linings and interlinings

···

All curtains are improved by the addition of a lining or interlining or both. They give body and added strength to the drape of the curtain and also improve the life of the fabric. Some linings are specially designed to contain feathers for items such as cushion pads and Continental quilts.

CALICO
Plain-weave cotton fabric, bleached or unbleached, and available in different weights. Mainly used as a casing for cushion pads, first-class calico can be made into inexpensive curtains and stencilled.

Calico

Polyester wadding

Cotton interlining

4

Sanforized buckram

Blackout

Downproof herringbone

COTTON SATEEN
Soft cotton fabric with a slight sheen. Comes in a wide range of colours and is used for lining curtains.

COTTON INTERLINING
Natural fibre interlining. Used like domette for interlining curtains.

BUCKRAM
Firm stiffening fabric made from cotton or jute. Heavyweight buckram is used to stiffen curtains, tiebacks and pelmets.

POLYESTER WADDING
Lightweight bonded fabric available in several weights. Used for quilting, plaited tiebacks and goblet pleats on curtains.

SANFORIZED BUCKRAM
Buckram treated with an anti-shrink finish. Used for making hand-made headings on curtains.

MAN-MADE INTERLINING
White synthetic interlining with soft, brushed surface. A cheaper alternative to domette.

BLACKOUT
Matt fabric which totally excludes the light. Ideal for lining bedroom curtains and blinds.

BUMP
A thick loosely woven cotton interlining. Suitable for heavy drapes.

DOWNPROOF HERRINGBONE
Plain-woven cotton with special downproof finish for cushion pads filled with feathers.

DOMETTE
Brushed cotton interlining for curtains and pelmets. A lighter weight alternative to bump, it gives a slightly padded effect and is suitable for interlining swags and tails.

Man-made interlining

Bump

Domette

Chintz   *Damask*   *Linen union*

ƒabrics: curtains and blinds

....

Almost any fabric can be used for curtains as long as it drapes well.
Curtains will always fall better and last longer if they are lined. There is
also a wide range of fabrics available which are suitable for making into
blinds, although very thick fabrics should be avoided.

CHINTZ
Fine cotton printed with
floral design and treated
with a semi-permanent
glaze. Suitable for curtains
and blinds.

TARTAN SILK
Finely woven tartan
pattern in lustrous silk. Use
in large amounts for
curtains to create a
dramatic effect.

Tartan silk   *Floral miniprint*   *Stripe*

Provençal print *Linen union* *Drill*

DAMASK
A classic Jacquard-woven fabric. Shiny and matt yarns are mixed together to produce the traditional damask design of foliage and flowers. Ideal for curtains in traditional interiors.

FLORAL MINIPRINT
Fine cotton printed in an all-over pattern of small flowers. Suitable for curtains and blinds in kitchens, bedrooms and bathrooms, particularly in small rooms.

LINEN UNION
Linen mixed with other yarns, such as cotton. The ratio of linen to cotton can be varied to achieve a number of interesting textures. Suitable for curtains.

STRIPE
A striped design works well for curtains or for Roman or roller blinds.

PROVENÇAL PRINT
Fine cotton printed with an all-over Provençal design. Comes in bright, clear colours, mainly with naturalistic motifs or a paisley pattern. Used for lightweight curtains in bathrooms, kitchens, bedrooms and for draping around beds.

COTTON SATEEN
Satin-weave cotton fabric with a polished finish. Used for lining curtains and blinds, and for making decorative contrasting binding and piping.

DRILL
A strong, hard-wearing fabric suitable for curtains and blinds. Looks good with contrasting binding.

INDIAN COTTON
Coarsely woven textured cotton made of uneven yarns. Suitable for making inexpensive curtains, and works well in informal settings.

SATIN COTTON
Satin-woven cotton with a soft texture. Comes in a good range of plain colours for lining and protecting curtains. Can also be made into inexpensive curtains.

Cotton sateen *Indian cotton* *Satin cotton*

Care and cleaning

Take care of your soft furnishings and they will keep looking good for years to come. Wash or dry clean fabrics as often as they need it, and don't forget always to follow the manufacturer's cleaning instructions. Treat stains as soon as they occur, using the appropriate method for the fabric. And don't forget the proverb 'A stitch in time saves nine'. If you discover a small hole or tear anywhere, mend it as soon as possible or later on you may find you have a major repair on your hands.

UPHOLSTERY

Shake out feather cushions every day and during the summer months give them an airing outside. Vacuum upholstery regularly to remove day-to-day dust and fluff. Direct sunlight will weaken fabrics and cause colours to fade, so try to position sofas and chairs away from the windows or filter sunlight with blinds and curtains. Protect any new upholstery by coating the fabric with a brand-name protective spray.

Fitted covers can be cleaned *in situ* with a brand-name upholstery shampoo. Always test the solution first on an inconspicuous piece of fabric. If you are unsure about cleaning, call in a firm of specialists.

Loose covers can generally be washed, but test the fabric first for colour fastness. Multi-coloured fabrics are especially vulnerable to colours merging. If you are unsure, have the covers dry cleaned. Cotton and linen covers will always shrink with washing. If the covers already fit the furniture tightly, they should be dry cleaned. Make sure that any piping cord was pre-shrunk before it was inserted into the covers, otherwise it will pucker the seams as it shrinks.

Covers can be stretched and pulled back into shape as they dry. In some cases the covers can be replaced on the sofa slightly damp and left to dry in place to give a smooth finish.

CURTAINS

All fabrics are sold with instructions on how to care for them, usually in the form of symbols from the International Care Labelling Code. You should always check this information carefully before cleaning a fabric.

To wash a pair of heading-tape curtains, remove the curtain hooks, untie the heading cords and gently ease out the gathers. Give the curtains a good shake, preferably out of doors, then wash them at the appropriate machine setting for the fabric. Sheer curtains should be washed frequently to keep them fresh and clean. If necessary, use a brand-name cleaning product that will whiten dull nets.

REPAIRS

Check over soft furnishings regularly and mend any small holes or tears as they occur before they turn into a major problem. Simple tears in loose covers can be repaired from the wrong side with iron-on patching tape. On fitted covers, slipstitch the edges together using a strong machine thread and an upholsterer's needle.

PATCHING A SMALL HOLE

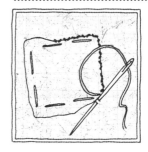 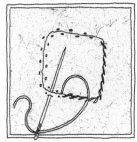

Slipstitch patch in place.   *Oversew edges on reverse.*

To patch a small hole you will need a piece of the same fabric slightly larger than the hole. Make sure that the new piece exactly matches the pattern or pile on the cover. If you do not have any spare fabric, it should be possible to cut away a small piece from the main fabric, such as from the hem, where it will not show.

Carefully trim away any frayed edges from around the hole. Place the patch right side up over the hole and tack in place. Thread the needle with matching thread and slipstitch the patch in position, pushing under the raw edge of the patch with the point of the needle as you sew. On the wrong side of the fabric, oversew the raw fabric edges to finish.

DARNING

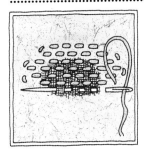 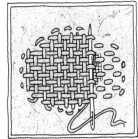

Work across worn area. *Weave thread under and over.*

Darning across a worn piece of fabric can help to give it added strength. Use a darning needle and matching thread. Begin and end about 1 cm (³⁄₈ in) around the edges of the worn area. Work rows of tiny running stitches across the worn area. When you have covered the whole area, work across it again, this time stitching in the opposite direction and weaving the needle under and over the first set of threads.

STAIN REMOVAL

The secret of success when dealing with stains lies in the speed with which you get to grips with the problem – the faster you treat a stain, the easier it will be to remove completely. One basic rule is to absorb or scrape off as much as possible before applying any form of treatment – for example, soak up liquids first by dabbing *lightly* with absorbent kitchen paper and scrape off solid matter with the back of a knife. For any stain that requires secondary treatment, decide whether to tackle it yourself or to leave it to a professional cleaner. Though more expensive, dry cleaning is the best course of action if you have a difficult stain on an expensive fabric or piece of soft furnishing.

SAFETY CHECKLIST

If you decide to go it alone, work through the following checklist first.

- Is the fabric washable or not? Most non-washable items require professional dry cleaning, although grease marks may be removed with a brand-name solvent.

- Can the fabric take the planned treatment? You cannot use hydrogen peroxide on nylon and flame-proof fabrics, for example. Vinegar, methylated spirits and commercial solvents will harm acetate fabrics.

- Is the fabric colourfast? Try out the required stain removal on a small concealed area, such as the underside of a hem. Sandwich the treated patch between two pieces of clean white cloth and press gently with a warm iron. If the colour comes out, leave further treatment to a professional dry cleaner.

- Have you read the instructions? Toxic stain removal agents must be handled carefully, and you must follow the manufacturer's instructions regarding their safe use. Wear rubber gloves, and work in a well-ventilated area. Keep away from naked flames. Never decant the contents into other containers. Store containers out of the reach of children and away from food.

FIRST AID KIT FOR STAINS

Have on hand in your store cupboard at least some of the following to ensure that you do not waste time in dealing with accidental spills.

Ammonia
Use for removing acid marks. Dilute 1 part household ammonia to 3 parts water and apply to colourfast fabrics only. Handle with caution. Do not use on wool.

Biological (or enzyme) detergent
This is a pre-wash soak to digest protein-based stains. Follow the manufacturer's instructions regarding the recommended length of time for soaking and suitable fabrics for treatment.

Bleach
Household bleach is useful for stains on white cotton and linen. Never use it neat. Dilute 5 ml (1 teaspoon) of bleach in 1 litre (2 pints) of water to dab on small stains. For a larger area, soak in a solution of 10 ml (2 teaspoons) of bleach in 10 litres (2½ gallons) of water. Rinse the fabric thoroughly before washing. Do not use on treated or delicate fabrics.

Borax
Household borax can be used – with care – for acid stains on most washable fabrics. Sponge or soak the fabric for no more than 15 minutes in a solution of 15 ml (1 tablespoon) borax dissolved in 500 ml (1 pint) of warm water, then rinse and wash as usual.

Glycerine
Glycerine softens stains, making them easier to remove. Dilute in equal parts with warm water. Work the solution into the fabric, leave for at least an hour and wipe off with a sponge and warm water.

Hydrogen peroxide
Hydrogen peroxide is a mild bleach. It is suitable for use on delicate fabrics such as silk and wool. Do not use on nylon or treated fabrics. Dilute 20-volume strength solution in the ratio 1 part peroxide to 6 parts of cold water. Soak delicate fabrics for up to 30 minutes. Whites can be safely left overnight.

Methylated spirits
Dab on methylated spirits neat to remove residual colour from a stain using a clean white cloth. Do not use on acetates, triacetates and non-fast colours. Observe safety precautions.

Proprietary grease solvents/dry cleaners
Brand-name solvents and stain removers in liquid, dab-on, paste or spray versions are available for selective household stains and are particularly effective on grease. Can be used on most surfaces, including upholstery. Always follow the manufacturer's instructions.

TREATING SPECIFIC STAINS

Before using any of the following methods, refer to the general information in the First Aid Kit For Stains in the previous column.

Blood
Washable items Rinse fresh stains immediately under the cold tap, then soak in strongly salted water, changing the solution frequently until the mark disappears. If it remains, soak overnight in biological detergent or try a solution of 10 ml (2 teaspoons) household ammonia to 500 ml (1 pint) of water and a few drops of hydrogen peroxide. Only machine wash once the stain has gone, as the heat will seal the mark permanently.
Non-washable items Sponge the stain using cold water with a few drops of ammonia added to it. Rinse with cold water and blot dry. If necessary, finish off with an upholstery spot-removal kit or take to a dry cleaner.

Candlewax
Washable items Freeze the wax by placing the item in the freezer or surrounding it with ice cubes. This will make the wax easier to break off. Sandwich the fabric between pieces of blotting or brown paper and press with a warm iron to melt the remaining wax. Keep moving to a clean area of paper and continue until no more wax appears. If a greasy mark remains, dab with dry cleaning fluid or methylated spirits to remove residual colour.
Non-washable items Melt the wax by holding a warm iron over the blotting paper. Do not press down on pile fabrics and, if possible, hold the iron against the wrong side with blotting paper at the front. Clean any traces of coloured wax with methylated spirits.

Chewing gum
Washable items If possible, put the article in the freezer, or dab it with ice cubes. The hardened gum will break off more easily. Dissolve the remainder by soaking in white vinegar or rubbing with methylated spirit before washing.
Non-washable items Harden as above then treat residue with methylated or white spirit (except for acetates or rayons). A proprietary chewing gum remover could also be used.

Chocolate
Washable items Scrape off immediately and dab with glycerine solution if the chocolate has been allowed to harden. Sponge on the reverse side of the fabric with soapy water containing a few drops of ammonia. Rinse, then pre-soak and wash in a biological detergent.
Non-washable items Scrape off as much as possible, then use a stain remover or dry clean.

Coffee
Washable items Sponge, then soak in warm water and biological detergent. If the stain persists, treat delicate fabrics by dabbing with a solution of 15 ml (1 tablespoon) borax to 500 ml (1 pint) of warm water. For white or colourfast fabrics, use diluted hydrogen peroxide.

Residual stains can be removed with dry cleaning solvent.
Non-washable items Sponge with clear water, then with the same borax solution as above. Rinse well, taking care not to over-wet the fabric. On acrylic fabrics, blot thoroughly, then dab with a clean pad dipped in a warm solution of biological washing powder (5 ml/1 teaspoon of powder to 1 litre/2 pints of water). Wring out until it is almost dry and wipe lightly in the direction of the pile.

Curry

Washable items Spoon up surplus, then rinse the stained area under the cold tap. Rub in a solution of equal parts glycerine and warm water, and leave on for an hour. Rinse, then pre-soak and wash in biological detergent. Bleach white fabrics with diluted hydrogen peroxide (1 part peroxide to 6 parts water) if necessary.
Non-washable items Sponge with a solution of 15 ml (1 tablespoon) borax to 500 ml (1 pint) of warm water. Rinse and blot well.

Fruit and fruit juice

Washable items Rub the stain with salt, rinse immediately with boiling water poured on from a height, then wash at a high temperature using biological detergent. If the stain persists, soak whites in a diluted solution of 1 part hydrogen peroxide to 6 parts water to which a few drops of household ammonia have been added. For acetates, use a solution of 15 ml (1 tablespoon) of borax to 500 ml (1 pint) of water. Dried-on stains can be softened before treatment with a solution of equal parts glycerine and warm water.
Non-washable items Sponge with cold water, then rub in a little solution of 1 part glycerine to 1 part water and leave for an hour before applying a suitable stain remover. For upholstery, shampoo the whole area.

Gravy

Washable items Rinse out in cold water, then treat with dry cleaning fluid to remove grease before washing.
Non-washable items Scrape off surplus with a spatula and wipe over with a damp cloth, provided the water does not watermark. Treat with a stain remover.

Ink

Washable items For ballpoint pen, dab the stain liberally with methylated spirits, then soak in a biological detergent, rinse and wash.

For felt-tip pen, rinse off water-soluble stains with cold water before washing. Rub a more permanent mark with household soap or glycerine or use methylated spirits if the fabric can take it.

For fountain pen ink, isolate the stain and rinse under cold water, then treat from the back of the fabric with liquid detergent and rinse again. Sponge remaining marks with equal quantities of lemon juice, ammonia and water.
Non-washable items For ballpoint pen, apply methylated spirits with a cotton bud to small spots on fabrics other than acetates and triacetates. Alternatively, use an aerosol stain remover.

For felt-tip pen, sponge water-soluble stains lightly with cold water, and treat with a stain remover when dry.

For fountain pen ink, take care not to spread the stain. Sponge carefully with cold water, blot well, then apply a spot remover, repeating as necessary.

Paint

Washable items For emulsion and water-based paint, scrape off any excess and rinse away all traces with cold water before washing in warm soapy water. Dried stains may be softened with methylated spirits or paintbrush cleaner, but test first as this may discolour the fabric.

For gloss and oil-based paint, treat immediately by dabbing with white spirit or paintbrush cleaner. Do not use this on acetate fabrics. Sponge with cold water and repeat if necessary before washing.
Non-washable items For emulsion and water-based paint, try using methylated spirits with caution (see above) on small stains, but for a larger area seek expert treatment.

For gloss and oil-based paint, test the fabric before applying white spirit or paintbrush cleaner, then sponge with cold water and repeat if necessary. Alternatively, try using a spot-removing kit.

Scorch marks

Washable items Rub the fabric under cold running water, then soak in a solution of 15 ml (1 tablespoon) borax to 500 ml (1 pint) warm water until the mark fades. Bleach heavier stains on white cotton or linen fabrics with a hydrogen peroxide solution, then rinse and wash as usual.
Non-washable items Lubricate the stain with equal parts glycerine and warm water. Leave for up to an hour, then sponge with warm water. For heavier marks, wipe over with a cloth wrung out in the borax solution. Rinse and repeat, taking care not to over-wet the fabric.

Urine

Washable items Neutralize the acid by sponging with a solution of 15 ml (1 tablespoon) of ammonia in 1 litre (2 pints) of cold water. Rinse thoroughly, then pre-soak and wash in biological detergent. Stubborn stains can be treated by soaking in diluted hydrogen peroxide solution.
Non-washable items Sponge first with cold water, blot dry, then apply a solution of 10 ml (2 teaspoons) of distilled white wine vinegar to 1 litre (2 pints) of water. Shampoo upholstery with a liquid dry cleaner to which a few drops of disinfectant have been added.

Wine

Washable items Pour white wine over a red wine stain and soak up with absorbent paper.
Non-washable items Use absorbent paper, changing it frequently, to blot up the stain, then sponge with warm water and sprinkle with talcum powder to absorb the remaining moisture. After 15 minutes, brush or vacuum off and repeat if necessary.

*f*abric: the basics

Here are some simple guidelines on the fabrics most commonly used for various soft furnishing jobs. Basic advice is given on how different fabrics should be cleaned, although you should always check the manufacturer's washing instructions on individual fabrics. There is also basic information on suitable needles and threads, and tips on how to sew difficult fabrics.

FABRIC	DURABILITY	LAUNDERING	SEWING	THREAD
Calico Firm plain-weave cotton *Uses*: Curtains, cushion pads, upholstery lining	Reasonably durable	Can shrink with washing – wash before making up	Easy to sew 80–90 sharp machine needle	Mercerized cotton No50, polyester-cotton, polyester, cotton
Chintz Glazed or polished cotton *Uses*: Curtains, blinds, pelmets, valances, bedcovers, cushions	According to quality	Can be washed – dry clean to preserve glaze	Easy to sew, but avoid unpicking as it will show 80–90 sharp machine needle	Mercerized cotton No50, fine polyester-cotton, fine polyester
Cretonne Plain- or twill-weave unglazed cotton *Uses*: Curtains, cushions, bedcovers	According to quality	Dry clean – can be washed with care	Moderately easy to sew 80–90 sharp machine needle	Mercerized cotton No50, fine polyester-cotton, fine polyester
Furnishing Cotton Plain-woven cotton fabric *Uses*: Curtains, blinds, valances, table linen, bedcovers, cushions	According to weight	Heavyweight cotton should be dry cleaned – light to medium weights can be washed with care	Easy to sew 80–90 sharp machine needle	Mercerized cotton No50, fine polyester-cotton, fine polyester, cotton
Flannel Soft, plain- or twill-weave cotton or wool fabric *Uses*: Curtains, wallcoverings	Reasonably hard-wearing	Dry clean or wash	Easy to sew 90–100 sharp machine needle	Mercerized cotton No40, polyester-cotton, polyester

FABRIC	DURABILITY	LAUNDERING	SEWING	THREAD
Lace and Net Fabric woven in open patterns *Uses*: Lightweight curtains, bed drapes, tablecloths	Reasonably hard-wearing	Can be washed	Easy to sew – tack open lace well before stitching 80 sharp machine needle	Mercerized cotton No50, fine polyester-cotton, fine polyester
Linen Union Linen mixed with other fibres *Uses*: Upholstery, curtains, pelmets, cushions	Hard-wearing	Dry clean	Reasonably easy to sew, tendency to fray 80–90 sharp machine needle	Mercerized cotton No50, fine polyester-cotton, fine polyester
Cotton Sateen Satin-weave cotton in range of colours *Uses*: Lining curtains, blinds, bedcovers	Extends life of curtains, blinds, bedcovers	Clean as for main fabric	Easy to sew 80–90 sharp machine needle	Mercerized cotton No50, fine polyester-cotton, fine polyester
Sheeting Plain-woven cotton or polyester - cotton mix *Uses*: Bedding, cushions	Hard-wearing	Washable	Easy to sew 80–90 sharp machine needle	Mercerized cotton No50, fine polyester-cotton, fine polyester, cotton
Silk Filament produced by larvae of silkworm *Uses*: Curtains, blinds, upholstery, cushions	Hard-wearing	Dry clean, although some silks can be hand washed	Reasonably easy to sew – tack if slippery	Silk, fine polyester
PVC Plastic-coated fabric with knitted or woven base *Uses*: Tablecloths	Hard-wearing	Wipe over with a damp cloth	Dust needle bed with talcum powder or stitch through tissue paper or use rollerfoot on sewing machine Hold with paper clips – do not tack 90–100 sharp or wedge machine needle	Mercerized cotton No40, heavy-duty polyester-cotton, heavy-duty polyester, nylon
Tapestry Heavy- woven fabric *Uses*: Upholstery, cushions	Reasonably hard-wearing	Dry clean	Reasonably easy to sew 90–100 sharp machine needle	Heavy-duty polyester-cotton, heavy-duty polyester
Velvet Fabric with closely woven cut pile *Uses*: Upholstery, curtains, cushions	Hard-wearing	Dry clean	Check pile all runs the same way Press over a needle board 90–110 sharp machine needle	Heavy-duty polyester-cotton, heavy-duty polyester

Sewing equipment

Before you start on any home furnishings projects, check that you have all the necessary equipment to do the job properly. Basic items include a tape measure, tailor's chalk, pins, a pair of sharp cutting scissors, and the right needles and thread for the fabric being used. Keep all your sewing equipment together in a handy place – a good-sized sewing box is ideal.

CUTTING EQUIPMENT

You will need several pairs of scissors in a workbox. Buy the best quality high-grade stainless steel scissors you can afford. Always keep scissors sharp and only use them for the job for which they were designed.

Dressmaker's shears
The handles permit the lower blade to lie flat while the upper blade cuts through the fabric. Choose 20 cm (8 in) blades for a manageable cutting length.

General sewing scissors
Choose a pair about 13–16 cm (5–6½ in) long for trimming seams and cutting threads.

Small sewing scissors
These are useful for snipping sharp corners and other close sewing work. The scissors should have fine sharp pointed blades about 10 cm (4 in) long.

Pinking shears
The blades have serrated edges for cutting a zigzag edge. They are handy for trimming and neatening seams. Do not use them for initial cutting out.

Thread clippers
These are held in the palm of the hand. Use them for trimming off thread ends as you work.

Rotary cutter
This is a specialist cutter with a sharp cutting wheel. Use it only with its special mat for cutting through several layers of fabric at once, such as in patchwork.

MEASURING AND MARKING EQUIPMENT

Accurate measuring is essential when making any soft furnishing.

Tape measure
Choose a non-stretch tape with metal ends with both metric and imperial measurements down each side. Tape measures are usually 150 cm (60 in) long.

Metre (yard) stick
A metre (yard) length of wood is useful for marking across fabric widths when cutting out large items such as curtains. A metre (yard) stick can be used with a set square to provide an accurate right angle.

Metal tape
Use a retractable metal tape to measure and mark positions accurately when putting up curtain tracks, pelmet shelves and so on.

Tailor's chalk
This is a specialist chalk for marking fabric. It is available in different colours so that it can be seen on various coloured fabrics. It is also available in pencil form. The chalk is easily rubbed off the fabric after stitching.

SEWING AIDS

Apart from pins, none of the following are essential items for the sewing box. However, they are all useful, not least the handy gadgets which are designed to do specific jobs.

Pins
There is a huge range of pins on the market. Always match the pin with the fabric you are sewing. The standard pin length is 26 mm (1 in), but longer pins – 30 mm (1¼ in) and 34 mm (1⅜ in) – are also available. Glass-headed pins are a good choice to use on open weave fabrics as they are highly visible. Make sure that the pins are sharp. Blunt ones will snag the fabric.

Thimble
Wear a thimble on the middle finger of the sewing hand to help push the needle through the fabric. Choose a steel thimble and check it is the right size to sit comfortably on the finger.

Tape and binding maker
A handy gadget that folds the edges of bias-cut strips into finished bias binding. Thread the strip through the maker and press the turned-in edges with an iron as they emerge.

Beeswax
Before stitching on buttons, run the working thread through beeswax to give strength to the thread and to prevent it from tangling.

Seam ripper (quick unpick)
If you make a mistake run this quickly through a seam to cut all the threads.

Needle threader
A useful gadget to help thread needles quickly and easily.

Tack stick
This is a special adhesive fabric stick which can be used instead of tacking to hold fabrics together ready for stitching.

SEWING THREADS

The success of a soft furnishing project is partly dependent on using the right thread. Always match the thread to the fibre and weight of the fabric. If you cannot exactly match the colour of the thread and fabric, choose a thread which is one shade darker than the fabric. This will be less noticeable on the finished item than a lighter shade. On printed fabrics, choose a thread that matches one of the main colours in the fabric.

Natural fibre threads
Pure cotton thread Cotton thread is strong and smooth, with a slight sheen. Use this thread for stitching pure cotton fabric.
Mercerized cotton thread A cotton thread that has been treated to make it lustrous and able to take colour.
Linen thread Strong thread used for sewing linen fabrics.
Silk thread Use this strong, lustrous thread for stitching silk and wool.
Tacking thread A loosely twisted cotton thread that is easy to break, making it quick to remove from fabric.

Synthetic and mixed threads
Polyester thread An all-purpose synthetic thread.
Cotton-wrapped polyester This is the most common all-purpose thread. The cotton gives a smooth finish to the strong polyester core.

NEEDLES

Needles are divided into type and size, so match the needle to the sewing. Needles have tapestry eyes, long eyes, round eyes or easy-threading eyes. Needles come in tapestry points, normal points, leather points or ball points.

Sharps
Needles with round eyes and normal points, they are used for general sewing and for tacking and gathering.

Betweens
Betweens have round eyes and normal points. They are shorter than sharps and are used for hand-stitching and fine sewing work such as hemming.

Straws
These are long needles with round eyes and normal points. They are useful for tacking and gathering.

Bodkins
Bodkins have flat or long eyes and blunt points. They are used for threading cords and ribbons.

Easy-threading needles
These needles have a slot above the eye into which the thread is pulled. They are designed for people who have difficulty with needle threading.

*F*rom top row down, left to right: small sewing scissors, measuring tape, selection of needles, tape and binding maker, thimbles, marking pencils, pins, needle threaders, thread, seam ripper, tailor's chalk, thread clippers, dressmaker's marking pen and dressmaker's shears.

$\mathcal{P}$eriod style

Textiles have played an important part in the decoration of homes throughout the ages, and when we look back at the styles that were once popular with our ancestors, we can see what a great influence these designs still have over modern fabrics and over the way that textiles are used around the home.

THE MIDDLE AGES

In the Middle Ages in Europe only the nobility had enough money to make their homes comfortable. Because much of people's lives was spent on the move, soft furnishings took the form of woven tapestries and embroideries, which were easy to transport and store. These could rapidly transform even the barest room, and provided much-needed insulation in draughty buildings designed more for defence than for comfort. Hung along walls, across doorways and around beds, they were generally made in rich, warm colours, and the finest examples depicted scenes from legend and daily life. From the twelfth century onwards, Italy became an important producer of fine silks and rich velvets, but plain linen or woollen materials still remained the most widely used textiles. Chairs were a status symbol used only by the master of the household; everyone else had to make do with stools or benches. Loose cushions provided a degree of comfort on the wooden furniture.

THE SIXTEENTH CENTURY

By the end of the fifteenth century, textiles in Europe had become much more elaborate, particularly bed furnishings. The bed was now one of the most important pieces of furniture in the home. Wealthy households spent a great deal of money on designs with intricately carved frameworks and had them hung with ornate fabric canopies in rich jewel-like colours, often embellished with gold, silver and lace trimmings. During Tudor times even modest households would hang wool and linen drapes from their beds; these hangings were often painted to resemble tapestries.

In earlier, more turbulent times windows had been regarded as a weakness in defence and had consisted of small, narrow slits, designed to let out smoke and fumes rather than to allow natural sunlight in. Houses began to be built with larger, glazed windows in the relative peace and prosperity at the end of the sixteenth century, and people soon began to exploit the decorative possibilities of draping fabric at these windows. In England curtains tended to be just a simple strip of narrow fabric, but the more style-conscious Italians and French were using rich velvets and brocades in strong, earthy colours to create far more elaborate curtain treatments.

Towards the end of the eighteenth century, Neo-classicism swept through Europe. This design for an arched recess (right) is very much of the period. It draws on Classical motifs for the decorative plasterwork, while the arch itself is embellished with fabric hung in deep swags and tails.

Chinese motifs on wallpapers and fabrics were popular in the seventeenth and eighteenth centuries in England (left). The style, known as chinoiserie, was inspired by the lacquerwork furniture, porcelain and other artefacts that had started to reach Europe from the Far East.

Upholstered chairs also began to appear in the sixteenth century, usually covered in fabric to match those on the walls, window and bed. Chairs tended to be arranged around the walls and were placed in the middle of the room only when in use. Tables were often draped with a carpet or with a piece of fabric.

THE SEVENTEENTH CENTURY

During the 1600s the increasingly sophisticated fabric treatments popular in France and Italy began to be taken up by the English, and in the latter part of the century the French court at Versailles exerted a strong influence on the style of interior decoration throughout Europe. Furnishings were designed to complement one another, and matching fabrics were deliberately chosen for walls, curtains and bed drapes. Another innovation was the use of damasks and watered silks to cover the walls – the forerunners of wallpaper. The bed remained a status symbol, and the wealthy would often spend more money on its decoration than on any other household item. Half-testers now started appearing, hung with lightweight silk curtains and valances. Although the drapery around the bed became rather lighter, the textiles were often heavily embellished with gold and silver thread and appliquéd motifs. Window treatments were also becoming more luxuriant. Paired curtains replaced single drapes, and pelmets and valances were arranged to hide the rings and poles. Gathered pull-up blinds began to appear, creating an effect similar to modern festoons.

The interiors of the New World owed much to the Old as each group of new immigrants introduced some of the style of their own country into the homes they built. In the eastern settlements Dutch, German and Scandinavian architecture predominated, but the influence of the late medieval English style was also strongly felt. To begin with, interiors were universally plain, with minimal use of textiles, but as the century drew to a close the more sophisticated upholstered furniture and fabrics that were appearing in

European fashions were adopted by the style-conscious. Much of the material was imported from Europe, but local craftsmen were quick to develop home-grown versions, allowing a distinctive American style to emerge.

THE EIGHTEEENTH CENTURY

The eighteenth century saw the dawning of fashions in interior design in our modern sense. Trend-setting architects and builders began to find inspiration in distinct sets of ideas – in nature, in exotic cultures or in the styles of the past – and to apply design concepts systematically to the creation of harmonious interiors. Fashion-conscious householders embraced the opportunity to display their wealth and their knowledge of the latest taste.

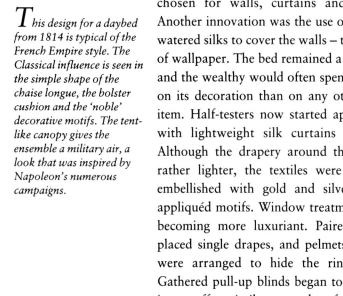

This design for a daybed from 1814 is typical of the French Empire style. The Classical influence is seen in the simple shape of the chaise longue, the bolster cushion and the 'noble' decorative motifs. The tent-like canopy gives the ensemble a military air, a look that was inspired by Napoleon's numerous campaigns.

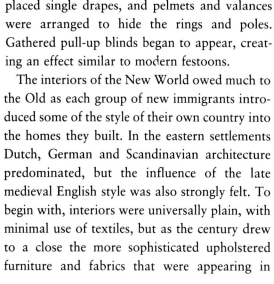

Rococo and Palladian

Early in the eighteenth century the informal look of the Rococo style, which took its inspiration from nature, was popular in continental Europe. Decorative motifs featuring flowers, leaves, animals and birds, interspersed with ribbons and arrows, adorned furnishings influenced by the Rococo. Meanwhile, imported Chinese artefacts were being imitated by textile and furniture makers in Europe to produce chinoiserie, also featuring many stylized naturalistic motifs. In England and in America, the Palladian style, following the architectural principles of Andrea Palladio, had far more influence on interiors than Rococo. This look, which followed the symmetry and proportion of classical Greek and Roman architecture, lent itself more readily to more

modest homes with traditional wood-panelled walls. Temple porticoes, circular stairwells and tall round-headed windows were typical architectural features of Palladianism. Gothic interiors derived from the medieval style of architecture were also popular for a short time in eighteenth-century England; and Chinese-style wallpaper, textiles and porcelain were occasionally used to decorate individual rooms.

The choice of fabrics had never been greater, with cotton chintzes and painted silks imported from the Far East. Italy and France continued to dominate the market in sophisticated damasks, velvets and brocades. Fabric was still required in great quantities for bed drapes and curtains, but the introduction of wallpapers meant that fabric was no longer used very much to cover walls.

Bed hangings were at their most sumptuous, with richly decorated canopies to which pelmets, curtains and gathered festoons were added. Most windows were fitted with pairs of curtains made from generous amounts of lightweight fabric and were topped with richly embroidered pelmets. Pull-up festoons made from light silks were now more widely seen, and other types of blind including roller and Venetian styles began to appear towards the end of the century.

Neo-classicism

The excitement over the discovery of ancient remains at the sites of Pompeii and Herculaneum in the latter part of the century gave rise to a wave of Neo-classicism through most of Europe. Motifs inspired by the art of ancient Rome and Greece included wreaths, laurels, swags, urns and trophies; favourite colour schemes were pale shades of green, yellow, blue and purple. The curtains at this time were very grand, with swagged pelmets and tails, often topped with Neo-classical motifs made from plaster. The choice of fabrics included silks and damasks in delicate floral designs; striped taffetas; velvet, voile and muslin. This revival of ancient architecture and interior styles was also readily adopted by America.

Empire and Regency

The years around 1800 saw the emergence of the Empire style in France, across the Napoleonic courts of Europe and (because of the large numbers of emigrating Parisian craftsmen) in America. The primary influence was that of Napoleon and his military career, in particular his Egyptian campaign. This second Neo-classical era produced a wealth of furniture, textiles and decoration copying the styles discovered on paintings and sculptures from Ancient Egypt and Rome. There were also designs reflecting military life, with folding camp furniture, tented rooms and a proliferation of martial emblems.

In England a slightly different style of interior design evolved – the Regency style, masterminded by Thomas Hope. Although this also found inspiration in ancient civilizations, its approach was simpler than that of the Napoleonic school, with less relief ornamentation. As with the Empire style, Egyptian motifs were popular, but in addition Roman, Turkish, Chinese and even Hindu elements appeared. The designs of ancient Greece, however, were most widely used, especially the classic key motif.

Curtains and drapes became even more inventive during this century. Styles ranged from simple drawn curtains, held in place with tiebacks, to elaborate drapes with voluminous swags and tails, often decorated with tassels and fringing. It was the fashion to display curtain poles, and these were often highly gilded with decorative finials inspired by classical motifs such as laurel wreaths, eagles or animals' heads. Intricately constructed and often festooned pelmets and valances were an alternative to decorative curtain poles. A multi-layered look which combined heavy outer curtains with light muslin or silk undercurtains became popular.

There was a vast selection of fabrics to choose from, including many different types of silk, taffetas, linen, wool velvets, sprigged muslin and cotton. Some fabrics featured patterns with human figures and animals. Trimmings such as fringes, tassels, rosettes and embroidered borders often adorned plain curtains. Colour schemes based on deep reds, greens and yellows were all the vogue.

Designs for furniture became much simpler, but beds were often still draped with elaborate canopies and pelmets. Chairs and sofas, often of dark mahogany or with ornate gilded frames, were comfortably upholstered and given silk covers in strong shades of pink, blue, green and yellow. These were often trimmed to match the curtain treatments in the room. Bolsters were now an essential feature of sofas and couches.

THE NINETEENTH CENTURY

The window treatments of the eighteenth century were very elaborate, and by the beginning of the nineteenth century they had become one of the most important elements in the design of a room scheme. Many of the styles developed around this time remained popular throughout the century, and even influence curtain designs of today.

American Independence

American homes at the turn of the nineteenth century saw many changes in interior decoration, and painted, papered or fabric-covered walls began to replace the more traditional wood panelling found in the homes of the earlier settlers. The homes of the wealthy kept abreast of fashions in Europe, adopting curtain treatments that included festoons and swags. The symbol of independence – the American eagle – was incorporated into carved wooden pelmets. Satin, velvet and silk damask were much in demand, particularly in shades of crimson, blue, yellow and green. Smaller householders took to stencilling walls, floors and fabrics to achieve similar highly decorative effects at a fraction of the cost. They took their design inspiration from their surroundings. Favourite motifs – among them flowers, fruit, stars, birds (and, of course, the American eagle) – were stencilled using natural dyes that copied the colours favoured by the wealthy, and included earthy reds, yellows, greens and blues.

The Victorian Era

Victorian furnishing fashions were largely eclectic and based on several different historical styles. The middle-class Victorian lady took her inspiration for furnishings from the many books and periodicals now published on the subject. Later in the century she could even visit one of the many department stores that had opened to choose her interiors.

Rooms would often be crammed with furniture, overloaded with ornaments, picture frames and bric-à-brac, and window treatments and furnishings were similarly decorated to excess. The predominantly dark greens, browns and reds were joined in mid-century by a new palette of garish synthetic colours produced by the new aniline dyes. The Victorians liked to mix contrasting colours and patterns together. The development of the Jacquard loom meant that increasingly complex designs could be woven into fabrics, and naturalistic patterns with fruit and flowers were very popular. The mass of furniture, sombre colours and heavily draped curtains combined with poor lighting to give an overall impression of gloom.

Curtains were anything but simple, and multi-layered treatments trimmed with fringing and braid became grander and grander. Light muslin or net curtains were used to filter out the light, and heavy outer dress curtains were swept back in dramatic draped effects. Roller blinds with decorated, cut and trimmed borders were sometimes used in addition to other curtains. Although some treatments featured highly ornate brass poles, elaborate pelmets were a popular alternative, and it was at this time that lambrequins (stiff pelmets that extended down the sides of the window) were developed. Drapes were not confined to the window – the Victorians used heavy curtains over doors and archways, around mirrors and even at the chimney piece. Bed treatments, on the other hand, gradually became less fussy towards the end of the century, when it was considered much healthier to sleep without layers of fabric all around the bed.

The Arts and Crafts Movement

Towards the end of the nineteenth century in England, a number of artists and designers – including William Morris and Charles Eastlake – rebelled against the excesses of design that marked the Victorian era. The Arts and Crafts movement, as it became known, took its inspiration from the Middle Ages, an era when it was believed artistic creativity had been part of everyone's daily life. Furniture was simpler in design and produced by hand by craftsmen. Unfortunately, although the initial concept was 'art for the people', many of the movement's products were so labour-intensive that this style was way beyond the means of the masses.

The Victorians loved to mix colours and patterns together wherever possible, and this design for a small sitting room from 1840 is no exception. Attention to detail was all important – note how even the curved edge of each pelmet point is 'finished' by a tiny bell. The highly decorated roller blind was a common feature of the period.

The distinctive Art Deco style of the 1920s and '30s is exemplifed by this Edward Thorne design for an 'ultra modern' bedroom. Plain outer curtains are softly draped Greek fashion, while the inner geometrically patterned curtains are hung straight to the floor. Clean curves characterize the dressing-table mirror, bed and armchair. Animal designs often appeared in Art Deco interiors. Here, a swan motif embellishes the furniture.

Although the trend for dark colours persisted, interiors began to lose their heavy draperies and profusion of furniture in preference for a lighter and less cluttered look. Simpler curtain treatments reflected the fact that smaller windows were being installed in new homes. Naturalistic designs were popular for fabric and wallcoverings; some of the most distinctive were those produced by Morris & Co, which featured stylized flowers and foliage, sometimes interspersed with birds or fruit. The taste for a simpler, more streamlined look also manifested itself in a vogue for all things Japanese at this time.

Art Nouveau

The next important phase of interior design was Art Nouveau, which emerged in the France of the 1890s. This completely new style was characterized by designs based on sinuous, flowing plant forms, and in its short life span of less than a decade it swept through Europe and America. Curtain treatments were now even simpler, and furniture designs were often elongated and decorated with flowing carvings of twisted tendrils and flowers. The peacock, whiplash and rose were favourite motifs.

THE TWENTIETH CENTURY

The twentieth century has seen many changes that have affected the way we live, and this includes the way we use fabrics in the home. As business thrived in the early part of the century, for example, fewer women chose to go into domestic service, favouring factory or shop work instead. As a result of this decline in home labour, simpler window treatments and other furnishings became popular. At the same time, technological advances brought the advent of artificial fabrics and washing machines, and the traditional heavy velvets and brocades were quickly replaced with easy-care cottons, viscoses and polyesters.

The Bauhaus

Germany saw the next major shift in design philosophy when in 1919 the architect Walter Gropius founded the Bauhaus school of design. Experimenting with materials such as tubular steel, leather, cane and canvas, the Bauhaus designers produced stark, modern furniture on strictly functional lines, much of it still popular today. Many of the abstract textiles they used had a naive, almost ethnic look. When the Bauhaus was closed down by the Nazis in 1933, many of its designers emigrated to America, where their style was more readily appreciated.

Art Deco

This distinctive style emerged in France in the mid 1920s. Its roots lay in the past, deriving inspiration from many sources including the eighteenth century, the Orient and primitive art. The furniture, often made from luxury materials such as ebony, ivory and lacquer, relied on fairly traditional forms, but exploited more modern two-dimensional and geometric patterns for decoration. Brightly coloured, patterned fabrics, plain-coloured satins and various furs and animal skins were used for upholstery. Armchairs and sofas had semicircular backs and square or rectangular bases with deep, smoothly rounded upholstery and large, soft seat cushions.

The trend for Art Deco continued into the 1930s. Walls were kept plain in colour, often black, white or yellow. Plain satin in white, beige or pale shades of grey, pink and mauve was used for upholstery, and geometric-patterned wool rugs were fashionable on floors. Curtains were mostly plain and usually hung straight to the ground without any form of pelmet. Occasionally they were draped in the style of ancient Greek interiors. Furniture shapes became more angular, with edges defined by simple piping.

Post-war Modernism

After the Second World War, American manufacturers began to invest heavily in new materials and technology. Fibreglass and plastic began to be used for moulded pieces of furniture, which were upholstered with rubber or foam and covered in a top fabric. The designs aimed for comfort and were often shaped to follow the contours of the body. Plain woven fabrics in natural colours were widely used to cover furniture, while leather was reserved for the more expensive ranges. Sofas and chairs tended to be made from square or rectangular blocks of foam attached to metal or wooden frames.

Interiors at this time were light and airy, with large windows. Decoration was very plain in style and curtains were simply straight drops of fabric with no pelmets or ties. The only pattern in a room was likely to come from rugs, scatter cushions or curtains. Paintings and ornaments were scarce.

The 1960s and 1970s

In the 1960s blues, greys and pinks emerged as key colour schemes. Upholstery was almost exclusively of moulded foam, covered in a variety of textured finishes – velvet or PVC – or nylon jersey. The 1960s through to the 1970s also saw the reappearance of natural materials like wood and leather, with textured fabrics in earthy shades of brown, beige and terracotta. This sophisticated look, which was imported from Scandinavia, was largely promoted by architects.

In complete contrast, some manufacturers adopted the brighter country-style colours of Scandinavia and popularized the use of bright reds, blues, yellows and oranges.

High Tech

High Tech rose to fame in the late 1970s and is a look which is still favoured today by those seeking an alternative to traditional approaches to interior design. Inspired by industrial design, it is a sparse, plain look which features sharp angles and solid colour rather than pattern. Metal, glass, rubber and plastic are the preferred materials and much of the furniture used in rooms of this style is recycled from industry – chairs made from car seats, beds from scaffolding and studded rubber flooring more commonly found in airports and public buildings.

Post Modernism

Not everyone was fond of the sterility of the modern design of the 1970s and a postmodernist approach resulted in the 1980s. The new movement, started in America and Milan, was initially quite outrageous and extreme in contrast to the sombre modernism it set out to flout. The Memphis group of designers in Milan developed a highly influential collection of furniture, fabrics, ceramics and glass in a new, relaxed style, with sometimes jokey overtones. Unusual colour combinations like contrasting pinks and printed laminates with bright, jagged patterns were also part of the look.

The Return to Traditionalism

Throughout the twentieth century there has always been an underlying trend for the 'antique' look. During the 1970s and '80s this grew in importance, and the 'country look', which put together stripped pine furniture and small-patterned floral fabrics, became popularized. With the gradual move towards greater authenticity in traditional design, more intricate curtain treatments, upholstery and bedding have come back into fashion.

Contemporary style

One of the greatest advantages for home owners today is the diversity of styles available. Whether your taste is for the simplicity of American country, the elegant Neo-classical interiors of the English town house, the stark, no-compromise look of the minimalist home, or an eclectic mix of all three, it is possible and perfectly acceptable to furnish your home in any way you choose. Each style has its own typical colour choices, furnishings and accessories, and it is important to follow certain guidelines to achieve a co-ordinated and authentic look. This section takes a glimpse at a variety of favourite contemporary styles and shows you how to re-create each style with the minimum of effort.

Fabric plays an important role in a room's decor and can provide the inspiration for the overall style (below). Here, pillowcases with strong floral motifs in blues and whites hint at a French provincial bedroom. The theme is carried through in the white cotton sheeting, pale quilted cover and lacy wall hanging at the head of the bed.

Traditional hand-made textiles with bright, earthy colours and vivid patterning are a classic ingredient in a number of stylish modern interiors (left).

american country style

American country style embraces the many different looks created by the first settlers. The overall style is one of functional simplicity, but the strong influence of folk-art traditions adds an element of individual, naive charm.

The homes of the early colonists were built from readily available timber, and tongued-and-grooved interior walls are a typical feature of the American country look. The wood was usually stained to mimic more expensive timbers, or painted in strong, flat colours such as deep blue-greens, ochre yellows and ox-blood reds. Stencils were developed as cheaper alternatives to the patterned wallpapers used by the wealthy settlers. Simple folk motifs like fruit, flowers, hearts and stars were popular choices.

The textiles available to the American settlers were very limited, and patterned designs were mostly hand-embroidered or stencilled onto hardwearing homespun cloths. Windows were simply dressed, usually with straight curtains with slotted or looped fabric headings hung from slender wood or metal poles. These styles can be easily copied today using plain calicoes and muslins, ginghams or rough hessians. Wooden Venetian blinds, plantation shutters and simple roller or Roman blinds make appropriate alternatives to curtains.

The Windsor chair is one of the classical pieces of American country furniture, and would have often been used with simple tied-on squab cushions. The rocking chair, invented in the New World, was also something of a national institution. For a more comfortable seating arrangement, it is perfectly acceptable to mix a variety of modern and traditional upholstered chairs and sofas, covering them in simple geometric and striped fabrics. Facsimiles of some of the old stylized floral and hand-blocked linen prints are also available today. Patchwork quilts and woven blankets were widely used by the settlers to add colour and pattern to plain furniture. Use them as throws over neutral-coloured upholstery, as wall hangings and tablecloths and to cover cushions.

Most of the early American furniture was based on Jacobean styles, but several independent religious communities such as the Shakers developed their own distinctive designs. Shaker style was a very disciplined and extremely functional look, and decoration had no place at all.

QUILTS

No American country bedroom would be complete without its patchwork or appliquéd quilt. The designs common to the religious sects like the Amish used large, bold geometric patterns in lavender blue, brick reds and strong earth colours, but more free-style multicoloured designs were also used.

Elements of the traditional American country style are easily incorporated into modern schemes (left). A large patchwork quilt, whether it's new or old, provides a colourful and eye-catching display. Painted furniture, which was introduced by early settlers from Holland, Germany and Scandinavia, adds another distinctive and individual touch.

The simple shapes of the perfectly made furniture are currently enjoying a revival, and it is relatively easy to buy reproductions to help you re-create an authentic Shaker look. One of the most characteristic features of these interiors is the continuous peg rail that runs around the top of the walls in a room, used to store all manner of things tidily off the floor. From it were hung the chairs when not in use, clocks, mirrors, brooms and baskets. Everything else was kept neatly out of sight in large cupboards and sets of drawers. You can buy copies of this peg rail today, or improvise by using battening set at head height around the walls with dowelling pegs or small doorknobs screwed in at regular intervals. Basic blue-and-white checked fabrics gave a minimal splash of colour to interiors, and soft furnishings like bedspreads and cushions may have been embroidered with the characteristic heart-in-hand motif.

Half-tester and open-post beds were most often found in the colonial homes. Although some of the beds in the homes of the very wealthy may have been richly dressed with swathes of fabric, country styles relied on simpler treatments. If you want to use a four-poster bed in your room, keep the drapery to a minimum – a simple throw of antique lace can look very effective, or leave the posts completely bare to show off the woodwork. Old linen, lace and netting are all suitable fabrics for colonial bedrooms and can be used for tablecloths, cushion covers and bedcovers.

Simplicity was the key to the Shaker lifestyle (left). In the bedroom, plain or checked fabrics were used to cover the bed and to provide basic wall coverings.

french provincial style

The French provincial style, with its rustic roots, is one that mixes practicality with a sense of graciousness. Although the differing climates in the north and south of the country result in slight variations in the choice of furnishings and interior colour schemes, the essence of the look is the same. Walls are left plain, sometimes with exposed brickwork. Plaster finishes are washed in white, cream or pale yellow, and woodwork may be stripped or painted with faded matt shades of smoky blue, green and even brown. There is a limited use of wallpaper in neutral floral motifs or pale stripes.

Furniture is typically from the eighteenth and nineteenth centuries – grand in style, but also very practical. Large upright cupboards called armoires are to be found in French country houses and are used for storing anything from china and linen to food. Rush-seated chairs are common, and upholstered furniture is very elegant, and usually of ample proportions. Deep armchairs and sofas are favourites, and can be upholstered in heavy tapestry fabrics, velvets or leather. If you want to create a gentler look use covers in neutral shades instead. There is a trend in France to use simple, shapeless loose covers made from crisp white linens and cottons. Held in place with basic ties, these covers look rather like dust sheets, and create a much more informal look. Chaise longues and daybeds are another popular feature in living rooms, and may be covered with plain silk or striped covers. In the southern areas of France, where the warmer climate allows more time to be spent out of doors, wicker and bamboo furniture is more common, used with plenty of large colourful cushions for comfort.

With the exception of homes in the south of the country, windows are generally large, allowing good views over the countryside or garden. Curtain treatments are kept reasonably simple to ensure that these views are not obscured. Venetian blinds and wooden shutters are very much in keeping with the French provincial look, but if you prefer curtains go for unlined sheers like muslin, lace or cotton in calming neutral white and cream. Don't bother with pelmets or valances, the French style is to hang curtains on slim wooden or dull brass poles.

The bedroom in a French provincial home is almost monastic in its simplicity, but nevertheless gives an overwhelming impression of warmth. With such sparse furnishings, the bed itself becomes the focus of the room, and can often appear oversized. The sheets and pillowcases should be of crisp white cotton or linen to look really authentic, and can be teamed with a plump duvet in plain white or fresh red and white or blue and white gingham. Large, comfortable pillows are usually square in shape. As an alternative to crisp, neutral fabrics for bed linen, you can opt instead for cheerful, brightly coloured designs with a definite feeling of the south. These intricately patterned fabrics reflect the colours of the sunny Provençal countryside – bottle greens, ochre yellows, faded blues and cherry reds. The paisley, geometric and naturalistic patterns have a distinctly Indian flavour, and can be mixed together very successfully to make a room positively glow.

Simple window treatments are typical of the French provincial style (left).

As an alternative to brightly coloured Provençal cloths, choose lace and cotton table linen in white or pastel shades (below).

PROVENÇAL PRINTS

Provençal cottons were first produced in the eighteenth century and were based on brightly printed cottons imported to France from India in the seventeenth century. Many of these original block-based designs are still used today, particularly small floral and paisley motifs in vivid hues.

Mediterranean style

The sun plays a major part in the life of Mediterranean peoples, and greatly influences the style and decoration of their homes. With such long hot summers the preference is for simple and practical furniture and furnishings and minimal decoration.

Inside the house the use of colour is often restricted to white and pastel shades that reflect the light and maintain the welcoming feeling of coolness. Exteriors, however, often take their inspiration from the abundance of colour in the surrounding vegetation and, of course, the sea, and bright blues, pinks, aquamarines, terracotta and yellows abound.

In colder climates it is possible to conjure a Mediterranean atmosphere by making use of these brighter, warmer colours. An all-over scheme based on such colours may be hard to live with – opt instead for neutral-coloured walls with touches of darker contrasting colours on woodwork and furnishings.

Fabrics have never been used in any great quantities in Mediterranean homes because they have never been much needed for keeping out the cold. The windows in traditional Mediterranean homes are usually small, designed to keep out the sun, and often have no curtain treatments at all, relying simply on wooden shutters. If curtains are used, they are generally simple and made from sheer fabrics or cotton lace that allow the free movement of air. You can re-create this look yourself with plain white cottons and wool for curtains or Roman blinds. Wooden louvred shutters or fine Venetian blinds would be appropriate, too. For a more colourful variation choose brighter coloured fabrics in checked, striped and even floral patterns.

The style of furniture is usually simple and very practical. Dark or painted wooden pieces are favoured, and have a rustic feel to them. Basket chairs and rush-seated chairs are popular choices, and can be easily moved outside when necessary. Upholstered furniture is likely to be covered in cool cotton fabrics, such as canvas, in shades of white. They are usually decorated with colourful cushions or hand-woven cotton rugs. A

FABRIC CHOICES

Colourful woven rugs are used for flooring and as wall hangings in Mediterranean homes. Lighter weight weaves in traditional designs or lacework are ideal as tablecloths or to cover scatter cushions. Choose white or off-white woven cottons for curtains and upholstery and to frame doorways. In the bedroom, hang muslin or a semi-sheer cotton round a simple four-poster bed. Transform an ordinary bed by creating a simple coronet and draped arrangement at the head of the bed.

To create a Mediterranean look, paint walls white or in shades of white, such as a hint of green, yellow or pink (left). Choose sturdy upholstery cottons in plain white or with a contrasting stripe for sofas and armchairs. Introduce colours and patterns with masses of scatter cushions.

seating more comfortable. Choose plain colours or prints featuring naturalistic motifs, such as birds, flowers or fruit.

The bedroom in a Mediterranean home must be cool and quiet, ideal for afternoon siestas as well as night-time sleep. Plain white or faintly colour-washed walls with bare polished floorboards will re-create an authentic look. The bed should be very plain, almost austere-looking (a basic wooden or iron bedstead is ideal), and dressed simply with fresh white cotton bed linen. If this seems too cold in a more temperate climate, opt instead for sheets and duvet in bright summery yellows, sky blues or sea greens. Crisp stripes or checks would again look equally effective in the bedroom.

In the bedroom, opt for crisp white bed linen and large pillows. A quilt made from a floral-patterned fabric is also in keeping with this style.

daybed covered in checked or striped cotton fabric would be very much in keeping in a Mediterranean-style interior.

While the midday sun usually drives the Mediterranean family indoors for lunch, the mild evening climate makes eating al fresco a common pursuit. Simple wooden tables are generally laid with a brightly coloured cotton tablecloth, and equally colourful tie-on cushions make wooden

Scandinavian style

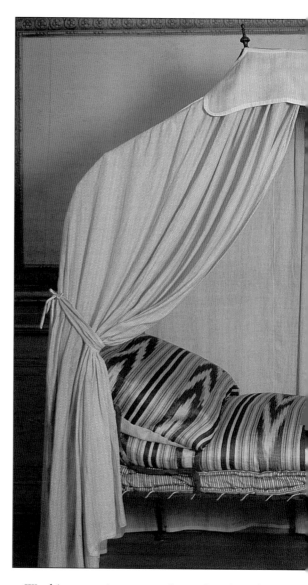

Scandinavian design has had a considerable influence on interiors in this century. The modern styling made popular first in the 1930s and then later on in the 1970s was based around pale-coloured wood and neutral colours. In this style, still popular to a certain extent today, furniture, floors and sometimes even walls and ceilings are restricted to pale woods. Fabrics in neutral shades or pale pastels are used for upholstery and simple window treatments; tufted or woven wool rugs in the same subtle shades add a touch of comfort to the plain wooden floors.

As nostalgia for the past has grown worldwide, a more traditional Scandinavian-style interior has increased in popularity. This takes its influences from both the charming folk art of the humble country cottages and the grander Neo-classical interiors of the eighteenth and nineteenth centuries. If you prefer the cool, elegant style of the Neo-classical interior, choose pale, almost faded colours for the walls of your room – grey-blues and greens, peaches, creams and pastel yellows are all suitable. Patterned wallpaper and borders can also be used, but stick to simple pale stripes or classical motifs for authenticity. Wood panelling is also appropriate for the walls in this style of interior. For the more rustic folk-art interiors, opt for wooden tongue-and-groove walls, painted in stronger shades of blue and green.

The flooring used for both the Neo-classical and the folk-art interiors is stripped wooden boards, bleached and sealed to a honey-blond, near-white tone. Simple striped rag rugs and kilims are perfect for the more rustic interiors, while classic oriental rugs add a more appropriate touch of warmth and colour in formal rooms.

Working curtains are rarely used in Scandinavian countries – windows may be shuttered, left bare or decorated with light dress curtains. For privacy you could use roller or Roman blinds made from pale neutral-coloured fabrics and sheers, or make up simple straight curtains in typically Scandinavian patterns such as stripes, checks or gingham. Choose natural textures and materials like cotton, linen, calico and muslin – soft pastel yellows and peaches add a warm, glowing look to a room, while blue and white mixes create a crisper, fresh look.

The furniture in the classic Scandinavian look is painted. In the grander interiors the style of furniture is elegant Neo-classical, painted in

An elegant canopied daybed in cool, delicate colours is typical of the Swedish Neo-classical style (left). In peasant-style interiors, use fresh ginghams in blue, red, yellow or green for curtains, bedcovers, bolsters and cushions (below).

sophisticated pale shades, with plain or subtly patterned upholstery seats. In the peasant-style interiors furniture is more basic in shape, and painted with much stronger, rustic colours like blue, green, red and yellow. Paint finishes and stencilling are often used on both types of furniture – use either delicate bows, swags and classical motifs, or more rustic free-style designs, depending on the look you are trying to create. The daybed is a classic Scandinavian favourite and can be used, if necessary, as both sofa by day and bed by night. For true authenticity paint it grey, blue or cream and cover it with a simple blue and white stripe or check fabric. Another typical Scandinavian touch is to add squab cushions to upright chairs – pastel-coloured fabrics or crisp stripes and ginghams work well.

As always, accessories help to bring the look together. Chandeliers and wall sconces with candle-style fittings make perfect choices for lighting in the Neo-classical interiors. Empire-style mirrors and gilt-framed pictures can be used to decorate the walls and simple dried flower garlands will brighten up bedroom and bathroom doors. Bolster cushions are the best choice for upholstered furniture – they add visual interest without too much fuss or unnecessary clutter. And to complete the Scandinavian style, install a traditional cast-iron heating stove in the corner of the room.

english country house style

The slightly eccentric nature of English country-house style mixes elegance with informality to create a timeless look with an air of faded glory. In this interior style colour schemes tend towards rich, mellow shades; fabrics are chosen for their traditional, sophisticated patterns, and antique furniture is a must. But the typical English country house is not a show-piece, but rather a well-used, slightly worn-around-the-edges family home, where a genuine love of the countryside and its traditional pursuits is much in evidence.

The decoration of walls, ceiling and woodwork must, of course, be appropriate to the age of the property, but as the proportions of rooms in the typical country house err on the large side, they demand a much grander treatment than smaller country cottages. Strong paint or wallpaper colours are a favourite choice, creating an uncompromising statement of taste, as well as providing the perfect backdrop for dark wooden furniture, collections of paintings, china and so on. The dining room, study or library in the country house would have often been decorated with deep shades of green, red, ochre and brown that gave them a definite masculine air, while the drawing room tended towards lighter, more feminine colours and furnishings.

Open fires help to create the cosy atmosphere associated with this interior style – the larger the proportions the better. Again, depending on the age and the location of the property, typical flooring would have been stone flags, marble or polished wooden boards. Richly decorated traditional and oriental-style rugs and carpets would supply touches of warmth and comfort.

The large scale of the windows in the English country house calls for elegant curtain treatments

that use generous amounts of fabric in either rich, plain colours or bold patterns and designs. Big windows like this look their best when topped with a pelmet or valance, and finished off with tiebacks, rope or tassels. Don't be tempted, though, to make the curtain treatments too intricate; the idea is to create a grand, yet informal, flourish at the windows.

The furniture in the true English country house is an eclectic mix of classic and antique pieces, collected over the years. To re-create the style

*F*aded grandeur and a cosy, cluttered air are the key elements of the English country house look.

yourself, look for good-quality English antique furniture. For authenticity, upholstered sofas and chairs should be in simple, classic shapes with generously sized seat cushions designed for comfort and for sophisticated elegance. Loose covers are more appropriate than fitted upholstery, and you can choose from a wide range of styles according to the mood you wish to create. Overblown flowery prints, crisp ticking stripes or plain colours are all in the right spirit. Richly coloured brocades and tapestries make a good choice for dining chairs which are less often used. In keeping with the slightly eccentric nature of the English country-house look, the arrangement of furniture in rooms can be very relaxed – almost haphazard. Plenty of cushions on sofas and easy chairs will add to the air of comfort. Hand-stitched needlepoint or embroidered covers look especially good. Embroidered samplers and needlepoint designs are also particularly effective when framed and used as pictures and fire screens around a room.

Colonial style

Colonial settlers in Africa in the last century created their own particular style of interior design that reflected not only classic English tastes, but also the local surroundings and life-styles they became accustomed to.

The intense heat of the African climate dictated, to a great extent, the type of decoration and furnishings that were most popular, and this is a look that can be easily re-created today. Walls should be painted rather than covered with wallpaper. Cool whites, creams and ivory help to create a light, airy feel in a room – but as an alternative you could opt for earthy tones like terracotta, olive and ochre, more reminiscent of the baked African landscape and native-style dwellings. Paint finishes such as colour washing look good in the Colonial home, helping to create an impression of either faded glory or rustic simplicity.

Wooden floors are appropriate for this interior style – it was easier to sweep the dry dust blown into the African house off floorboards than off a closely woven carpet. Carpet made from sisal, jute or similar natural fibres would also be an authentic choice; a splash of colour and pattern can be added with a few simple kilims or striped mats. Choose rich earthy reds, browns and greens to be in keeping with the overall look.

Heavy ornate curtains have no place in the Colonial home. Plain wooden plantation-style shutters, wooden Venetian blinds and cane roller blinds are much more appropriate. To soften the appearance of the window, use simple curtain treatments in sheer fabrics, or choose roller or Roman blinds in neutral cottons like calico.

The typical furniture in a Colonial home would have been made from rattan or wood.

Basket chairs with high backs, hammocks and wooden steamer-style loungers were favourite choices for the veranda, where colonials would sit to escape the heat of the day or relax in the evenings after dinner. Wooden directors' chairs were also popular, as they could be folded up and transported when on safari. Mix a selection of this furniture in with more conventional upholstery to create the Colonial look. And opt for large, comfortable sofas and armchairs covered with natural fabrics like cotton or linen. Depending on the look you want to create, choose either

made from pure cotton or linen is most appropriate, and you can either underpin its crisp simplicity by using a plain white bedspread, or add a splash of colour and pattern with an ethnic blanket or throw.

Pay attention to detail if you want to create a more authentic Colonial room. Large ceiling fans are the perfect accessory for this look, as are intricately carved wooden folding screens and leather travelling trunks. For decoration and ornamentation, use plenty of traditional-style woven African baskets, tribal patterned pottery and native wooden carvings. And to give you more of a feel of the jungle, add an exotic touch with large parlour palms, rubber plants and cheese plants.

To re-create the Colonial style, use ethnic textiles for upholstery, scatter cushions and tablecloths (left). These also make effective and dramatic wall hangings. Enforce the Colonial mood with inexpensive native baskets and pottery.

plain colours like cool ivory, vibrant earthy reds, browns and greens; or richly patterned kilim-style fabrics. You can even add a fun touch to the room by using animal print fabrics for less prominent pieces of furniture.

In the bedroom you can continue the theme by draping swathes of sheer muslin around the bed to imitate the mosquito nets that would have been essential in the Colonial household. The bed itself should be a simple wooden design, one with an intricately carved headboard or a more basic woven rattan headboard. Crisp white bed linen

A few well-selected tribal carvings are all you need to create the right air of authenticity in a Colonial-style interior (left).

english town house style

The traditional style of the English town house has its roots in the Georgian and Regency eras of the mid eighteenth and early nineteenth centuries – a time when craftsmanship and design were at a peak. Although the rooms in these terraced homes were not particularly spacious, the high ceilings and large windows helped to create a feeling of elegant grandeur.

The fireplace would have formed the focal point in a traditional town house room, and is a good starting point for an authentic reproduction of the look. To be in keeping with the period style, opt for a white marble Adam-type surround, with steel fender and grate. Hang a large gilt-framed mirror or painting above the fireplace, and use the mantelpiece for display – fresh, cut flowers, a gilt clock, small pieces of china or figurines are all appropriate accessories.

Pale background colours are a good choice for the walls in a town house. Pastel shades of green, yellow, blue and peach offset the darker wooden furniture that is typical of the style, but you can add textural interest to plain walls with a paint effect such as marbling, dragging or ragging, which were all popular in the Georgian era. If your decorating skills do not stretch to paint techniques, there are plenty of wallpapers available that mimic these finishes. Wallpapers with discreet geometric patterning are also appropriate for the town house look; for a bolder design statement, choose either a Regency stripe paper or one with a traditional oriental pattern.

In the past, traditional and oriental rugs would have been thrown over simple polished wooden floorboards. These days it is perfectly acceptable, especially in drawing rooms and bedrooms, to opt instead for fitted carpets in soft, muted

shades, adding oriental rugs for decoration where appropriate. In a hallway or bathroom marble or wooden flooring can make a spectacular alternative. If the real thing is out of your price range, consider painting floorboards with a stencilled paint effect.

The window treatments for this interior style are typically fussy and very formal. If you are lucky enough to have tall, elegant windows, make the most of them by hanging full-length curtains, trimmed with fringing or braid, and topped with swags and tails or an elaborately shaped pelmet. For rooms with smaller proportions you can re-create an authentic town house look by using Austrian or festoon blinds with their pretty ruched shaping or classic Roman blinds. Plain damasks, stripes, large-scale floral fabrics or chinoiserie designs make excellent choices for windows.

Furniture for the town house is essentially very traditional in style. Antique or good reproduction pieces in hardwoods like mahogany, yew or rosewood are appropriate, especially in the style of Chippendale, Hepplewhite or Sheraton. Elegant daybeds and 'Grecian couches', with their classically shaped serpentine back and sides, would add a touch of authenticity. Suitable fabrics for upholstery include ornate damasks and brocades; favourite patterns are floral and oriental, as well as stripes.

*E*arly Georgian homes favoured strong, dark colours, and walls or wooden panelling were often painted in brown or olive green (left). Swagged and tailed curtains were popular, as were simple paired curtains hung from wooden or metal poles.

*P*iles of starched white lace and linen cushions create a crisp, elegant look in this town house bedroom (left). Antique shops generally have a good selection of old lace panels to choose from, or you could use pieces of new Chinese lace to make up cushions like these. Framed prints of classical friezes complete the look.

Oriental style

Fascination with oriental design began in the eighteenth century, when the first examples of porcelain, fabrics and furniture were brought back by explorers to the East. This fascination has continued ever since, and while a truly authentic Chinese or Japanese room may not always fit in with modern day-to-day Western lifestyles, it is simple enough, and perfectly acceptable to incorporate ideas from these two interior styles to create your own individual oriental look.

When it comes to the decoration of walls there are several different options to choose from. If you prefer the minimalist quality of the Japanese home you should stick to pale wood panelling or painted walls in soft neutral shades of white and cream. For a less severe look, more influenced by Chinese designs, go for combinations of blue and white – the classic colours of oriental porcelain. Many oriental-style wallpapers are available in these colours, from simple geometric patterns to highly decorative designs featuring the traditional motifs of willow trees, fishermen, bridges, bamboo groves and waterfalls; or you could use an oriental-style stencil to add decoration to plain painted walls. A third, more dramatic Mandarin-style interior can be created by choosing deep russet reds for walls. Again, several wallpaper designs suited to this look are available, which may even incorporate ornate gilt patterning.

Floorboards in the simple Japanese room are left plain or are covered with natural rush or sisal matting. Where the influence of Chinese design is stronger you should opt for one of the thick rugs typical of the country, with their large floral designs in pastel shades of beige, pink and blue.

More dramatic room schemes can take a plain deeply coloured carpet or one with a bold all-over oriental pattern.

Window treatments can differ considerably, depending on the type of look you are trying to create. Simple cane roller blinds would be a good choice for a Japanese room, or you could re-create the typical sliding paper blinds by sticking opaque paper to a delicate wooden framework. For a softer look choose silk or chintz fabrics to make up more formal curtain treatments. Depending on the interior style you are trying to create, you could opt for traditionally patterned blue and white fabrics, soft pastel shades or richly coloured and patterned fabrics hung from ornate gilded poles.

In the minimalist Japanese interior, furniture is also kept to the bare essentials. For true authenticity seating should be at or near floor level, simple in design and style. The futon is classically used for sleeping on, and can double up as seating during the day. For other oriental interiors modern bamboo – or pieces of antiqued fake bamboo – furniture looks perfect. Cane chairs coated in shellac to bring out the grain and give a shiny mirror finish are also appropriate, or you can go for the more dramatic look of red and black lacquered furniture, painted with oriental motifs. Screens are another typical furnishing – from the simple paper and wooden designs of Japan, to the more intricately carved wooden pieces of China. Classic porcelain, embroidered silk hangings and bonsai trees can be used to complete your oriental room.

A Japanese-style bedroom is calm and uncluttered. Colours are kept to a minimum – neutrals for the walls and floor with black accents on the woodwork and furniture. Cover a low bed or futon with plain white or cream bed linen in natural cottons.

english country cottage style

The unpretentious style of the English country cottage is characterized by simple, homely furnishings chosen as much for their practicality as for their charm. The small proportions of the cottage interior rule out any grand decorating schemes, and features should always be in keeping with the architectural style of the building itself. The dappled effect of colour-washing is ideal for genuine old walls, and will re-create the uneven qualities of rough plaster in a more modern interior. Neutral shades like buttermilk and stone give a light, airy feel; fresh pinks, yellows and greens re-create the mood of summer; and the warm tones of brick red, bottle green and ochre evoke a cosy wintery mood. In a tiny cottage room pattern is best kept to a minimum on the walls, but in a more spacious home all-over floral wallpapers can look very striking and effective.

Window treatments can be as simple as you like – in a true country cottage heavy, ornate drapes would not only look totally out of place, but would also obstruct the daylight. Fresh floral cottons, brightly coloured ginghams, heavy tapestry weaves or warm velvets can also be used to create an authentic country look; and sheer muslin, voile and antique lace make good choices for the bedroom and bathroom. Swags and tails are unsuitable for the humble proportions of the cottage window, but you can make good use of neat pelmets or prettily gathered valances. A plain wooden or metal pole, however, can look equally appropriate and will stop the effect from becoming over-elaborate.

It is quite acceptable for furniture to have a slightly battered appearance, so scour the local second-hand and antique shops for chairs and sofas in an eclectic mix of traditional shapes. By

using loose covers in matching or co-ordinating fabrics you can draw individual elements of the room together and give old furniture a new lease of life at the same time. Floral patterns in any size evoke the country cottage feel, but you could also make use of checked or plain fabrics. Decorate with plenty of cushions and wool throws, and for a really authentic look add lace or hand-embroidered antimacassars.

Nothing looks better in the country cottage bedroom than an old brass bedstead, and antique and reproduction versions are both relatively easy to get hold of. But it is how you dress the bed that really adds authenticity. Crisp white cotton or linen sheets are a must, and look particularly good when edged with delicate antique lace. In the past all beds would have been covered with bedspreads, painstakingly made by the women of the household. Choose patchwork, quilted or crocheted designs to re-create the look yourself, and add a layer of warmth with knitted blankets or fat feather eiderdowns. Window treatments can have a slightly more feminine look than in other areas of the home. Pretty lace panels, frilly-edged curtains or even softly ruched Austrian blinds are all in keeping with the country-cottage feel. Small bedrooms often look good when the walls, ceiling and windows are treated as one, with wallpaper and fabric in the same pattern.

*C*hoose pretty floral-print curtains in fresh colours for country cottage windows (above). Add a matching frill to soften the leading edges.

*O*pt for traditional designs in the English country cottage, such as this classic, comfy armchair. Loose covers are ideal for transforming old pieces of furniture – again, go for large or small floral prints.

*M*inimalist style

Minimalist interior styles are not for the faint-hearted, and certainly not for those who like to live amid a homely clutter and untidiness. As the name suggests, this style is one where both decoration and possessions are kept to the barest minimum, colour is limited to neutral creams and whites, and furniture, upholstery and equipment are all made of pure, uncompromising materials such as natural wood, stainless steel and chrome, leather and marble.

Taken to its extreme, the minimalist style is empty, with little or no visual distractions afforded by accessories, pictures or soft furnishings. However, since this look requires a somewhat fanatical self-discipline alien to most of us, it can be adapted into a slightly softer version while holding on to certain basic principles. Start by painting walls in neutral shades. Stark white can be too much in a large expanse, so for something that is easier on the eye opt instead for soft ivory, or the palest shades of pastels like grey, blue or beige. Polished wooden floorboards add a touch of colour and warmth. These can be left totally bare for an authentic touch, or softened slightly with the addition of rugs in traditional or modern designs; opt for neutral colours to maintain the calm, serene look of the interior.

As you might expect, window treatments for the minimalist interior are extremely plain and unfussy. Venetian blinds in plain white, steel or wooden finishes are probably the most appropriate – their slats can be closed to hide the untidy outside world from view, and create interesting abstract patterns on the floor as they filter sunlight through. Other suitable window treatments include paper or cane blinds, and translucent

neutral-coloured sheer fabrics made into very simple straight curtains.

One of the main principles of the minimalist look is to create a feeling of space, and for this reason furniture should be kept to the bare essentials. In a small room one simple sofa (upholstered in a plain neutral-coloured fabric, black or tan leather) and a couple of individual chairs is plenty. Avoid occasional tables altogether where possible for a true minimalist look, but if you are unable to do without one, choose a single, really beautiful design in glass or wood. Possessions like books, records and so on should be hidden from view in either built-in cupboards or a single plain piece of freestanding furniture. And in the bedroom a futon mattress to sleep on is the perfect choice – during the day it converts into a stylish simple sofa or can be folded away altogether into a cupboard for a totally uncluttered look.

The only accessories that the minimalist style will allow are single pieces of unusual modern or classical sculpture, an occasional isolated picture, and perhaps one or two striking houseplants, preferably with their own interesting and un-usual characteristics – like the yucca with its slightly surreal spiky leaves. Lighting is, of course, essential in any interior and can be used to create interesting visual effects. In the true minimalist interior, however, it should be dis-creet and unobtrusive – uplighters, downlighters and halogen spots are appropriate.

In this archetypal minimalist interior, window treatments are restricted to a plain cotton Roman blind and a series of simple but unusual window covers that can be swung open and closed.

TEXTURES AND PATTERNS

*U*se fabrics to introduce subtle textures and patterns into the minimalist interior. Textured natural weaves or self-patterned fab-rics in linen, cotton or wool are all appropriate, preferably in cream or white. Canvas and coarse cottons which have slight variations in the weave are also suitable, particularly for covering sofas and chairs.

*e*clectic style

Eclectic-style interiors are for those people who like to mix and match ideas to create a highly individualistic look, and for the real devotees it is as much a hobby as simply a decoration style. The lover of eclectic interiors has a nostalgia for the past and spends a lot of time collecting memorabilia of all kinds to display. This memorabilia may be put together in the most unlikely combinations – Art Deco furniture may sit alongside 1960s upholstery; a Georgian console table may be used to display a collection of childhood metal toys. Owners of these interiors like to break the rules and often do so in a joking, flippant manner.

With their inability to settle on any one particular style, devotees of the eclectic look are often highly sensitive to changes in the design climate and will readily incorporate elements of a new look into their homes alongside existing ones. Eclectic enthusiasts may, in fact, play an important part in popularizing innovations in mainstream design. They, for instance, were the first to recognize the beauty of Victoriana and Art Deco, helping to make them the sought-after collectors' items that they are today. Inspiration for new looks may come from all kinds of sources – a film, an exhibition or simply an individual's enthusiasm for a particular style.

While some eclectic interiors are individual to the point of being bizarre, there is no need to take things to such extremes. You can achieve a very successful look simply with a strong colour sense, an eye for display and the knack of seeing potential in unlikely items – for instance, shabby-looking furniture from junk shops that can be transformed with a lick of paint or new uphol-stery. Colour and pattern play an important part

in the eclectic look. Colours can be frivolous and even theatrical – strong shades of yellow, red, green and blue, for example, make the perfect backdrop for displaying objects. Patterns can be mixed in profusion, especially when you are trying to achieve a really dramatic look. Colour can also be used to link different elements of the room scheme together – for instance, a haphazard collection of junk-shop wooden chairs could all be painted in the same colour or decorated with a matching stencilled motif. Window treatments and soft furnishings are treated in the same way as other elements of the eclectic look, and may be a mix and match of several different styles from the past and present.

The important thing to remember when trying to re-create an eclectic interior is that things do not have to be perfect. The look can be built up slowly over many years as your collection of memorabilia grows, and when you tire of items you can simply replace them with new pieces suited to your mood at the time.

*E*thnic textiles, native artefacts and antique nineteenth-century furniture all work well together in this spacious, modern living room (left).

*T*his amusing pastiche on earlier window treatments (below) may be too individual for some tastes, but it is an excellent example of what can be achieved using simple and inexpensive materials and a bold approach.

Curtains

• •

Two very different treatments combine to striking effect in this bedroom (left). The toile de jouy Roman blind has, like the walls, been bound in deep red braid, and the heavy cream fabric used for the curtain contrasts well. The classic goblet heading has also been bound with red braid and trimmed with a smart twisted rope.

Simple neutral-coloured curtains can create a chic, sophisticated look (left). Use anything from cheap calico to more expensive fabrics. A fixed heading, slotted onto ordinary track, allows you to drape the curtains back in soft, elegant folds.

For a luxurious alternative to a standard shower screen, make up a full-length curtain to hang along the side of the bath (right). A separate plastic lining hooked on the inside of the curtain will make it more practical.

Curtains are an important element of any interior design scheme, and often form the focal point of a room. They immediately give a 'lived-in' look, and they can be used to create many different moods, from the elegance of swagged drapes to the rustic simplicity of sprigged cotton hung from rings on a wooden curtain pole. Curtains are also very practical: they provide privacy from the outside world, give effective insulation against both noise and the cold, and help to keep out the light (something that is of prime importance in a bedroom, for example).

The shape of the curtains and the fabric you choose will largely depend on personal taste, but it is important that both should suit the style and

*P*lain, full-length curtains in a bedroom are softened by a valance with an asymmetrical hemline and a smocked heading (right). The trim on the curtains picks up the colour scheme in the rest of the room.

proportions of the room where they are to be hung. Lavish, floor-length curtains with elaborate detailing, for instance, may be perfect in a town house with tall windows, but would look out of place in a country cottage with low-beamed ceilings. Similarly, crisp, tailored drapes in a plain fabric would be more at home than floral drapes in a masculine or modern room.

Curtains always look best hung to the floor rather than to the bottom of the windowsill. Curtains should always be long enough, and can either touch the ground or hang 2.5 cm (1 in) or 5 cm (2 in) above the floor. The only exceptions are curtains for deeply recessed cottage windows or bay windows, but even here there are more successful ways of treating such areas than with sill-length curtains. Roman blinds or festoon blinds work well, and dress curtains can always hang on the side.

*W*ith a rich, heavyweight fabric in a bold textural weave (right), keep the curtain treatment simple to show the material to its best advantage. Here, these fringed kelim curtains are hung from a classic wooden pole and draped softly to the sides of the window, held back by a thick rope tie.

These simple curtains hung on a pole are lifted out of the ordinary by the goblet heading and smart contrasting trim.

ETHNIC DESIGNS

E thnic, hand-woven or printed textiles are often highly patterned and come in a wonderful range of rich, deep colours. Used as inexpensive curtains, they will add a touch of theatre to a room, especially when half-drawn across a pair of tall, imposing windows or French windows. Such ornate fabrics look best if they are given simple curtain headings, such as a standard curtain heading or pencil pleats. Keep trimmings simple, too.

Curtains effectively 'dress' a window, and in the same way as clothes they can be cleverly used either to enhance or disguise certain features. If you have a window that looks out over a beautiful view, choose a curtain treatment that acts as a frame, leading the eye through to the view beyond. An unusually shaped window can be enhanced by opting for a treatment that outlines and defines the line of the frame. A small circular window, for example, could have a fabric-covered template of the shape which slots into place at night, allowing the maximum amount of light in during the day. When a window looks over-wide, you can compensate by taking the curtains up to the cornice and right down to the floor, or draping them so that they cover part of the glass even when the curtains are drawn back; in the same way, if a window appears too narrow you can make it look wider simply by extending the curtain rail beyond the frame.

The effect is stunning, but the treatment couldn't be simpler (right). Lengths of sheer fabric are artfully draped over curtain poles to frame part of the window area and to let in the maximum amount of light.

Transform a lightweight curtain with a simple cased heading (above) by adding a decorative border and trim to the lower edge.

Using full-length curtains on a tiny window tricks the eye into believing that the window itself is larger (right). Here, the curtains also give the room a better proportion.

There is a huge choice of fabrics suitable for curtains available today, with patterns, textures and weights to suit all tastes and pockets. Curtains do require quite a lot of fabric, so to avoid making costly mistakes it's always a good idea to take several small samples home to look at against other furnishings, paints and wallpapers before making your final decision. Be imaginative with your choice, but generally speaking classic colours and designs are very easy to live with and will stand the test of time much better than some bright, modern prints which may date very quickly. There are no set rules when it comes to choosing fabrics for specific curtain styles, but as a guide, damasks, heavy silks, velvets and linens all work well in traditional,

A pretty, feminine window treatment can be achieved using delicate layers of fabric (above). Here, lace curtains are placed behind floral chintz curtains; the half nets at the window also provide privacy.

For an understated look, hang floor-length lace curtains on a simple wooden pole with finials (right). Roller blinds could also be installed at the windows to pull down at night.

ALL WHITE

White as a home furnishing colour became popular during the 1920s and 1930s as a reaction against the use of over-rich colours in the previous centuries. An all-white colour scheme is wonderful used on its own or as a background to other furnishing colours. White has the effect of expanding a room, as it reflects bright light off surfaces and furniture. It emphasizes subdued tones of pale wood, and makes any bright colours stand out.

Corded and tasselled curtain tiebacks (above) can be found in most department stores and come in a wide range of colours and trimmings.

Traditional shaped tiebacks made of stiffened fabric are easy to make and trim. Add braid or piping to the outer edge, or sew on a large bow.

*T*his distinctive and formal window treatment is designed to frame the view beyond (right). The top area is softened by the introduction of a shaped pelmet with trumpets and bows, and is finished with a deep contrasting fringe.

formal treatments; richly textured, densely woven cloth is a good choice where insulation is important; fresh floral chintzes look perfect in country-style rooms and feminine interiors; and pale-coloured, self-patterned fabrics lend an elegant, sophisticated air in either classically styled rooms or those with modern decoration.

Fortunately, beautiful window treatments can be achieved without the use of expensive fabrics – even plain calico and ticking can appear opulent given the right finishing touches. Using a pelmet or valance is an effective way of emphasizing the style of a window. For instance, a softly pleated valance with a frilled edging is pretty and feminine; elaborate swags and tails, on the other hand, are elegant and formal. Even the style of heading you choose can greatly alter the appearance of drapes. Casual curtains can have simple gathered, bunched or slotted headings. Highly decorative French pleat or goblet

*A*dding colourful, patterned linings to plain curtains can look very stylish (above) – make sure that the curtain fabric is caught back to show off the design on the lining.

*T*hese pleated curtain valances (left) suit this bedroom well – the deep cream fringing and binding cleverly pick up not only the colours in the curtains but also the colours in the rest of the room.

*T*hese pencil-pleated valances (above) have been given longer sides to keep them in proportion with the windows, and are finished with a linen fringe.

CURTAIN VALANCE

A cleverly cut valance or swag defines the outline of a window. A valance is made from unstiffened fabric and it must be made in the same fabric as the curtains. The gently swagged or gathered fabric can have braid or a fringe to soften the edge and echo the trimming on the leading edges of the curtain underneath.

A self-bordered fabric gives an instant decorative effect to curtain treatments (right), especially when it is used on a valance. Here, the bordered fabric has also been made into tails which frame the curtain.

headings are a good choice for grander curtains. Lining a curtain is recommended if you want to protect the main fabric from strong sunlight and improve insulation. But it can also be used to add a decorative and luxurious touch to curtains. Why not consider using a bright contrasting colour or co-ordinating pattern that tones with the main fabric? Other very effective details include binding the edges of curtains with ribbon, fringing or cord, and using thick rope or matching fabric tiebacks to drape open curtains into full deep swags.

You can add a touch of fun to your curtain treatment by choosing either a traditional or modern curtain pole, depending on the style of the

Windows that look out over a beautiful view should be given special treatments that lead the eye beyond (below). A fringed swag and tails have been used here to form a frame for this leaded hall window. The bold floral fabric and plain velvet lining are in keeping with the country cottage feel.

Swags and tails at the windows complement the grand style of this living room (above). Such elaborate window treatments can be toned down and softened for less ornate rooms.

room. Classic wooden poles are often finished with carved finials in motifs taken from nature, such as acorns, pineapples and honeysuckle, while neo-classical inspired finials include urns and medallions. Wooden poles can be stained to look like mahogany, pine or rosewood, or they can be given a decorative paint finish. Finials for traditional metal poles include the fleur-de-lys and arrow heads. Chrome-finished steel poles look good in a contemporary room, or choose a wrought-iron design for a modern interior.

SWAGS AND TAILS

Proportion is the key when adding swags and tails to a window treatment. The high drama of a grand swag can only be produced in a room with tall, well-proportioned windows. The room must be able to contain the large areas of fabric needed for this type of arrangement – small rooms will only look smaller if the window area is allowed to be swamped with fabric.

*I*t does not work to have standard curtains with a fitted window seat (right). When drawn they may create an ugly crumpled look along the tops of the cushions. A smarter alternative is to fit a decorative pelmet or valance and place dress curtains that frame the shape of the window, creating a focal point.

*F*ull-length swags and tails can also be used to frame French windows and doors (right). Cording and tassels provide simple but effective trimmings.

tracks and headings

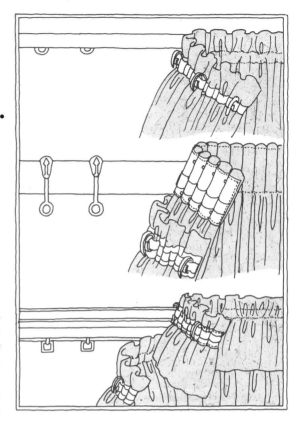

Curtains can make an important contribution to the decor of a room, so it is important to choose the right curtain track and curtain heading tape for the look you want. The curtains themselves are not difficult to make, but accurate measuring and cutting, and straight stitching, are essential.

CURTAIN TRACKS

There is a large range of curtain tracks from which to choose. They can blend into the background or be an additional decoration at the window. Tracks can either be fitted to the wall or, if there is insufficient space above the window, to the ceiling. Before you buy a curtain track, check that it can be easily fitted and can support the weight of your curtains. You should also make sure that you will still be able to open the window easily when the track and curtains are in position.

Curtain tracks are made in plastic, aluminium or steel, and most can be cut, bent or moulded to fit any window shape. Tracks are sold with the necessary fixtures and fittings. For more elaborate window treatments, combination tracks are available to hold valances and even swags and tails, as well as curtains.

Lightweight plastic or aluminium tracks for sheer and lightweight fabrics can be wall- or ceiling-mounted and are quickly cut to size with a small household saw. Multipurpose plastic or aluminium tracks can be easily bent round bow or bay windows. The hooks are mounted over the front of the track so you can hang a separate lining behind the curtains. Concealed tracks are the best type for curtains with deep headings, as the hooks hang down below the track. These tracks can be painted or covered in the same fabric as the curtains to blend into their surroundings. Steel curtain tracks are very strong and should be used when hanging heavy interlined curtains. They may need to be professionally installed if chosen for bay or bow windows. Combination tracks are made up of a series of

tracks and rails which can be slotted together to hold valances and curtains one in front of the other at the window.

FIXING A CURTAIN TRACK

The position of the curtain track above a window will influence the look and feel of the room.

*M*ake a window look longer by hanging the track higher above the frame (above). To add width, extend the track at each side (above right), and add height and width to make the window seem larger overall (right).

*P*encil-pleat headings (opposite) are one of the most popular headings for curtains.

SEE ALSO:

CONTEMPORARY STYLE   49

FABRIC FILE   9

A *curtain hung from a pole can provide an effective room divider. To create an interesting and dramatic visual effect, use contrasting fabric for the window areas.*

A longer-than-average curtain track over a small window will not only create the illusion of a wider window, but also means that the curtains can be drawn back to let in the maximum light. Give the impression of height by hanging the track above the window.

Always follow the manufacturer's instructions which come with every track. Position the tracks at least 5 cm (2 in) above the window and, depending on the curtain fullness, between 15 cm (6 in) and 40 cm (16 in) beyond the window on either side. If you cannot drill above the window because of a concrete lintel, fix a wooden batten, which only needs a few screws, above the window and attach the track to the batten with as many screws as necessary.

CURTAIN POLES AND RODS

Curtain poles are usually only used for straight curtain runs, although they can be fitted round bays and bows in sections. Poles are readily

available in wood, brass and ornate cast iron. They can be bought in sets or you can mix and match different components together. Decorative finials can be purchased separately and fixed to the end of plain poles.

Before buying a pole, try to visualize how it will look in its eventual setting. Make sure that you have sufficient brackets to support long poles or ones carrying heavy curtains.

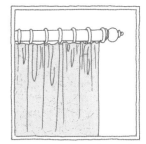

Curtain poles come in wood, brass and ornate cast iron. Each large curtain ring has a smaller ring attached at the base for holding curtain hooks.

Wooden poles can be plain or varnished in various shades of brown mahogany wood or in a small range of other colours. Alternatively, they can be painted or varnished at home. Brass or brass-finish poles can be smooth or reeded; narrow brass rods are a good choice for hanging sheer or net curtains with a cased heading. Curtain tracks fronted with half a pole to give the impression of a pole are also available. A simple smooth flat rod is often used for hanging valances; it can also be used for curtains with a cased heading, but they cannot be drawn.

Tension rods, made of plastic or metal, can be used across a recessed window – the internal spring holds the rod in place so no fitments are needed, making it easy to adjust the position.

Hinged portière rods are used for hanging curtains over doors – ideal for draughty rooms. As the door opens, the rod lifts the curtain out of the way.

FIXING POLES AND RODS

Again, follow the maker's instructions. Curtain poles are held on brackets fixed about 10 cm (4 in) in from the finials. The outer curtain rings are held between the bracket and the finials to hold the curtain in place when it is drawn.

ACCESSORIES

Of the range of accessories for tracks and poles, the most popular is a cording set which enables you to draw the curtains easily using a pulley cord. Draw rods, sold in pairs, are fitted behind

*T*aking curtains across the whole wall in a room creates a dramatic sense of theatre (above). During the day these triple-pleated curtains are elegantly tied back to reveal the windows and create interesting shapes in the drapery.

*M*ulti-layered treatments that mix pelmets, blinds and curtains work best on windows with large proportions (right).

the leading (centre) edge of the curtains and used to draw the curtains back and forth across the window. Electronic opening sets are also available, which can be operated on a time switch (useful for holiday security) or from an armchair using a hand-held remote control unit.

Overlapping arms can be added to some tracks so that a pair of curtains can overlap in the centre rather than meeting edge to edge.

CURTAIN HEADING TAPES

A heading tape determines the hang of a curtain. It is made of a strong material and stitched across the top of the wrong side of the curtain. It has integral cords which are pulled up together to pleat the curtain top. There are a variety of different types available in a range of widths to suit both long and short curtains. Before you buy any, check that the pleating effect will be compatible with the chosen fabric.

Standard heading tape: forms a softly gathered curtain heading.

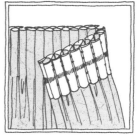

Pencil-pleat tape: creates crisp, uniform pleats for a tailored look.

Standard heading tape This 2.5 cm (1 in) wide tape gives a curtain a gentle pleated effect. It works best on curtains covered by a valance or pelmet or with lightweight fabrics in kitchens or bathrooms, where a structured curtain top is not necessary. You will need 1½ times the track length in fabric to achieve this heading. There is also a combined standard heading tape with two sets of cords. Pull up one set for traditional gathers, and the opposite set to create neat cluster pleats.

Pencil-pleat tape The most popular curtain heading tape, this can be bought in a good range of depths to suit most curtains. The fabric is pulled up into tailored pencil pleats. You will need 2 to 2½ times the track length in fabric.

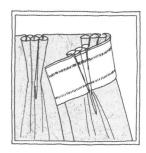

Triple-pleat tape: pulls up into a series of fan-shaped pleats.

Triple-pleat tape Also known as French-pleat tape, this tape is available in a range of depths.

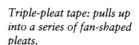

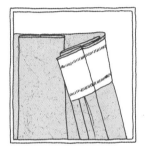

Cartridge-pleat tape: forms cylindrical pleats.

Box-pleat tape: creates neat, tailored pleats.

Cartridge- and box-pleat tape With these two heading tapes the fabric is pulled up to form cartridge or box pleats along the curtain top. With both these tapes you must make sure that the pleats will match in the centre. You will need 2 times the track length in fabric for these tapes.

*F*or a tailored look (left), stick to plain-coloured curtains with simple, classic headings such as triple pleats. Mounting curtains on a box-shaped track also helps to give a neat finish to the edge nearest the wall.

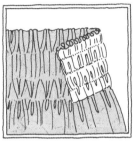

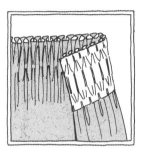

Smocked tape: pulls up to form traditional smocking.

Tudor ruff tape: creates a soft, ruffled effect.

Decorative tapes Choose from a range of totally different effects, such as smocking and ruff designs. These heading tapes look marvellous combined with sheer and plain fabrics. You will need 2 times the track length in fabric for these tapes.

The fabric is pulled up into groups of three fanned pleats. Work a few handstitches across the base of the pleat sets to give a professional touch. When making a pair of curtains, make sure that the groups of pleats will match across the centre of the curtains – begin each one half way between a set of pleats.

Triple pleats can also be formed with a plain heading tape and long pleat hooks. The hooks slot into pockets on the tape which pleat up the fabric. You will need 2 times the track length in fabric for these headings.

CHOOSING THE RIGHT FABRIC

Proper furnishing fabric is essential for hard-wearing curtains. Dress fabric can be used for unlined curtains provided it has a certain amount of body and is a suitable width. Choose a fabric that will not fade too quickly and make sure it drapes well. Check that any pattern or motifs are printed straight across the fabric.

If possible, buy a large sample of fabric before you commit yourself and hang it beside the window to see what it looks like in your room in artificial and daylight.

If you are unsure of your fabric estimates, ask the shop to check your calculations.

Goblet-pleat tape: forms goblet-shaped pleats spaced evenly apart.

Goblet-pleat tape For goblet pleat tape, you need twice the track length in fabric. You also need to evenly space the pleats across the centre of a pair of curtains. The fabric pulls up into cylindrical pleats with tapered stems, forming goblets.

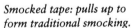

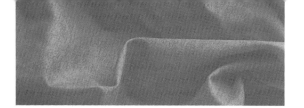

Unlined curtains

· ·

Unlined curtains are simple to make and ideal for kitchens and bathrooms, where the window covering needs regular washing and where eliminating light is of secondary importance. Unlined curtains will not hang as well as lined ones and will not provide the same insulation. Check that you make a right-hand and left-hand curtain when making pairs of curtains.

Materials

- Furnishing or dress fabric
- Curtain heading tape and hooks
- Matching sewing thread
- Cord tidy (optional)

Measuring up

- When measuring a window for curtains, always use a steel or wooden rule to measure, always fit the curtain track in position before you begin to measure for curtains, and give yourself adequate space to work so that the fabric widths and final curtain can be laid flat.

- Measure the length of the track, A. Multiply A by the fullness needed for the chosen heading, usually between 1½ and 3 times the finished curtain width, to find B.

- Divide the fabric width, usually 122 cm (48 in), into B to find the number of widths needed using the chosen heading. Divide this number by two when making a pair of curtains. If the figure is over half-way between two widths, round it up to the next full width. If the figure is under half a width extra, add a half width to each curtain, positioning the half widths at the outer edges, where they will be less obvious.

- Decide on the curtain length, C. Measure from the hook suspension point on the track down

SEE ALSO:
· ·
CONTEMPORARY STYLE   49
· ·
FABRIC FILE   9
· ·
SEWING GUIDE   200
· ·

Measuring windows for curtains.

to the sill, radiator or floor and subtract 1 cm (⅜ in). Add an extra allowance for hems and headings, depending on the type of curtains.

- Multiply C by the number of curtain widths required to make both curtains to find the required amount of fabric. If the fabric has a prominent pattern repeat, add one extra pattern repeat per fabric width.

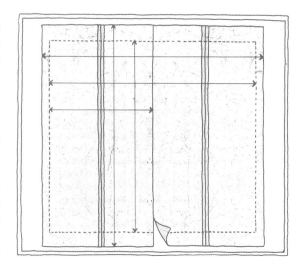

Basic unlined curtain: measure the curtain fabric carefully and recheck all your calculations before marking and cutting out.

Cutting out

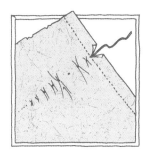

Straighten the raw edge of the fabric before cutting out curtain lengths.

- Straighten the raw edge of the fabric before you begin to cut out the curtain lengths. For some woven cottons and mixtures, just snip into the fabric for about 2.5 cm (1 in) and tear across the fabric. For wools and linens, snip across the selvedge, pull out a loose weft thread gently across the fabric width and then cut along the gap formed in the fabric.
- *Plain fabric* Use a large set square, or other square object, against a metre (yard) stick to make sure you cut out the fabric at right angles to the selvedge edge. Measure the first length up from the straightened edge on both sides of the fabric and mark. Hold a metre (yard) stick across the fabric matching up marks and mark a line across. Cut along the marked line. Cut all subsequent widths in the same way. For half widths, fold one full fabric width in half lengthways matching selvedges together. Press along fold. Unfold the fabric and cut along pressed line.

Cut out the fabric following the grain.

Match the main pattern on the hem edge.

- *Patterned fabric* Always cut out the fabric following the grain; if the pattern is large and printed badly off-grain, then cut out following the fabric pattern. Position the main pattern or motif on the hem edge of the curtain –

incomplete patterns are less obvious in the gathered heading. Mark along the base of the pattern repeat. Measure the hem allowance below this line and cut across the fabric at this mark. Measure from the cut edge to the correct length for the curtain on each side of the fabric and mark. Match marks together and cut across the fabric. Reposition the cut fabric length next to the uncut fabric, matching the pattern exactly across the edges. Cut across the uncut fabric for the second length. Cut all the fabric lengths in the same way. Cut out any half fabric widths in the same way as for plain fabric.

Create a dramatic effect by draping curtains of different fabrics in symmetrical sweeps across a window. To re-create this look you will need to use good-quality heavyweight fabrics that fall naturally into soft, full folds. The curtain in the foreground is purely decorative and can be left unlined.

1 Cut out fabric widths as described, allowing 18 cm (7 in) for base hem and heading and 4 cm (1½ in) at each side for side hems. Either cut off selvedge edges or snip the selvedge edges both sides of each width at regular 4 cm (1½ in) intervals to release the fabric and prevent puckering.

2 Pin, tack and stitch fabric widths together with flat fell seams. To make sure that patterned fabric is exactly matched across the seamlines, tack the fabrics together from the right side with ladder stitches. When all seams have been tacked, fold fabrics with right sides together and stitch seams in the usual way.

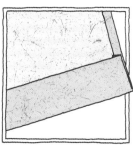

3 Turn in 2 cm (¾ in) down each side edge of curtain and press. Turn up 7.5 cm (3 in) across hem and press. Mitre base corners. Measure twice the base hem width and mark at side edges with a pin. Measure twice the side hem width and mark at base hem edge with a pin.

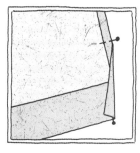

4 Press in the corner from pin to pin.

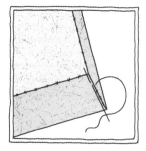

5 Turn up hem for 7.5 cm (3 in) and turn in side for 2 cm (¾ in) over the pressed-in corner to form a neat mitre. Slipstitch side and base hems, and across each mitred corner. Do not mitre corners on sheer fabrics as the turned-in corner will show through to the right side – just form a neat straight corner and then stitch.

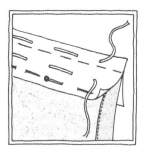

6 Turn down curtain top by width of curtain heading tape, trimming off excess fabric as necessary. Cut a length of curtain heading tape to curtain width plus 8 cm (3½ in). Place heading tape to wrong side of curtain top at required position, making sure raw edge of curtain is covered.

7 At the leading centre edge of curtain, pull out cords on wrong side of tape for 4 cm (1½ in) and knot. Turn under tape end in line with edge of curtain. At outside edge, pull out cords from right side of tape. Turn under tape end, avoiding cords, in line with curtain edge.

8 Pin, tack and stitch heading tape in place, catching down cords at inner edge but leaving them free on outer edge.

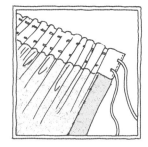

9 Gently pull up cords fully from outer edge, then ease out gathers until curtain measures correct width. Knot cords together and wind up excess cord and hold on a cord tidy at curtain edge. Do not cut off cords, as the heading tape will need to be released when laundering the curtains.

10 Slot hooks through heading tape about 8 cm (3½ in) apart, with a hook at each end.

VARIATION: A DETACHABLE LINING

Detachable linings are made in the same way as unlined curtains. A special lining tape is fitted to the top of the lining curtain – in the most commonly used type, the raw fabric edge is slotted between the halves of the tape and stitched in place. The lining is hung by hooks slotted first through the lining tape, then through the main curtain heading and onto the track.

If the curtains are long, you may have to add small ties, press fasteners or strips of touch-and-close fastening tape to hold the bottom half of the lining against the curtain.

Stitch the raw edge of the fabric between the halves of the lining tape.

lined curtains

Linings add body and weight to curtains as well as excluding light and improving insulation. A lining will also extend the life of a curtain, by protecting it from light, dust and dirt, so pick a good quality fabric. A poor quality lining will wear badly and need replacing before the curtain fabric. Cotton sateen is the most commonly used curtain lining. It is a tightly woven fabric and available in white and neutral shades as well as a good range of colours. Either choose a colour that blends with or matches the curtain colour or go for a neutral tone.

Thermal linings are a good choice for older homes, which may have draughty windows. They keep the heat in during the winter months and out during the summer. There are different types to choose from, usually in plain colours with silvered or thickened backing.

Blackout linings are also available. Neutral in colour, as well as having thermal qualities, they totally exclude all light so are a good idea for bedrooms of small children and night workers. This type of lining will also help to reduce outside noise.

It may be necessary to add weights to the corners of the curtains to help them keep their shape and hang well. Corner weights are made in a range of sizes and look like buttons with two central holes.

Materials

- Furnishing fabric
- Furnishing lining fabric
- Corner weights (optional)
- Curtain heading tape and hooks
- Matching sewing thread

SEE ALSO:

CONTEMPORARY STYLE 49

FABRIC FILE 9

SEWING GUIDE 200

UNLINED CURTAINS 92

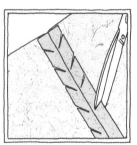

Heavy lined curtains provide extra insulation, especially at a large window area.

Making up

2 Cut out and stitch lining widths together as before (*see* Unlined Curtains), but do not snip into seam allowance.

1 Measure and cut out sufficient fabric widths for each curtain (*see* Unlined Curtains). Pin and stitch widths together with plain flat seams. Match any pattern across seamlines and across a pair of curtains. If necessary, tack widths together with ladder stitch. Press seams open and clip into selvedge at regular intervals.

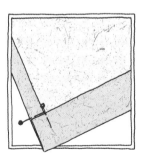

3 Press under a 5 cm (2 in) hem down both side edges of curtain. Mark where side hem falls on base edge with a pin. Turn up a single 10 cm (4 in)

hem along base edge and press. Mark where base hem falls at side edge with a pin. Unfold hems and mitre base corners by pressing in each corner from pin to pin (*see* Unlined Curtains).

4 Refold hems over pressed-in corner. Herringbone stitch the hems in place all round curtain, side edges and base edge.

A contrasting patterned lining can look very stylish – to display it, the leading edges of the curtains should be caught back slightly.

5 If necessary, handsew a weight inside the corner of each hem, stitching it to the hem only so that the stitching will not show on the right side.

6 Lay curtain fabric flat, wrong side up. Place lining centrally on top, with wrong sides together, matching top edges. Pin the two layers together down centre of curtain. Turn back lining over pins and lockstitch both fabrics together to just above hem. Turn back lining, and if necessary add further rows of lockstitching on either side of centre, spacing rows about 40 cm (16 in) apart.

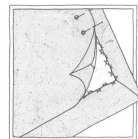

7 Trim down side edges of lining, to match side hem edges of curtains. Turn under 2.5 cm (1 in) on side edges of lining; pin. Turn under 5 cm (2 in) on base edge of lining, mitring the base corners. Slipstitch lining to fabric down sides and along base edge.

8 Treat both fabrics as one when adding heading tape. Stitch heading tape to top edge of curtain in the same way as for unlined curtains (*see* Unlined Curtains). Pull up heading tape cords and hang curtains.

RECYCLED LININGS

Good-quality lining can be recycled from old curtains and reused to line curtains for smaller windows. Unpick the lining from the old curtain and wash. Cut away the worn sections along the seam and hem lines, then join and cut the lining for the new pair of curtains. Alternatively, use the old curtain fabric as a lining. This will help to cut the cost of a new pair of curtains.

VARIATION: INTERLINED CURTAINS

Adding an extra layer of material between the curtain fabric and the lining gives a professional finish to a curtain as well as providing extra insulation at the windows. Interlining is available in various weights. The heaviest, bump, is a coarse-woven brushed cotton. Domette, which is either bleached or unbleached, is also brushed cotton but not so thick. A bonded synthetic interlining is also available, which, although probably easier to work with, is less effective.

Interlinings are lockstitched to the wrong side of the fabric before the hems are turned. Cut the interlining to the finished size of the curtains. After the interlining has been lockstitched to the fabric, hem and add the lining as before.

$h$andmade heading

Handmade curtain headings are generally based on the goblet or French pleat. However, simple gathered headings, box pleats and even pencil pleats can be created by hand. Before heading tapes were readily available, these styled headings were all pleated by hand. This handmade goblet heading can be trimmed with decorative braiding to finish.

Materials

- Furnishing fabric
- Furnishing lining fabric
- Matching sewing thread
- Strip of stiffening such as buckram
- Tailor's chalk
- Curtain hooks

Measuring up

- Fix the curtain track in position at the window before measuring for the curtains.

- For the curtain length, measure from the track to the required length, adding 14 cm (5½ in) for heading and hem. For the width of the curtains, measure the curtain track and multiply by 2. For both curtain widths, add 4 cm (1½ in) for each side hem and 3 cm (1¼ in) for each seam if joining fabric widths together to gain the required curtain width.

- For the lining, you will need the same amount of fabric as for the main curtain fabric.

SEE ALSO:

FABRIC FILE   9

LINED CURTAINS   95

SEWING GUIDE   200

Making up

1 Cut out fabric widths to required size. Seam together to make each curtain to size. Cut out and make up the lining in the same way. Lockstitch lining to wrong side of curtain and complete hems (*see* Lined Curtains).

2 Cut a strip of stiffening slightly deeper than the goblet-pleat depth, approximately 10–12 cm (4–5 in), and the same width as the finished curtain. Press down hem allowance along top edge of curtain.

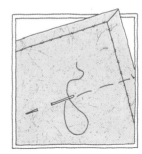

3 Turn back top edge of lining and slip stiffening inside and tuck underneath curtain hem. Trim stiffening so edges are level with side and top edges of curtain. Turn under top raw edge of lining, 1.3 cm (½ in) below curtain top; pin and slipstitch to curtain. Tack across curtain underneath edge of stiffening.

4 You will need to work out how many pleats and the size of spaces between the pleats for each curtain. Divide the width measurement of the prepared flat curtain in half, subtract 5 cm (2 in), and then divide the remaining space into even spaces between 10 cm (4 in) and 12.5 cm (6 in) to give the number of pleats.

5 Calculate the space needed between each pleat: take the half-width measurement less 5 cm (2 in) as before, and divide by the number of spaces needed – for example, if there are 4 pleats, you will need to allow for 3 spaces.

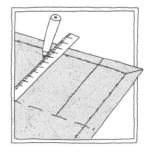

6 Using a ruler and tailor's chalk, mark 5 cm (2 in) in from each edge and then mark the position of each pleat and space with vertical lines on the wrong side of the fabric. Each vertical line should be the same length as the stiffening fabric.

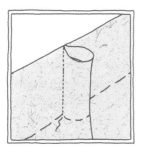

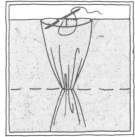

7 At each pleat position, bring the two vertical lines with wrong sides together, forming a single large pleat. Pin and stitch from top edge of curtain to base of stiffening. Check that stitching is at right angles to curtain top. Stitch each pleat in the same way.

9 To form the goblet shape, fan out the top of the pleat. Catch top edge of pleat to top edge of curtain, 1.3 cm (½ in) on either side of centre stitching line. Position a hook at each pleat.

8 Pinch and fold together the base of each pleat, creating three or four smaller pleats, and work a few hand stitches over the base of the pleat.

VARIATION: HANDMADE TRIPLE-PLEAT HEADING

To create triple pleats, increase the size of each pleat to approximately 15 cm (6 in). Form each pleat into three smaller pleats at the top of the curtain and catch to the curtain top with a few hand stitches at both ends of the stiffening. At the lower edge of the stiffening, pinch the pleats firmly together and stitch in place.

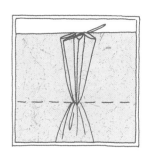

A SIMPLE LACE HEADING

*S*how off a piece of heavy cotton lace on a very simple lightweight curtain. Fit a slim curtain rod across the window. The curtain should measure the same width as the rod plus 4 cm (1½ in) for seams, and the length from the rod to the floor plus 7 cm (2¾ in). Remember to deduct the depth of the lace section from the curtain fabric length. Lay the lace over the top of the curtain, about 1 cm (⅜ in) overlapping, and pin and stitch round the lower edge, following the line of the lace design. Trim away the excess fabric and lace and stitch along the outline again, covering the raw edges with zigzag stitch. Turn under a double 1 cm (⅜ in) hem down each side edge and a double 3 cm (1¼ in) hem, mitring the corners. Turn over a narrow double hem at the top edge of the lace to form the top heading and stitch. Handsew small curtain rings along the top edge and thread onto the rod.

Café curtains

As café curtains only fit over the bottom half of the window, they are generally used in kitchens, where they give some privacy but also let in plenty of light through the top half of the window. The top heading of these curtains can be finished in different ways. To create a scallop heading, as here, the top edge of the curtain is folded over to form a self facing.

If you need to join curtain widths together to achieve the chosen width, stitch together with flat fell seams.

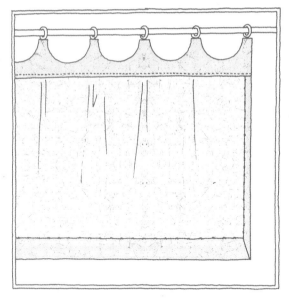

Café curtain with scalloped heading: hang from a narrow wooden or brass curtain rod.

Materials

- Paper for pattern
- Strip of interfacing
- Furnishing fabric
- Matching sewing thread
- Curtain rings

Measuring up

- The finished width of the curtain is generally the same width as the curtain pole, but it can have fullness added if liked, about 1½ to 2 times the width of the pole. Add 4 cm (1½ in) for each side hem. Measure finished depth of curtain and add 7.5 cm (3 in) for base hem. Decide on the scallop depth and allow an extra 7.5 cm (3 in) for the facing. The interfacing should be a 6.5 cm (2⅝ in) strip the same width as the curtain.

Making up

1 Cut out a piece of paper to the finished width of the curtain by the depth of the scallop plus 7.5 cm (3 in). Fold in half widthways.

(1¼ in) apart in between. Slightly increase the size of the scallops or tabs to take up any left-over space. Cut out the pattern.

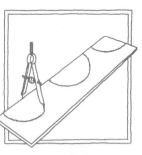

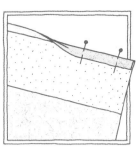

2 Use a small plate, saucer or pair of compasses to mark the scallops, about 10 cm (4 in) wide and 3 cm (1¼ in) apart across the pattern. Leaving 4 cm (1½ in) at the side, position the centre of the first scallop over the centre fold and the others spaced about 3 cm

3 Cut out a strip of iron-on interfacing to the depth of facing, 7.5 cm (3 in) less 1 cm (⅜ in) and the width of the curtain. Fuse to the wrong side of curtain 1 cm (⅜ in) below curtain top. Turn down 1 cm (⅜ in) hem over the interfacing; pin and stitch.

SEE ALSO:

CONTEMPORARY STYLE   49

FABRIC FILE   9

LINED CURTAINS   95

SEWING GUIDE   200

UNLINED CURTAINS   92

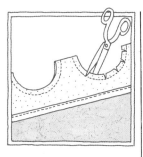

4 Turn right side of facing to wrong side of curtain; pin. Place pattern to top folded edge, matching centres. Mark round scallops. Stitch all round marked outline. Trim off excess fabric, leaving 6 mm (¼ in) round scallops and snipping into fabric round curves. Turn right side out and press.

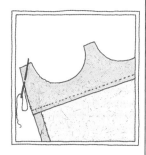

5 Turn in a double 2 cm (¾ in) hem down each side of curtain and turn up the base hem (*see* Unlined Curtains). Slipstitch in place. Slipstitch side edges of curtain and facing together.

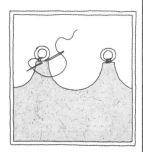

6 Buttonhole stitch a curtain ring to centre of each tab.

VARIATION: CAFÉ CURTAIN WITH TABS

As an alternative to a scalloped heading, tabs can be made from contrasting fabric or ribbon and set in between the curtain and a plain straight-edged facing.

Measure round the curtain pole with a cloth tape measure to gauge the correct length of the tabs; remember to allow 3 cm (1¼ in) for turnings plus enough space for the tabs to move freely along the pole. For each tab you will need two pieces of fabric twice the length of the finished tab height, plus 3 cm (1¼ in) for seams; decide on the width and add 2.5 cm (1 in) for side seams. For example, for a tab 5 cm (2 in) wide and about 11.5 cm (4½ in) long, you will need two pieces of fabric, each measuring 7.5 × 24 cm (3 × 9½ in). The tabs should be spaced about 15 cm (6 in) apart.

Materials

- Furnishing fabric
- Contrasting fabric or ribbon for tabs
- Strip of interfacing
- Matching sewing thread

Making up

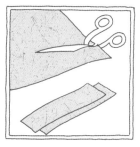

1 Cut out café curtain to size as before, omitting extra for facing, but adding 1.5 cm (⅝ in) for top seam. Cut out the required number of tabs.

2 Place tab pieces in pairs, with right sides together; pin and stitch side edges. Trim and turn right side out.

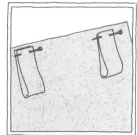

3 Fold tabs in half widthways and position raw edges together at each marked position across curtain top, with one placed just in from outside edge. If using ribbon, cut to correct length, fold in half and place as for tabs.

4 Cut a straight fabric facing, 10 cm (4 in) deep and as wide as the curtain, plus 2 cm (¾ in) for side hems. Fuse a strip of interfacing to the wrong side of facing. Turn under side and base edges of facing for 1 cm (⅜ in); pin and stitch. Place facing centrally to right side of curtain over tabs. Pin and stitch top edge of facing, catching in tabs. Turn right side out and press. Finish curtain hems as before.

- For the top casing, measure round the rod or pole and double the measurement. For a covered wire, allow for twice its circumference.

Making up

1 Cut out sufficient curtain widths in fabric. Pin and stitch widths together with flat fell seams. Turn under double hems on side and base edges; pin and stitch.

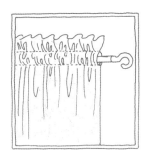

2 Turn under a double hem the required depth, along top. Pin and stitch across close to fold edge. Stitch across again, close to hem fold. Thread with covered stretch curtain wire and hang at the window.

A simple and economical way to hide shelving and storage areas – choose any lightweight fabric for the curtaining and thread curtain wire through the cased heading.

Café curtains are ideal for kitchen windows and are best made in a lightweight cotton.

CASING FOR SHEER CURTAINS

A simple cased heading may be all that is needed at the top of a plain sheer curtain. Casings can be added to both the top and the lower edge of a sheer curtain if the curtain is to be held against a window or behind a glass-fronted cupboard door. Extra fabric can be added above the casing and this will form a frill when the casing is gathered up on the curtain wire or curtain rod.

Materials

- Sheer curtain fabric
- Matching sewing thread
- Covered stretch curtain wire

Measuring up

- Measure in the same way as for unlined curtains (*see* Unlined Curtains), allowing 2.5 cm (1 in) for each side hem and 8 cm (3½ in) for base hem.

Arched window

● ●

If an arched window needs to be curtained, it will look best if the curtain follows the line of the arch. This type of curtain will not draw back from the window, but may be draped back during the day with a tieback.

Materials

- Furnishing fabric
- Specialist touch-and-close pencil-pleat curtain heading tape
- Matching sewing thread

Measuring up

- For the curtain length, measure from the highest point of the window to the chosen length, adding 18 cm (7 in) for heading and hem. For the curtain width, measure the widest part of the arch and add 8cm (3½ in) for side seams.

- For the self-adhesive 'grip' half of the touch-and-close tape, measure round the arched part of the window frame. For the pencil-pleat half of the tape, measure the width of the curtain and double the amount.

SEE ALSO:
● ●
FABRIC FILE   9
● ●
SEWING GUIDE   200
● ●
UNLINED CURTAINS   92
● ●

Making up

 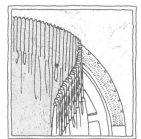

1 Fix the self-adhesive 'grip' half of the touch-and-close tape round the arched part of the window frame. Snip into the top edge of the tape so it curves to fit round the window.

2 Cut out and make up the curtain in the same way as for unlined curtains (*see* Unlined Curtains). Leave base hem unstitched and stitch the heading tape half of the touch-and-close tape across the top of the curtain.

3 Pull up gathering cords on heading tape and fit curtain in place by pressing heading tape to 'grip' tape round window.

4 Pin across base of curtain at chosen length. Remove curtain from window and ungather heading tape before marking and trimming hem edge. Trim off excess fabric, leaving 15 cm (6 in) hem allowance. Turn up hem and stitch as for unlined curtains. Replace gathered curtain at window, pressing tapes together.

ARCHED WINDOWS

Articulated tracks are available for arched windows. Fix the curtain track in place round the window, following the manufacturer's instructions. Alternatively, fix screw eyes into the wooden frame all round the window, spacing them approximately 4–6 cm (1½–2½ in) apart. Add a curtain heading tape to the top of the curtain. Pull up. Fix hooks into the heading tape at the same intervals as the screw eyes round the window and slot together.

Shower curtains

• •

Shower curtains are easy to make and there is a wide range of speciality fabrics available. Shower curtains can be hung either following the edge of the bath or to form a cubicle round the shower area. Stitching can weaken plastic fabrics, so fabric widths should be joined with French seams, which will be stronger and more watertight. Do not pin or tack shower curtains as this will make unnecessary holes; instead, hold the fabric pieces together with small pieces of adhesive tape or paper clips. For a more decorative effect, a second, outer curtain can be attached to the top of the shower curtain, which then remains outside the bath.

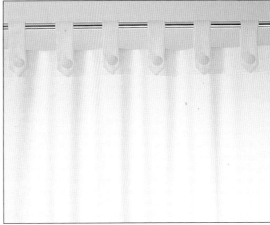

A range of headings can be used for shower curtains. Here, a tab heading is finished with matching decorative buttons.

Materials

- Shower curtain rail with clip-on rings
- Shower curtain fabric
- Matching synthetic sewing thread
- Adhesive tape or paper clips
- Eyelet kit with 1 cm (³⁄₈ in) diameter eyelets

Measuring up

- Measure the length of the shower rail and allow for 1½ times this measurement for the curtain width. Measure from the base of the shower rail to halfway down the side of the bath or to the base of the shower tray for the curtain length, plus a 17 cm (6½ in) allowance for hems.

Making up

1 Fix shower rail in position following the manufacturer's instructions. Cut out as many fabric widths as necessary to the correct length. Stitch fabric widths together with French seams. Turn in 2.5 cm (1 in) hems on side and base edges. Turn in base corners diagonally across corner point. Refold hems for 2.5 cm (1 in) to form a double hem. Hold in place with adhesive tape or paper clips. Stitch hems all round.

adhesive tape or paper clips. Stitch across hem and across each end. Following the manufacturer's instructions, fix the eyelets through the triple hem, spacing them about 12–15 cm (5–6 in) apart.

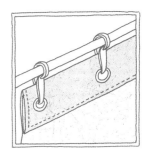

3 Hang curtain by slotting clip-on rings through eyelets and attaching to rail.

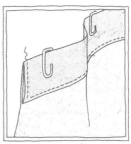

2 Turn down top edge for 4 cm (1½ in) three times, to form a triple hem. Hold in place with

SEE ALSO:
• • • • • • • • • • • • • • • • • •
FABRIC FILE   9
• • • • • • • • • • • • • • • • • •
SEWING GUIDE   200
• • • • • • • • • • • • • • • • • •

jardinière curtain

This simple one-piece net curtain with a deep base frill curves up gently in the centre. The frill, about 12–18 cm (5–7 in) deep, is stitched to the right side of the curtain and the stitching is covered with ribbon or braid. The curtain is suspended from a covered curtain wire or a thin curtain pole.

Materials

- Curtain pole or covered stretch curtain wire
- Sheer curtain fabric
- Matching sewing thread
- Dressmaker's marking pen
- Narrow ribbon, cord or braid

Measuring up

- Measure the length of the curtain pole or wire and allow twice this measurement for the curtain width. Measure from the wire to the sill for the curtain length. Deduct the frill depth and then add 7 cm (2¾ in) for top heading and base seam.

- Allow twice the curtain width for the frill width and add 2.5cm (1 in) hem allowance to the chosen depth.

SEE ALSO:

CONTEMPORARY STYLE   49

FABRIC FILE   9

SEWING GUIDE   200

Making up

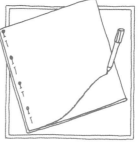 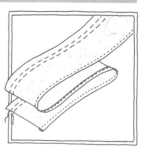

1 Fix a covered wire or curtain pole across the window inside the frame. Cut out as many fabric widths as necessary to the correct length. Pin, tack and stitch lengths together with a narrow flat fell seam. To shape lower edge of curtain, fold curtain in half widthways and pin edges together. Using a dressmaker's marking pen, draw a line from the outer edge of the curtain base across and up to the centre fold in a gentle curve. Check the effect, then cut along marked line. Unfold curtain.

3 To make frill, turn under a double 6 mm (¼ in) wide hem all round outer edge; pin and stitch. Run two rows of gathering stitches 3.5 cm (1¼ in) below top edge. Lay curtain flat, right side up. Position frill on right side of curtain. Pull up gathers evenly to fit curtain; pin and stitch in place through centre of gathers. Pin ribbon, cord or braid over stitching, turning under ends in line with side edges of curtain; topstitch in place along both edges of ribbon.

4 Thread wire through top casing and hang at the window.

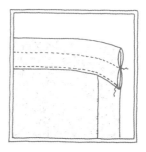

2 Turn under a double 1 cm (⅜ in) hem along side and lower edges of curtain; pin and stitch. For top casing, turn down a double 2.5 cm (1 in) hem. Pin and stitch across hem base. Stitch across hem again to form a casing wide enough for the wire. The fabric above the casing will gather up into a frill.

Cross-over curtains

These sheer curtains are made from two identical frilled curtains layered one on top of the other and swept back separately across opposite sides of the window. The fabric above the casing gathers up into a frill. A pair of tiebacks in matching or co-ordinating fabric will hold the curtains neatly on either side of the window. The curtains can hang on a thin curtain pole or a covered wire. Alternatively, make up the sheer curtains as for ordinary curtains, but with a cased heading, and tie them back with ribbon or decorative tiebacks.

Materials

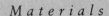

- Curtain pole or covered stretch curtain wire
- Sheer fabric
- Matching sewing thread

Measuring up

- Measure the length of the curtain pole or covered wire and allow for 2½ times this measurement for the curtain width. Measure from the pole to the sill for the curtain length, deduct about 8 cm (3½ in) for frill and then add 16.5 cm (6½ in) for top casing and seams.

- For each 11.5 cm (4½ in) wide frill strip allow twice the length of the combined measurement of both sides and base edge of each curtain.

SEE ALSO:

CONTEMPORARY STYLE   49

FABRIC FILE   9

SEWING GUIDE   200

Making up

1 Fix curtain pole or covered wire in position at window following the manufacturer's instructions. Make up two curtains, each one in the same way. Cut out sufficient fabric widths, to the required length, to make up the curtain width. Pin and stitch the widths together with flat fell seams.

2 Cut out the frill strips. Pin and stitch short edges together into one long length with flat fell seams. Turn under a double 6 mm (¼ in) hem on side and lower edges of frill forming neat base corners; pin and stitch. Run two lines of gathering stitches along top edge of frill.

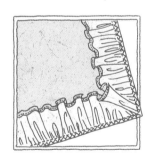

3 Position frill on curtain with right sides together. Pull up gathers evenly so frill fits side and base edges of curtain. Pin and stitch. Trim down seam allowances and zigzag stitch raw edges together to neaten.

4 Place curtains right side up, one on top of the other. Form the top casing with both curtains. Turn down top edges for 8 cm (3½ in). Turn under raw edge for 1 cm (⅜ in); pin and stitch across hem. Stitch across hem again 3 cm (1¼ in) above first row of stitching to form casing for pole or wire.

5 Thread pole or wire through casing and hang at window. Make up two tiebacks from the same fabric, adding frills as necessary. Pull back each curtain across the window and secure with a tieback.

tiebacks

· ·

Tiebacks are practical, holding the curtains back from the windows to let the maximum amount of light flood into the room. They are also decorative and can be made in a variety of styles and a huge range of shapes. A heavyweight interfacing or buckram, either sewn or fused in place, is used to stiffen them.

Piping and frills can be added to the outer edge of a tieback – simply make up the covered piping cord or frill and attach round the outer edge in the same way as for a cushion cover. Tiebacks can be quilted and the edges bound with matching or contrasting binding. Tubes of wadded fabric can be plaited to make soft tiebacks. By using a length of the same decorative heading tape that is used for the curtains, an attractive curtain tieback is quickly and easily created. Rosettes of fabric can be stitched to the end of the tieback for a more elaborate effect.

TRADITIONAL SHAPED TIEBACK
· ·

These plain tiebacks have the traditional shape with gently rounded ends. The outer edges can be finished in a variety of ways depending on the curtain style.

Materials

- Paper for pattern
- Furnishing fabric
- Heavyweight interfacing
- Four curtain rings
- Matching sewing thread

SEE ALSO:
· ·
CONTEMPORARY STYLE   49
· ·
FABRIC FILE   9
· ·
SEWING GUIDE   200
· ·

Measuring up

To find the finished length of the tieback, measure round the drawn-back curtain.

- Using a cloth tape, measure round the drawn-back curtain at the point chosen for the tieback to find the finished length. This depends on the amount of fullness you want to have. Decide on the width, generally between 10 cm (4 in) and 15 cm (6 in). Add 1.5 cm (⅝ in) seam allowance all round.

- Cut out a piece of paper to the finished length and depth of the tieback. Fold in half widthways. Working from centre fold, gently curve up base line to form a rounded edge. Cut out the pattern and unfold. Pin it round the curtain to gauge the effect and adjust its size and shape if necessary.

PLAITED TIEBACK

A simple three-strand plait is formed with wadded tubes of fabric and fastened at each end to form an attractive tieback.

*T*raditional tiebacks can be trimmed with frills or piping along the outer edge.

Materials

- Furnishing fabric
- Medium-weight wadding
- Four curtain rings
- Matching sewing thread

Measuring up

- Measure round the curtain as before. You will need six strips of fabric and six strips of wadding, each one 1½ times the finished tieback length and 13 cm (5⅛ in) wide.

Making up

 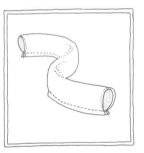 

1 Cut out six strips of fabric and six strips of wadding. Tack one strip of wadding to wrong side of each strip of fabric. Fold each strip in half lengthways, right sides facing; pin and stitch long edge. Trim and turn right side out. Press with seams over centre. Turn in raw edges at each end and slipstitch together to close.

2 For each tieback, place three tubes with seams underneath. Overlap one end of each, and stitch together to hold. Plait the three tubes into a conventional plait. Overlap these ends in the same way and handstitch together.

3 Handsew a curtain ring to each end of plait as before.

Making up

1 Using pattern, cut out four pieces of fabric, adding 1.5 cm (⅝ in) seam allowance all round, and two pieces of interfacing.

2 Pin one interfacing centrally to wrong side of one piece of fabric. Herringbone stitch interfacing to fabric, picking up only one thread of fabric with each stitch. If using an iron-on interfacing, fuse it centrally to wrong side of one piece of fabric.

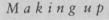

3 Place a second piece of fabric to first with right sides together; pin and stitch together all round following outline of the interfacing and leaving an opening in base edge for turning. Trim edges, clip curves and turn tieback right side out. Turn in opening edges and slipstitch together to close.

4 Handsew a curtain ring to each end of tiebacks, so the rings just overlap the ends.

TIEBACK WITH HEADING TAPE

Stitching a length of heading tape to the wrong side of a strip of fabric is a quick way to achieve a decorative tieback for plain curtains or a matching tieback on curtains with a similar heading.

Materials

- Furnishing fabric
- Decorative curtain heading tape
- Four curtain rings
- Matching sewing thread

Measuring up

- Measure round the curtain as before and double this measurement. You will need two pieces of fabric to this length plus 5 cm (2 in) by the depth of the heading tape plus 8 cm (3½ in).

- For the heading tape, you will need two pieces the same length as the fabric lengths plus 5 cm (2 in) to neaten.

Making up

1 Cut out two pieces of fabric to the required size and two pieces of heading tape. Press in long edges of fabric for 4 cm (1½ in). Press in short ends for 2.5 cm (1 in), forming neat corners.

of fabric, matching tape ends to ends of fabric; pin and tack. Stitch tape to fabric, catching down knotted cords at one end, but leaving them free at the other end.

2 Knot the cords at one end of heading tape. Turn under tape ends for 2.5 cm (1 in). Place tape centrally over wrong side

3 Pull up cords to pleat up fabric. Tie cords together. Wind up excess cords and catchstitch to end of tieback. Handsew on curtain rings as before.

ROSETTES

Two frills of different widths are layered together with a self-covering button as the centre.

Materials

- Furnishing fabric
- Self-covering button
- Matching sewing thread

Measuring up

- You will need one piece of fabric 56 × 12 cm (22 × 5 in) for the outer frill, and a piece 40 × 10 cm (16 × 4 in) for the inner frill.

Making up

1 Pin and stitch short edges of outer frill together into a ring. Press seam open. Fold in half lengthways with wrong sides together. Run a gathering thread round the raw edges, taking larger-than-average stitches; pull up tightly to form a rosette and fasten off.

2 Make up inner frill in the same way.

3 Cover button with fabric. Place inner frill over outer frill, matching centres; handsew together in centre, then stitch covered button over centre to finish.

$\mathcal{P}$elmets

. . . .

Pelmets are an attractive way of concealing curtain tracks and tops of curtains, and can also be used to fill the dead light between the window and the ceiling. The pelmet box itself – a wooden shelf, which can also have a front shaped panel – is usually covered with a stiffened piece of fabric. Traditionally, fabric pelmets are a sandwich of fabric, stiffening and lining or they can have an additional layer of interlining to give a soft rounded appearance.

For the stiffening, use either the traditional buckram or a modern self-adhesive stiffener. The backing of the self-adhesive version is marked with both a measured grid to help to plot your own design together with a few suggestions which can be copied.

Pelmets are generally one-sixth of the curtain length, so allow for about 5 cm (2 in) of pelmet per 30 cm (12 in) of curtain.

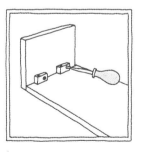

Pelmets: braiding in a contrasting colour accentuates the shape of a pelmet.

fabric pelmet. Decide on the depth and cut a piece of brown paper to this size. Fold paper in half widthways. Mark design along lower edge and cut out; unfold pattern. (By folding the paper the design will be centrally placed on pelmet.) Temporarily fix to edge of shelf to check for shape and size. Remove and adjust as necessary.

Materials

- 100 × 10 mm (4 × ⅜ in) softwood
- Four corner joints and small angle brackets for fixing, complete with screws
- Spirit level
- Paper for pattern
- Furnishing fabric
- Furnishing lining fabric
- Self-adhesive pelmet stiffening
- Sew-and-stick fastening strip
- Matching thread

Measuring up

- The pelmet shelf should be between 10 cm (4 in) and 15 cm (6 in) deep and 10 cm (4 in) longer than the curtain track.

- Make a pattern of front of shelf. Measure round the edge of the shelf from wall along return, front, second return and back to the wall. This will be the length of the finished

Making up

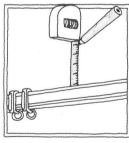

1 Cut out shelf from 100 × 10 mm (4 × ⅜ in) softwood, then cut out two returns – the sections which are fixed to each end of shelf. Screw two corner joints to the end of shelf and to the return, matching all edges. Repeat at opposite end.

2 Mark position of pelmet on wall 5–7.5 cm (2–3 in) above curtain track. Fix small angle brackets to wall, about 30 cm (12 in) apart, using spirit level to check they are in a straight line. Screw pelmet shelf centrally onto brackets.

SEE ALSO:

CONTEMPORARY STYLE   49

FABRIC FILE   9

LINED CURTAINS   95

SEWING GUIDE   200

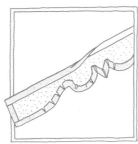

3 Using the pattern, cut one piece of fabric and one of lining, adding 1.5 cm (⅝ in) seam allowance all round. Centre any pattern or fabric design. If pelmet is longer than fabric width, cut and join widths together with plain flat seams. Position the seams equally on either side of a central width. Make up lining in the same way.

4 Using the pattern, cut out one piece of pelmet stiffening. Lay fabric wrong side up. Peel off backing from one side of stiffening and press onto centre of fabric. Peel off backing from other side of stiffening and press seam allowance over edge and onto stiffening.

Stylish tartan curtains have been given shaped pelmets covered in the same fabric to emphasize the bold effect.

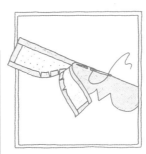

5 Press in seam allowance all round lining. Position lining over pelmet, wrong sides together, matching outer edges. Slipstitch folded edges together all round outer edge.

6 Position the 'sew' half of the fastening strip along top edge of wrong side of pelmet; stitch in place. Fix 'stick' half along shelf edge. Press pelmet in position.

VARIATION: A PADDED PELMET

Buckram replaces the self-adhesive stiffening and a layer of interlining is added to the wrong side of the fabric to give a slightly padded effect.

Materials

- Pelmet shelf as before
- Paper for pattern
- Furnishing fabric
- Furnishing lining fabric
- Buckram
- Curtain interlining
- Sew-and-stick fastening strip
- Matching sewing thread

Making up

1 Cut out fabric and lining as before. Using the pattern, cut out one piece of buckram and one piece of curtain interlining.

2 Place interlining to wrong side of fabric and lockstitch in position in the same way as for curtains (*see* Lined curtains). Place buckram centrally on top of interlining. Dampen edge of buckram and press fabric edges over onto it.

3 Press under seam allowance all round lining and lay over pelmet with wrong sides together. Slipstitch folded edges together all round pelmet. Add fastening strip to the top of the pelmet and to shelf as before. Press pelmet in position.

VALANCE

A valance is, in this context, a soft pelmet which hangs from a separate track in front of the main curtain track, covering the top edge of the curtain. The top edge of the valance is gathered up with curtain heading tape in the same way as a curtain; there is a variety of decorative heading tapes available especially for valances. Valances, like pelmets, are generally one-sixth of the curtain length.

Materials

- Furnishing fabric
- Furnishing lining fabric
- Heading tape
- Matching sewing thread

Measuring up

- Measure the curtain track in the same way as for curtains (*see* Unlined Curtains) to work out how much fabric you need for the chosen heading tape.

Making up

1 Cut out fabric widths to the required measurements and join together. Make up lining and stitch the two together in the same way as for lined curtains (*see* Lined Curtains).

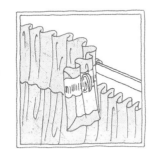

2 Attach the heading tape and pull up in the same way as for curtains (*see* Unlined Curtains). Hang on the valance track.

A gathered valance is given definition by the addition of a rope trimming at the top and fringing along the lower edge.

SUCCESSFUL TRACKS

Check your curtain track to see whether a valance track can be added to the front. There is a selection of valance tracks now available that can be quickly clipped onto the curtain track, eliminating the need to buy a complete curtain track system when you want to add a valance.

lambrequin

· ·

Lambrequins are similar to pelmets in that they are made from stiffened fabric, but as well as covering the top of the window, they also fit down the sides of the window. As with pelmets, the edges can be shaped and decorated with braid or ribbon. Lambrequins can cover curtains or blinds and are generally supported on a pelmet shelf above the window.

Materials

- Pelmet box
- Paper for pattern
- Adhesive tape
- Buckram
- Furnishing lining fabric
- Curtain interlining
- Furnishing fabric
- Matching sewing thread
- Sew-and-stick touch-and-close fastening tape
- Spray adhesive

Measuring up

- Fix the pelmet shelf in position above the window first.

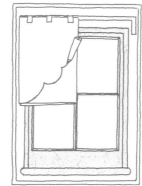

*P*lace the paper pattern to one half of the pelmet shelf and mark the design of the lower edge of the lambrequin.

SEE ALSO:
· ·
CONTEMPORARY STYLE   49
· ·
FABRIC FILE   9
· ·
SEWING GUIDE   200
· ·

- Measure the length of the pelmet box, including the returns (sides) for the lambrequin width. Decide how far down the window the lambrequin should extend and measure to this point from the top of the pelmet box for the lambrequin depth. Cut a piece of paper to the required size and fold in half widthways. Attach the paper pattern to one half of the pelmet shelf with strips of adhesive tape. Mark the shape of the lower edge of the lambrequin carefully on the pattern, so that the lambrequin 'frames' the window gently. Remove the pattern and cut out along the

marked line. Unfold the pattern and tape it to the shelf to check it against the window.

- You will need one piece buckram to the pattern, one piece of lining plus 1.5 cm (⅝ in) allowance all round, one piece of curtain interlining plus 1.5 cm (⅝ in) allowance all round, and one piece of main fabric plus 2.5 cm (1 in) allowance all round.

- For the touch-and-close fastening tape, you will need one strip the same length as the top straight edge of the pattern.

Making up

1 Using the pattern, cut one piece of buckram and one of lining, adding 1.5 cm (⅝ in) allowance. Cut one piece of interlining, adding 1.5 cm (⅝ in) allowance all round, and a piece of fabric, adding 2.5 cm (1 in) allowance all round.

2 Position 'stitch' half of touch-and-close fastening tape on right side of fabric piece along top straight edge, placing inner edge of tape 2.5 cm (1 in) from top edge of fabric. Pin and stitch along inner edge of tape only.

3 Using spray adhesive, secure buckram centrally to curtain interlining. Moisten the edges on wrong side of buckram; bring interlining edges over buckram and press down. Snip into interlining so it lies smoothly over curves.

4 Using spray adhesive, secure interlined side of buckram centrally to wrong side of fabric. Moisten exposed buckram edges and bring fabric edges over to wrong side; press in place. Start turning over fabric edge with touch-and-close fastening tape along top straight edge, then work round side and shaped edges, snipping into fabric edges round curves and corners.

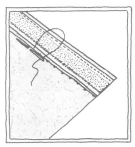

5 Position lining centrally, right side up over wrong side of lambrequin. Turn under raw edges and slipstitch to fabric all round. Along the top edge, tuck the top edge of lining under the touch-and-close fastening tape. Slipstitch free edge of tape to lining.

6 Glue or handsew any trimmings in place on right side of lambrequin. Secure opposite half of touch-and-close fastening tape along front edges of pelmet box. Press lambrequin in position.

*P*elmets like this Moorish-style lambrequin form a strong focal point in a room.

Swags and tails

● ●

Swags and tails are the most ornate window treatments and are therefore usually reserved for formal surroundings. A simple draped curtain can, however, look pretty above plain sheer curtains or over an uncurtained window. For this type of window treatment, choose fabrics that will drape well and match or tone them with the decor of the room.

Swags and tails are fixed above the window on a pelmet shelf. Generally, tails fall between half and two-thirds of the way down a window – remember to make up a pair of tails, one left and one right.

Materials

- Pelmet shelf as before (*see* Pelmets)
- Paper for pattern
- Furnishing fabric
- Furnishing lining fabric
- Sew-and-stick fastening strip and sew-and-sew fastening tape
- Drawing pins
- Matching sewing thread

Measuring up

- For the swag – the centre of the arrangement – measure the length of the pelmet shelf and add 40 cm (16 in), for swag length.

- For the swag depth, multiply the required finished depth by 2½ to allow for the pleats. Draw this rectangle on a sheet of paper. Extend the base line outwards for 10–15 cm (4–6 in) on either side. Join these outer marks to the ends of the top line with a gentle curve. Extend the pattern at the base centre by 10 cm (4 in). Join up the outer base edges to the centre mark, with a gentle curve. Add 1.5 cm (⅝ in) seam allowance all round, then cut out.

SEE ALSO:

CONTEMPORARY STYLE 49

FABRIC FILE 9

LINED CURTAINS 95

SEWING GUIDE 200

- For the tails, measure the finished width, including the return, and triple the measurement, to allow for pleats. Mark this width on a sheet of paper. Then mark the required length: the inner edge of each tail should be about the same length as the finished swag, the outer edge about twice the length. Join up the marks to create the pattern and add 1.5 cm (⅝ in) seam allowance all round, then cut out.

Making up

1 Using the swag pattern, cut out one piece of fabric and one piece of lining.

2 Place fabric to lining with right sides together. Pin and stitch together all round, leaving an opening centrally in one side for turning. Trim and turn right side out. Slipstitch across folded edges to close opening. Mark pleats about 12–15 cm (5–6 in) apart on either side of swag.

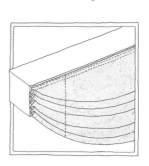

3 Stitch 'sew' half of fastening tape along top edge of wrong side of swag and stick opposite half to shelf edge. Press top edge of swag in place. Pleat up swag along each marked line and fasten to shelf at each side with a drawing pin. Check the effect. Pin fabric pleats together at each side. Remove from pelmet shelf and stitch across the end of each swag to hold the pleats in position. Fix to the shelf.

4 Using the tails pattern, cut out one piece of fabric and one piece of lining. Place fabric to lining with right sides together; pin and stitch together all round, leaving an opening in one side for turnings. Trim and turn right side out. Slipstitch folded edges together across opening. Repeat, reversing pattern.

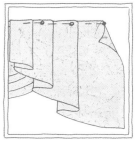

5 Mark the positions for pleats along top edge of tail, working from outside edge. First mark position for shelf return – the section between wall and shelf front – then mark

*P*aying attention to detail is the key to creating successful swags and tails. Try using a contrasting lining and decorative trimmings to give emphasis to the edges of curtains and valances.

pleat arrangement. Temporarily pin tails to each side of the pelmet shelf. Pleat up fabric, following marks, and pin in place; check for effect.

6 Remove tails from pelmet shelf; tack and press pleats in position. Cut a length of sew-and-sew fastening tape and stitch one half along top edge of wrong side of tails – this will hold pleats in position.

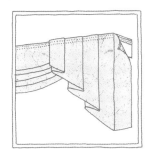

7 Stitch opposite half of fastening tape across top of swag; this will be hidden by tails. Press tails in position on either side of swag. Use a short length of sew-and-stick fastening tape to attach tail sides to the pelmet shelf returns.

A SIMPLE DRAPE

A draped sheer swag and tail arrangement can be simply created over a curtain pole using just one long fabric width. Find the middle of the fabric length and hang it over the centre of the pole in a generous loop. Let the two sides hang to the floor or fall in a heap of arranged fabric at each side. Hold the curtain to the pole with short strips of touch-and-close fastening tape. When using a one-way design, remember to make a centre seam so that the fabric will be the right way up on each side.

Blinds

*R*oman blinds (opposite) made in a warmly coloured tartan fabric add a splash of colour and design to an otherwise simple window treatment. Interest has been added by sewing a strip of tartan horizontally across the top of the blind to create a false pelmet.

*T*o cover a series of small windows (below), such as in a conservatory, individual roller blinds are a good solution, especially when they are held together visually by a lambrequin.

Blinds come in several styles to complement different-shaped windows, room schemes and types of fabric. Roller and Roman blinds have the plainest shapes. In a lowered position both styles cover the window with a flat rectangle of fabric; where they differ becomes apparant when they are raised. Roller blinds roll up tightly around a wooden or metal roller at the top of the window, leaving only a slim cylinder of fabric visible. Roman blinds are corded at the back and fitted with a number of horizontal wooden battens that allow them to be pulled up into a series of neat folds. Both types of blind can be used effectively on their own in modern or traditional room settings which require a simple, stylized look; but they can be equally successful as the

*A*plain Roman blind (above) at an end-of-corridor window is given definition and interest by the addition of a bound edge in bright blue and white gingham.

practical layer (providing privacy and shade) in window treatments which have elaborate pelmets and dress curtains to produce a multi-layered look. Roller blinds are a good choice for awkward sloping windows and skylights. They can be held flat either by slotting them behind poles or mounting them on tracks running along the edges of the windows.

Roman blinds can be made from a wide range of fabrics, from the more expensive linens and chintzes to cheaper cottons, calicoes and ticking. However, avoid very thin sheer fabrics, which are not strong enough to make firm folds. Cotton is generally the best fabric to use for a roller blind, but it must be stiffened so that it hangs correctly. It is possible to buy some ready-stiffened fabrics, but you can do the job yourself relatively easily using a special liquid available from most department stores. Once treated, the fabric can be sponged clean, which makes this type of blind a particularly good choice for kitchens and bathrooms.

Where there is no room for curtains at a window (below) and the decor is clean and uncluttered, the obvious choice is to use a roller blind.

COVERING BAY WINDOWS

One solution when covering a deep bay of windows is to use a set of independent blinds. The amount of fabric needed for a long run of curtaining can look overwhelming. Blinds, on the other hand, will fit neatly into each window area. They can be lowered at the same level across the bay or raised at different heights to let in varying amounts of sunlight.

*L*eave the lower edge of a roller blind plain or go for more decorative edgings such as scallops, curves or points.

*T*he crisp, tailored look of Roman blinds (above) can be emphasized by using a discreet pattern such as stripes or a simple geometric design – a style that suits almost any kind of interior scheme.

*C*hildren's rooms (left) are another area where roller blinds often work best at windows – especially if the blinds are made in a brightly coloured, patterned fabric, and preferably one that has been treated so that it can be wiped clean with a damp cloth from time to time.

A ruched Austrian or festoon blind offers a softer, more luxuriant window treatment. Unlike roller and Roman designs, these blinds require fabric at least twice the width of the window, which is gathered onto curtain heading tape and corded to pull up into deep swags. Austrian and festoon blinds create a very similar effect at a window and because of this are often confused, but they are in fact quite different. An Austrian blind falls like a curtain when lowered, ending in deep, permanently ruched swags along its base. It can be made with different headings, ranging from pencil and goblet pleats to simple French headed pleats. A festoon blind, on the other hand, has extra fullness in its depth and width and is permanently ruched from top to bottom, leaving gathers of fabric even when lowered.

With their decorative shaping, these blinds are ideal for dressing up a very plain window. You can use almost any plain fabric to make them up, from opulent silks to cheaper cottons and ticking. Fabrics with very large patterns should be

*B*linds can be used not just as window treatments, but as screens or room dividers too. In a child's room, Roman blinds can be hung in front of a built-in bed, and the blinds quickly let down at night to make a snug area. Teenagers may prefer to leave the blinds down during the day to close off the bed so that the rest of the room can be treated as a separate living room.

*B*linds (below) make an excellent choice for conservatories and sloping glass. The Roman blinds in this room have been mounted on a special tracking that follows the sloping shape of the windows and ensures that they pull up to form crisp, neat folds.

*A*blind (right) is always a good choice for a small window and the treatment can be highly decorative. Here, a Roman blind with a shaped lower edge is framed by a generous length of the same fabric twisted into a swagged heading and tails.

avoided, however, as they easily look overpowering when combined with the already fussy nature of the blind. In general it is best to line Austrian and festoon blinds, but unlined versions made in sheer fabrics make an excellent alternative to net curtains. Because of the generous amounts of fabric used to make them up, Austrian and festoon blinds look more in proportion when hung at big windows.

Somewhere between the style of an ornate Austrian blind and the plainness of a Roman blind is the relatively new London blind. When lowered this style of blind covers the window in a flat rectangle of fabric, ending in one or more simple ruched scallops. The heading at the top appears flat, but is made with inverted pleats that carry the cording that pulls the blind up. They can be made up in many types of fabric, plain or patterned.

Dark-coloured fabrics (right) with geometric or paisley patterns and a deep fringed trim instead of frills give Austrian blinds a more masculine look.

Austrian blinds (below) can look more tailored – the trick is to use fewer cords to pull up the blind, which will give a less ruched effect at the window.

AUSTRIAN BLINDS WITH VICTORIAN STYLE

*T*he Victorians liked to use fabrics with deep, rich colours and lots of pattern for window treatments, and these will also work well for an Austrian blind in a traditional setting. For an even more authentic touch, add some form of trimming such as a frill or braid all the way round the blind, or add a long, heavy fringe to the lower edge.

Whatever style of blind you choose, it's often the finishing touches that make all the difference, and help to give a blind a really special look. The hard edges of a plain roller blind, for instance, can be emphasized with a contrast binding or braiding. For a more decorative look, try using a scalloped or wavy-shaped edging along the bottom and trim it with fringing. Roman blinds can also be trimmed in a contrast fabric or fringing – for a particularly striking effect, inset the contrasting binding about 15 cm (6 in) from the edges of the blind. Austrian and festoon blinds lend themselves more readily to frilled edgings, which can be used down the sides as well as at the top and bottom. Alternatively, add a decorative braid or deep fringing to give a more masculine touch.

Pelmets and valances are best used in conjunction with curtains, although a shaped lambrequin, which extends down the sides of a window, is a good choice with a roller blind, for example, helping to hide the unattractive cylinder mechanism from view.

A frilled edge (left) works particularly well with festoon blinds, as these blinds are deeply swagged even when fully extended.

For a crisper looking festoon blind (right), go for a patterned fabric in tartan, gingham or stripes in untreated cotton, satin cotton or chintz.

roller blind

Roller blinds must be the simplest window covering to make. They consist of a length of stiffened fabric attached to a wooden roller suspended on brackets. The blind is raised and lowered by means of a spring mechanism fitted into the roller, and assisted by a lath slotted through a hem at the base of the blind. The lath also helps to keep the fabric lying flat and straight. Specially stiffened fabric is available in a range of plain colours and prints for making roller blinds. If you want to match an existing scheme, furnishing fabrics can be used but must be stiffened before being made up. Roller blinds can be made in cotton or chintz, or in lace or sheer fabric to substitute for net curtains. The only fabrics to avoid are loosely woven fabrics, which have no substance, or heavyweight fabrics, which would be too bulky wound round the roller. The lower edge of a roller blind lends itself to a number of decorative finishes, particularly shaped edgings.

Materials

- Roller blind kit, the chosen size or longer: consisting of a wooden roller, brackets end cap, pin, wooden lath, cord holder and acorn
- Furnishing fabric, medium-weight, closely woven cotton
- Fabric stiffener, either liquid solution or aerosol stiffener, if applicable
- Dressmaker's marking pen, set square and metal ruler
- Matching sewing thread
- Double-sided adhesive tape
- Staple gun with 6 mm (¼ in) staples or hammer and small tacks

Measuring up

- To calculate the correct width for the roller: if the blind is to hang inside the window recess, measure the exact width from one side of the recess to the other, using a metal ruler (not a cloth tape). Deduct 3 cm (1¼ in) to allow for the blind mechanism.

- If the blind is to hang outside the window, measure across the window and allow an extra 5 cm (2 in) on either side so the blind will totally cover the window and block out the light.

- For the blind fabric width, measure the exact width of the roller, excluding the end fixtures. There is no need to allow for side hems as the stiffened fabric will not fray. For the blind fabric length, measure from the roller to the sill and add 30 cm (12 in) for the casing and for the roller to be covered with fabric when fully extended.

  If the blind is hanging outside the sill add another 5 cm (2 in) to the length.

Note: If the fabric needs stiffening, see step 4 before buying or cutting out.

SEE ALSO:

CONTEMPORARY STYLE   49

FABRIC FILE   9

SEWING GUIDE   200

1 Buy a roller blind kit to the exact width you need or, if the length required is in between two kit sizes, buy the larger size and cut to fit.

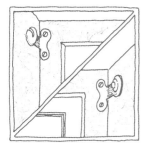

2 Screw brackets in position, ensuring that they are equally placed on either side of window. Make sure the round pin-hole bracket is on the right-hand side of the window and the square slot bracket is on the left-hand side. On recess windows, position brackets about 3 cm (1¼ in) down from top of recess to allow for thickness of rolled-up blind. When hanging the blind outside the recess, fix brackets about 5 cm (2 in) above window.

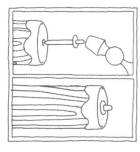

3 Measure the exact distance between the two brackets and, if needed, cut the bare end of the roller to fit. Fit the end cap over the cut end. Hold roller horizontally and hammer pin into roller through hole in cap. Place roller in brackets .

The choice of fabric can make an important contribution to the overall look of a room. Bold black and white stripes create a dramatic statement; here, they coordinate perfectly with the striking black and white flooring.

4 If the fabric needs stiffening, this must be done before you cut the blind to the finished size as the fabric may shrink. If you are unsure of the fabric, test a sample or spare piece to gauge whether it will shrink and its reaction to the stiffening solution. Stiffen the fabric following the manufacturer's instructions and press well.

5 Working on a smooth, flat surface, measure and cut fabric to size, using a set square to make sure that all the sides are absolutely square.

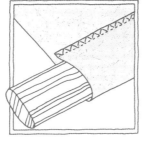

6 Neaten lower edge of the fabric with zigzag stitch. Turn 4 cm (1½ in) to wrong side along base edge; tack, then stitch across to form a casing for the lath. Cut the lath 2 cm (¾ in) shorter than the width of the blind. Slot the lath through the casing and stitch across the ends.

COPING WITH LARGE WINDOWS

Roller blinds work best on small or medium-sized windows. Try to avoid joining fabric widths together as this will form bulk and hinder the rolling up process. If you do need to join fabric to gain the correct width for a large window, place two pieces of the same size on either side of a central panel of fabric. Use a flat fell seam or a plain flat seam. When using a plain seam, press open and stitch down again on either side of the seam. Trim the fabric close to the stitching. In all cases match any pattern across the seams.

7 Measure across the lath to find the centre and mark. Thread the cord through the acorn and knot. Pull the opposite end through the cord holder and hold at the back of the lath to check for length. Knot the cord and trim off any excess. Screw the holder centrally to the back of the lath.

8 Fix the fabric to the roller. The roller may have a line marked across its length to indicate the position for the fabric. If not, mark a line with pencil along the roller. Stick a length of double-sided adhesive tape along the roller, carefully following the marked line.

Choose from a wide range of shaped edges to give a decorative finish to roller blinds.

9 Lay the blind flat, right side up. Lay the roller across the blind top with the spring mechanism on the left. Remove protective cover from tape and press the fabric onto tape, making sure that it is straight. Fix the fabric to the roller using either staples or small tacks, with one at each end of the roller and the rest evenly spaced about 2 cm (¾ in) apart in between.

10 Roll up blind by hand and slot into brackets. Pull blind down. Remove from brackets and re-roll. This increases the tension, so the blind will spring back when pulled. Replace in brackets.

VARIATION: ROLLER BLIND WITH A SHAPED EDGE

A shaped edge will add a professional touch to a plain roller blind. The shaped edge can either hang below the lath casing or incorporate loops through which a decorative pole can be slotted, taking the place of the bottom lath. To allow for the decorative edge, the lath casing has to be moved higher up the blind. This can be achieved in different ways:

- On plain fabric blinds the casing is formed above the allowance for the shaped edge, by stitching a large tuck, wide enough to hold the lath, across the blind on the wrong side. Allow for this extra fabric on the blind length when cutting out.

- On patterned fabric blinds a separate casing is made from a strip of plain or matching fabric, again wide enough to hold the lath. The fabric strip is topstitched across the wrong side of the blind, above the decorative edge.

Materials

- Paper for pattern
- Fabric bonding material (option)

Making up

1 Measure the width of the blind and cut a piece of paper to this length by the depth of the shaped edge, between 10 and 15 cm (4 and 6 in). Fold the paper up like a concertina into equal sections the size of the chosen pattern. Mark the chosen pattern – a decorative scallop, shallow curves or points – along the lower edge of top section of folded paper. Cut out through all layers. Unfold paper to form the pattern.

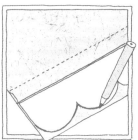

2 Lay pattern on wrong side of blind just below the casing. Mark round decorative edge. The edge can be cut and left plain or finished with zigzag stitching. If necessary, stiffen with another layer of main fabric fused to the wrong side with a layer of fabric bonding material. Fix in place, then mark, cut and stitch round shaped edge.

$r$oman blind

Roman blinds have a smart tailored appearance. When the blinds are lowered, they hang flat against the window, but pull up to form well-defined, evenly spaced horizontal pleats. Roman blinds should always be lined. To help keep Roman blinds looking sharp, a wooden lath is slotted through a casing stitched in the lining only, on either side of each pleat. The raising cords are threaded through rings stitched to these casings and the whole blind is mounted on a length of wooden battening. Try to avoid joining widths of fabric together to gain the blind width. If the window is extra wide, it is preferable to place two blinds side by side, but only if there is a central vertical frame between them. If you have to join fabric together to gain the correct width, stitch two similar-sized sections on either side of a central panel of fabric. Use plain seams and seam the lining together in the same way.

Materials

- Suitable curtain fabric, firmly woven cotton furnishing fabric
- Lining fabric
- Nylon cord
- Dressmaker's marking pen, set square and metal ruler
- Matching sewing thread
- Wooden laths 3 mm (⅛ in) thick, one for each casing, as long as the blind width plus an extra lath for the base of the blind
- Wood battening 5 × 2.5 cm (2 × 1 in) with fixing brackets and screws, cut to same width as blind
- Small plastic rings, two rings for each casing
- Two screw eyes
- Staple gun with 6 mm (¼ in) staples or hammer and small tacks
- Cleat with fixing screws

Note: Roman blind kits are available, but only for a soft-folded version, which is made with tapes and does not include laths.

SEE ALSO:

CONTEMPORARY STYLE   49

FABRIC FILE   9

SEWING GUIDE   200

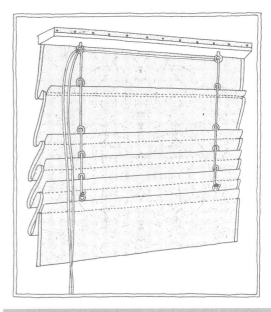

Measuring up

- If the blind is to hang inside the window recess, measure the inside width and height, using a metal ruler. This will be the finished size of the blind. Roman blinds look better, however, hung outside the recess.

- If the blind is to hang outside the recess, measure from chosen height to the sill level and add 5 cm (2 in) all round to totally cover the window. This will be the finished size of the blind.

- For either measurement, add 3 cm (1¼ in) to each side, 3 cm (1¼ in) to the length and 5 cm (2 in) to the top for seam allowances.

- The lining should be same size as the finished blind, including the allowances, plus 6 cm (2½ in) for each casing between the pleats. To calculate the number of casings needed, divide the main fabric horizontally into equal sections about 25 cm (10 in) wide, for each pleat. The number of pleats equals the number of casings.

- For the nylon cord you will need two lengths each measuring twice the blind length plus one blind width.

Making up

1 Cut main fabric and lining for blind to required sizes.

2 Lay main fabric wrong side up. Mark a line 5 cm (2 in) down from top edge, and another line 3 cm (1¼ in) up from base edge. Divide remainder of fabric horizontally into equal sections about 25 cm (10 in) apart and mark across blind for position of each casing. The last line should be about 25 cm (10 in) from the top line. Use a set square so the lines will be at right angles to the

3 Lay lining flat, right side up. Using set square, mark first casing line at base edge as on main fabric, then draw parallel line 6 cm (2½ in) above this. This marks the first casing. Mark next line about 25 cm (10 in) along, matching spacing on main fabric. Draw in next

blind edge and parallel to the blind top. Turn in and press a 3 cm (1¼ in) hem on side and base edges of fabric.

parallel line 6 cm (2½ in) above this. Repeat along full length of lining. Turn in and press 4 cm (1½ in) to wrong side on both side edges of lining. Press in 3 cm (1¼ in) on base edge.

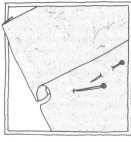

4 The casings are formed on the right side of the lining. Match the first pair of parallel lines with wrong sides together; pin and stitch across, forming a casing on the right side of the lining. Repeat, to form a casing at each marked position.

5 Lay main fabric wrong side up. Position lining centrally over main fabric, wrong sides together, matching base and top edges. Pin and tack together across marked lines on fabric, just above each casing. Work up the blind, then tack top edges together.

6 Stitch across front of main fabric, along each marked line. Avoid accidentally catching in the casings. Leave the base edges open to add the final lath at the end. Slipstitch lining to fabric along both side edges, leaving casings open. Zigzag stitch fabric and lining together across top edges.

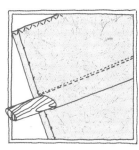

7 Cut laths 2 cm (¾ in) shorter than blind width. Slide a lath through each casing; slipstitch across ends of each casing to close.

8 Handsew a plastic ring to both edges of each casing 10 cm (4 in) in from outer edges of blind. Fasten a length of cord to right-hand ring at base of blind. Take cord up the blind through rings and leave hanging. Thread second length of cord up left-hand rings in same way.

9 The battening is screwed onto brackets above the window or in the recess at the chosen height. Fix bracket at each end. If the blind is long, fix two extra brackets evenly spaced in between. Check that the brackets are level using the battening and a spirit level.

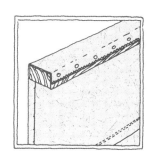

10 Fold top of blind over top edge of battening. Make sure blind is hanging straight; fix to back of battening using either staples or tacks.

Place staples at each end and the rest evenly spaced about 2 cm (¾ in) apart.

11 Fix two screw eyes to underside of battening in line with plastic rings on blind. Screw battening to the brackets at the window.

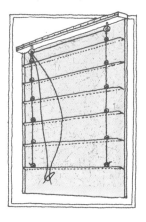

12 To complete cording the blind, take the left-hand cord up through the screw eye above it and through the screw eye to the right, leaving the cord hanging on the right-hand side of the blind. Thread the right-hand cord in the same way. Trim cords level with base of blind and knot together.

13 Let the blind hang down and position the last lath between the base edges, so it rests on the sill; slipstitch folded edges of fabric and lining together to hold the lath in place.

14 Screw a cleat beside the window on the right-hand side. Wind both the cords together round the cleat in a figure of eight to secure.

BATTENING TREATMENTS

- If you prefer, sew-and-stick fastening tape can be used to fix the blind to the front edge of the battening.

- The battening can be painted to match the window surround or covered in matching fabric before the blind is fixed in place (*see* London Blind).

Austrian blind

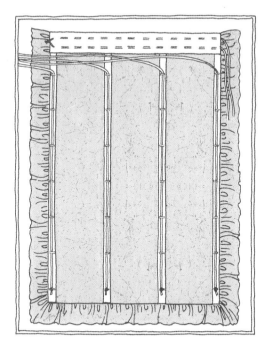

Austrian blinds gather up into softly-shaped ruches, but when they are lowered, they hang almost flat against the window like a curtain. However, as they are usually recessed into the window, they require less fabric than curtains. The blind is raised and lowered on cords. These run up through rows of looped Austrian blind tape stitched in vertical rows across the back of the blind and are held on a specialist blind track that has easy-to-thread cord holders. The blinds are headed with a pencil-pleat or French heading tape. As an alternative, Austrian blinds can also be hung from a standard curtain track mounted to a length of battening held above the window on brackets. In this case, a screw eye will have to be positioned to the underside of the battening above each tape position to carry the cords. Austrian blinds are generally made up in light-weight curtain fabrics, and they will hang better and exclude more light if they are lined. In this version, the blind is outlined with piping covered in a plain fabric and a double frill made in the same fabric as the blind. It would also look pretty with a deep fringe or ruching at the base.

Materials

- Austrian blind track or length of battening plus fixing brackets and screws combined with standard curtain track. If using battening, a screw eye will have to be added to the underside at the top of each tape.
- Lightweight curtain fabric, firmly woven furnishing fabric
- Lining fabric
- Covered piping cord
- Pencil-pleat curtain heading tape
- Austrian blind tape
- Nylon cord
- Matching sewing thread
- Tailor's chalk
- Cord tidy
- Cleat with fixing screws

SEE ALSO:

CONTEMPORARY STYLE   49

CURTAINS   86

FABRIC FILE   9

SEWING GUIDE   200

Measuring up

- Following the manufacturer's instructions, fix the Austrian blind track above the window at the chosen position. If the blind is to hang inside the window recess, fix the track to the recess ceiling. Or, fix the battening in place, adding a length of standard curtain track to the front.

- For the main fabric and lining, measure the length of the track and allow 2½ times this measurement for the blind width (this includes the seam allowance for the side seams). For the length, measure from the track to the sill and add 50 cm (20 in) so the blind will still have some fullness when lowered over the window. This also allows for top hem and base seam.

- For a double frill 7.5 cm (3 in) wide, you will need strips 18.5 cm (7¼ in) wide cut from across the fabric width; multiply two lengths of the blind plus one width by 1½ to find the ungathered frill length.

AUSTRIAN BLIND TRACK

An Austrian blind track carries cord holders which can be moved along the track and fixed above each length of Austrian blind tape. A cord lock holds the cords in position at the side of the track, so the blind can be fixed at different heights. Austrian blind kits are available with both types of tape, cord, cleat and fixing screws, screw eyes, acorn and cord tidy.

- For covered piping cord, allow two lengths of the blind plus one width.

- For pencil-pleat heading tape, allow for the blind width plus 5 cm (2 in) for neatening the ends.

- For the Austrian blind tape, first decide on the width of the finished scallop and multiply 2½ times to give the approximate space between the vertical tapes. Divide this amount into the blind width to give the number of tape lengths required. Allow for the blind length plus 5 cm (2 in) for each vertical tape length.

- For the nylon cord, allow twice the blind length plus one width for each length of vertical Austrian blind tape.

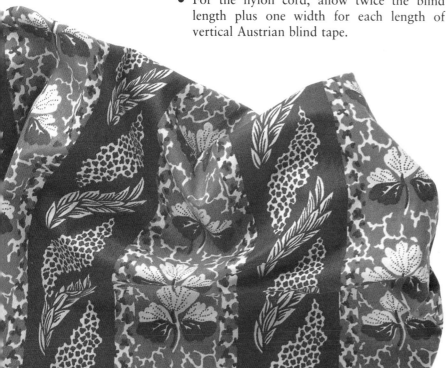

Making up

1 Cut one piece of main fabric and one piece of lining to the measurements required. If necessary, sew fabric widths together with plain flat seams to achieve the width needed for the blind, matching any pattern. Press seams open. Generally, the seams will be hidden once the fabric is gathered.

2 The double frill is made by folding a strip of fabric in half so the raw edges are gathered up together. Pin and stitch frill strips together with plain flat seams to form a strip 1½ times finished frill measurement. To neaten raw ends, fold frill in half lengthways with right sides together; pin and stitch across ends, then trim corners and turn right side out. Tack top raw edges together and press along folded edge.

3 Lay main fabric right side up. Position piping down side, along base edge and up remaining side of fabric with cord facing inwards. Stitch line on piping should be 1.5 cm (⅝ in) in from raw edges of blind. Begin and end piping 2 cm (¾ in) down from top raw edge. Tack in place.

4 Divide frill into four equal sections and mark; each section will be gathered separately. Work two rows of gathering stitches in each section, beginning and ending gathers at each mark.

5 Divide side and base edges of blind into four equal sections and mark. Matching marks, pin frill to blind over piping, with frill facing inwards and raw edges together, beginning and ending 2 cm (¾ in) down from top raw edge. Pull up frill gathers evenly in turn, to fit in each section. Pin and tack frill in place.

6 Position lining to main fabric with right sides together, raw edges matching; pin and stitch side and base edges of blind, taking 1.5 cm (⅝ in) seam allowance, using a zip or piping foot attachment, and catching in piping and frill. Trim and turn fabric right side out. Press side and base edges. Tack top edges of fabric and lining together.

7 Add the Austrian blind tapes. Lay the blind flat, lining side up. Cut the first two lengths of Austrian blind tape as long as the blind, making sure that the first loop will be 5 cm (2 in) up from the frill seam. Position the tapes vertically on the fabric, alongside the frill seam at each side. Make sure that the loops of the tapes align across the blind; tuck the lower ends under by 1.5 cm (⅝ in). Pin and stitch tapes in place.

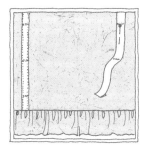

8 Divide remaining width into evenly spaced sections between 30 cm (12 in) and 50 cm (20 in) wide (the finished scallops will be just under half this size). Pin and stitch lengths of tape at these positions, making sure that the loops on each length of tape align across the blind.

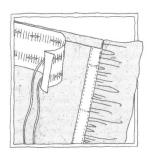

9 To stitch on the heading tape, turn down top edges together, including tape ends, by 2 cm (¾ in) in line with end of piping and frill. Position pencil-pleat heading tape to top edge of

blind covering raw edges and the raw ends of Austrian blind tape.

10 On the left-hand side, knot the gathering cords together and turn under the tape end in line with the blind edge. On the right-hand side, turn under the tape end in line with the blind edge, leaving the cords hanging freely on the right side. Pin and stitch heading tape in place close to outside edges of heading tape.

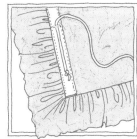

11 Cut a length of nylon cord for each length of Austrian blind tape, twice the length of the blind plus one width. With blind wrong side up, knot the first length to the first loop above the base seam on the left-hand tape and run through all the loops on the tape above it. Thread all the tapes in the same way.

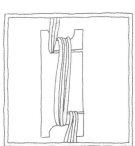

12 Pull up the heading tape evenly to fit the curtain track. Wind up the surplus cord onto a cord tidy and attach to one

side of the heading tape. Hang the blind on the track, positioning one curtain hook at each end and the remaining hooks in between, about 7.5 cm (3 in) apart.

13 Lock the cord holders above each tape position. Thread all the cords through all the cord holders on the track towards the right-hand side of the window. Trim the cords level with the base edge of the blind. Knot the cords together just beyond the cord lock with the blind at sill level. Plait the remaining lengths of cord together and knot at the end.

14 Fix a cleat at the right-hand side of the window. Pull up the blind and wind the cords round the cleat in a figure of eight to secure.

Austrian blinds lend themselves to soft decorative touches, such as a frill all the way round or a frilled or fringed lower edge. Notice how this blind has been designed to pull up into three deep swags with a tail either side, which gives it a better proportion at such a large window.

london blind

London blinds are plain and flat and pull up into softly draped blinds. They have two inverted pleats at each side, folded over a row of Austrian blind tape. The cords that raise and lower the blind run through both lengths of Austrian blind tape. They are best lined. If you wish to join fabric widths together to cover extra wide windows, position a seam on each side of the blind, behind the tape positions.

Materials

- Suitable curtain fabric, firmly woven cotton furnishing fabric
- Lining fabric
- Wooden battening 50 × 25 mm (2 × 1 in) with fixing brackets and screws, to width of blind
- Austrian blind tape (*see* Austrian Blind)
- Nylon cord
- Matching sewing thread
- Tailor's chalk or marking pencil
- 2 cm (¾ in) wide sew-and-stick fastening tape, for fixing, the length of the battening
- Two screw eyes
- Cleat with fixing screws

Measuring up

- If the blind is to hang inside the window recess, for the blind width measure across the recess and add 3 cm (1¼ in) for seam allowance, plus 60 cm (24 in) for pleats.

- For blind length, measure from the top of the recess to the window sill and add 3.5 cm (1⅜ in) for hem and heading allowances.

- If the blind is to hang outside the window recess (the same as for a Roman blind, *see* Roman Blind), add 5 cm (2 in) to the finished blind size all round then add the same allowances as above for seams, hems and pleats.

SEE ALSO:

CONTEMPORARY STYLE   49

FABRIC FILE   9

ROMAN BLIND   127

SEWING GUIDE   200

- For Austrian blind tape, allow for twice the blind length.

- For nylon cord, measure twice the blind length plus one width and double the measurement.

Making up

1 Cut one piece of fabric and one piece of lining to the correct size. Place fabric on lining with right sides together, matching raw edges. Pin and stitch side and hem edges, taking 1.5 cm (⅝ in) seam allowance. Trim seams and across corners and turn blind right side out. Press with seam to edge. Tack top edges together.

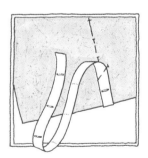

2 Add the Austrian blind tapes. Lay the fabric flat, wrong side up. Measure 30 cm (12 in) in from each side edge and mark down the whole length of the blind. Cut two lengths of tape to the length of the blind, making sure that the first loop on each length is 5 cm (2 in) up from the hem edge. Turn under 1.5 cm (⅝ in) of tape and position centrally over each marked line, with the folded edge just above the hem edge. Pin, then stitch down both edges of tape and across the lower ends. To avoid puckering, start stitching at the same end of the blind each time.

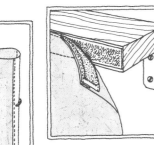

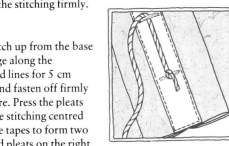

3 To form the inverted pleats, lay the fabric flat, right side up. Mark 15 cm (6 in) on either side of the right-hand tape, down the whole length. Fold the fabric along the centre of the tape, right sides facing, matching the marked lines together. Pin and stitch down the matched lines from the top edge for 10 cm (4 in) only, working a few stitches in reverse to secure the stitching firmly.

4 Stitch up from the base edge along the matched lines for 5 cm (2 in) and fasten off firmly as before. Press the pleats with the stitching centred over the tapes to form two inverted pleats on the right side of the blind. Repeat, to form an inverted pleat of the same size over the left-hand tape.

5 Fasten the blind to the battening. Turn the top edge of the blind, including the ends of the tape, to the wrong side just

under the width of the fastening tape. Position the 'sew' half of fastening tape to wrong side of blind with top edge against top edge of blind and covering raw edges. Trim the ends to match the edges of the blind. Pin and stitch the fastening tape in place along both edges and across ends.

6 Screw the battening into the ceiling of the recess or to the wall on brackets (*see* Roman Blind). Press 'stick' half of fastening tape to front of battening. Press the two halves of the fastening tape together to secure blind in position. Fix two screw eyes into the underside of the batten, matched exactly above each tape position.

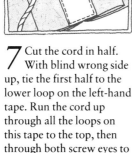

7 Cut the cord in half. With blind wrong side up, tie the first half to the lower loop on the left-hand tape. Run the cord up through all the loops on this tape to the top, then through both screw eyes to hang on the right-hand side of the blind. Tie and thread the second length of cord

up the second length of tape and through the screw eye above so the cords hang together. Trim ends level with base of blind and knot together.

8 Fix a cleat at the right-hand side of the window. Pull up the blind and wind the cords round the cleat in a figure of eight to secure.

COVERING THE BATTEN WITH FABRIC

*C*over the battening with fabric or paint to match the window surround. To cover the battening with fabric, wrap the wood like a parcel and stick the edges in place on the wrong side with clear adhesive.

*L*ondon blinds are a more tailored version of Austrian blinds. For a really crisp finish, the edges can be bound or trimmed with braid.

festoon blind

. . . .

Festoon blinds, like Austrian blinds, ruche up into soft folds when raised at the window, but whereas Austrian blinds lie almost flat against the window when lowered, festoon blinds are designed to remain attractively ruched even when fully extended. Festoons require such a large amount of fabric that they cannot be pulled up totally clear of the window, and they are traditionally made up in sheer fabrics and used as an alternative to net curtains. Festoons are gathered at the top using pencil pleat heading tape and are drawn up vertically by cords looped through rings on special festoon blind tape stitched at intervals across the back of the fabric. Festoon blinds are hung at the window either on a specialist blind track or on a length of standard curtain track fixed to a piece of battening held at the window on brackets.

Festoons look best either with a frill running down the sides and base, or with a bound edge sewn all the way round. This festoon blind has a single base frill and is bound on all edges.

Materials

- Austrian blind track (*see* Austrian Blind), or length of battening plus fixing brackets and screws combined with standard curtain track. If using battening a screw eye will have to be added to underside at top of each tape.
- Sheer cotton or cotton-mix fabric
- Transparent pencil-pleat curtain heading tape (suitable for sheer fabrics)
- Festoon blind tape
- Contrasting fabric for edging
- Nylon cord
- Matching sewing thread
- Cord tidy
- Cleat with fixing screws

SEE ALSO:

AUSTRIAN BLIND   129

CONTEMPORARY STYLE   49

CURTAINS   86

FABRIC FILE   9

SEWING GUIDE   200

Measuring up

- Fix the blind track at the window (*see* Austrian Blind). For the fabric, measure the width of the track and allow 2½ times this measurement. For the length, measure from the track to the sill and allow for 1½ times this length.

- For frill, join together strips 13.5 cm (5½ in) wide cut from across fabric width, to make up strip measuring twice width of blind.

- For pencil-pleat heading tape, allow for blind width plus 5 cm (2 in) for neatening the ends.

- For festoon blind tape, decide on width of finished scallop – between 20 cm (8 in) and 30 cm (12 in) – and multiply 2½ times to give approximate space between vertical tapes. Divide space equally into blind so that all scallops are same width apart. Allow for the blind length plus 5 cm (2 in) for each tape length.

- The edging should be about 6 cm (2½ in) wide; allow twice the blind length and twice the width plus 2.5 cm (1 in).

- For the nylon cord, allow twice the blind length plus one width for each vertical tape.

Making up

1 It is best to cut the blind fabric to the correct size from one piece. If you need to join fabric widths together to gain the blind width, stitch lengths together with French seams. Alternatively, stitch lengths together with plain flat seams and position them so they will go behind one of the lengths of festoon blind tape.

2 Turn under a 3 cm (1¼ in) wide hem on both side edges; pin and tack in place. The raw edges will be covered by lengths of tape.

3 The festoon tapes are stitched vertically across the back of the blind, spaced equally at 2½ times the width of each finished ruche. Position the first two lengths of tape 2.5 cm (1 in) in from the side edges of the blind to cover the raw hem edges. Cut same length as blind, making sure that the first ring on each length is 5 cm (2 in) up from lower edge.

4 Draw out gathering cords on wrong side on base of tape and knot. Place on blind with rings facing inwards. Pin and stitch in place with a single central row of stitching, catching side hems at the same time.

5 Divide up area between two outer lengths of tape evenly and mark positions for remaining tapes, usually between 50 cm (20 in) and 75 cm (30 in) apart. Pin and stitch a length of tape along each marked line in the same way as before, making sure rings align horizontally.

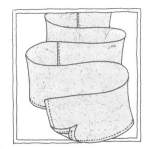

6 To make the frills, stitch 13.5 cm (5½ in) strips together with French seams. Turn under a scant double 1 cm (⅜ in) hem on side and base edges of frill; pin and stitch all round the hem.

7 Work two rows of gathering stitches across the raw top edge of frill, one on either side of stitching line. Place frill to blind with wrong sides together. Pull up gathers evenly to fit. Pin and stitch 6 mm (¼ in) from raw edges, catching in ends of tapes.

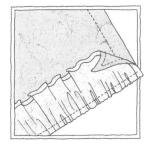

8 Refold with right sides together and seam to edge. Pin and stitch, taking 1 cm (⅜ in) seam allowance to complete French seam, again catching in tapes.

9 Turn down top edge of fabric to depth of heading tape. Pin and stitch binding fabric in place round all edges of blind, starting and ending at a corner. Position heading tape just below bound edge covering raw fabric edge; pin. Trim festoon blind tapes so they will tuck under heading tape by 1 cm (⅜ in), making sure first that tape threads are free to pull up. Stitch heading tape in place in same way as before (*see* Austrian blind).

10 Draw up heading tape cords until blind fits window width. Knot cords together and wind surplus cords onto a cord tidy and hang in heading tape.

11 Pull up each of the festoon blind tapes evenly in turn, until blind is correct length for window. Wind up surplus cords and knot at the top of each tape length. Hang blind on blind track, as for Austrian blind.

12 Cut the nylon cord into lengths, each one twice the blind length plus one width and cord the blind, as for Austrian blind.

13 Fix a cleat at the right-hand side of the window. Pull up blind and wind cords round cleat in a figure of eight.

FESTOON BLINDS

Sheer fabric is suitable for festoon blinds, as the featherweight fabric will ruche into deep folds across the window. For a lovely old-fashioned look, add a deep frill of old lace across the lower edge of the blind. Light, sheer festoon blinds can be hung straight onto the window frame by using a heading-and-grip tape combination. The 'grip' half of the tape is stuck to the window frame and the heading tape is stitched to the top of the blind. Once the blind is complete, the heading tape is gathered up and pressed onto the 'grip' tape, where it will be held firmly in position.

Covers and cushions

· ·

Covering seats and cushions with fabric is one of the easiest ways to add decoration and interest to the rooms in your home. Most traditional upholstery is a specialist job, best left to the professionals, but smaller-scale projects, such as basic cushion covers or covering drop-in seats, are well within the amateur's reach.

The shape of a sofa or chair will dictate, to a certain extent, the style of covering that you choose. Upholstered furniture with strong, curved lines generally looks best fitted with a tight cover to show off the shape, while squarer designs often look good in basic loose covers that fall in soft folds or finish in kick or box pleats, or in a gathered skirt. A simple fringe is an effective

Scatter cushions can be made in almost any fabric to match the decor of your room (left). Leave them plain, or trim with piping, cord or a border or frill.

Pretty chintz and embroidered cushions can be arranged on a bed during the day to provide a splash of colour (above).

On this modern sofa, well stuffed cushions have been arranged so that they form interesting sculptural shapes (right). To achieve a similar effect, use rectangular cushions with a soft filling such as down that can be easily moulded into shape. Plump up the cushions, then simply form them into two peaks with the side of the hand.

CUSHIONS

Cushions are one of the oldest forms of home furnishings. Originally, fur skins were thrown over hard stone benches to provide a more comfy seat. These were gradually replaced with layers of fabric and eventually, with the addition of padding, the cushion was born. Nowadays, even the cosiest seat is improved with extra scatter cushions, providing extra padding behind the neck or back. Also use them as an economical and effective means of introducing new colours, patterns and textures into your scheme.

These country-style cushions (left) have been cleverly made to co-ordinate with the tablecloth and napkins. The large floral motif from the fabric has been cut out and appliquéd onto the centre of plain cream cushion covers. Further decoration has been added with a floral frill around the edges.

alternative. For something altogether more informal, drape a shawl, rug or length of fabric over the furniture. (This is also a good way of discovering whether a proposed fabric works with other furnishings in the room.) Cheap junk-shop dining chairs can be transformed with slip-over loose covers in all shapes and styles, and pretty wooden or cane chairs can be made more comfortable with the addition of a squab cushion held in place with ties at the back. Loose covers, of course, have the advantage of being easy to remove and clean, and are a good way of extending the life of fitted covers. It also makes it possible to have different covers for one piece of furniture for different times of the year – something in a light, colourful fabric for the spring and summer months, for instance, and another cover in a warm, rich fabric for the autumn and winter months. On a more modest scale, the same idea could be applied to cushions, and would certainly be cheaper!

*W*indow seats can be easily made with a simple box cushion and lots of separate cushions to give support and comfort to the back (below).

*W*ell-tailored loose covers can transform an old sofa (right). Add some new scatter cushions to match or contrast with the sofa fabric and the new look is complete.

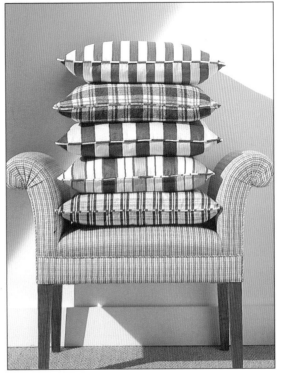

*S*tripes and checks can be mixed and matched to great effect (left). This stack of square cushions have a common theme of green that links them all together. To give a professional finish, use contrasting piping around the edges.

Scatter cushions are the perfect way to introduce variations on a colour theme (right), and to bring in different shapes and patterns on sofas.

A similar effect to these smart loose covers for dining room chairs can easily be achieved using suitable, inexpensive fabric (right). Piped edges will give a more professional look. Finish with simple ties to hold the covers in place.

Cushions can be given many different types of decorative edgings (below), including flat self borders, scallops, lace and broderie anglaise trims.

When it comes to choosing the fabric for a loose cover, bear in mind the amount of wear and tear it is likely to encounter. Glazed chintzes or silk damasks may be fine for a little-used bedroom chair, but something more hardwearing like a linen or upholstery weight twill would be a better choice for the sofa in a family sitting room. If you plan to remove the covers for cleaning, check that the fabric is colour-fast and non-shrinkable – this will apply to any trimmings or braids used on the cover as well. Plain fabrics or small all-over patterns won't tie you to specific colour schemes in a room and will also be easy to work with and ensure minimum wastage. Large or busy patterns may be more difficult to live with and are harder to sew – motifs should always be centred on the various sections of a chair or sofa, which will inevitably involve wastage. All upholstery fabrics must pass the standard flame-resistant tests; fabrics that don't pass these tests should be used with a suitable barrier cloth for safety.

One of the easiest projects for an inexperienced sewer to tackle is making cushions, and

Change a plain upright chair into something special (right) by adding a simple loose cover embellished with bows on the top corners, and a deep gathered skirt edged in contrasting green piping around the chair seat.

An all-in-one loose cover on a junk shop chair will give it a more tailored look (below). Here, bright yellow piping and matching covered buttons enliven this otherwise plain cover.

fortunately cushions are also one of the most versatile and inexpensive furnishing items in the home. At one end of the scale, large floor cushions can replace more traditional forms of seating, while at the other end, small cushions not only make a seat more comfortable and provide support for the back, but also add a splash of colour to break up the lines of a chair, sofa or bed. Virtually any fabric is suitable for cushions, from delicate white lace, crewel embroidery and silk, to velvet, linen and heavy tapestry. Fabric designs don't have to match the furniture they sit on: try a combination of co-ordinating coloured fabrics with different textures, shapes and trimmings to introduce variety and interest into a scheme.

*T*ransform an old upright chair with an all-in-one loose cover (left). Add a frill with a contrasting bound edge and paint the legs to match the trim.

*S*eparate, fitted slip-over covers for an upright chair back and seat are easy to make (left). Here, they are attached to the chair with large ribbon ties.

*B*olsters provide firm armrests at each end of a sofa (left) and can also be used to provide support for the back.

The shape of a cushion and the way it is trimmed makes a very important contribution to its decorative effect in a room. Square and rectangular cushions are probably the most versatile shapes, and in addition there are round and bolster shapes, which are useful as armrests and headrests, especially on beds. In most cases it is better to opt for generously sized cushions – too many small pads can look lost on a large bed or sofa. As with so many soft furnishing projects, it is the trimmings that add individuality. The variations on cushions are endless – choose from simple bound edges, frills, braiding or fringing and scallops. And don't forget it's not just the edgings of cushions that can be embellished: you might like to appliqué a design onto the pad of a cushion, or make the cover from patchwork or a favourite piece of cross stitch or antique lace backed with a plain fabric.

*N*eat, slip-over covers on the back and seat of a chair (above) can simply be held in place with a series of ties tied into bows.

*F*abric covers can be used to transform chairs of all shapes and sizes (left). Here, an array of striped fabrics have been used for squab cushions and given a variety of decorative edges, from simple piping to valances in long and short gathers, scallops and box pleats.

Scatter cushions

. . . .

Scatter cushions can be grouped together any-where, adding a touch of colour and pattern on sofas, beds or chairs. The covers are easy to make; use either a furnishing or strong dress fabric. Cushion pads are available in different shapes and sizes, or they can be made in the same way as the covers but without any decorative edging. For a really good fit make the cushion cover slightly smaller than the cushion pad.

SQUARE CUSHION COVER

A square cushion cover is one of the easiest coverings to make.

Materials

- Square cushion pad
- Suitable fabric
- Matching sewing thread

Measuring up

- To measure the cushion pad, place the tape measure seam to seam and allow a seam allowance of 1.5 cm (⅝ in) to all edges.

Making up

1 Cut out two pieces of fabric to the chosen size, including 1.5 cm (⅝ in) seam allowance to all edges.

2 Place the fabric pieces with right sides together. Pin, tack and stitch round the four corners and three sides,

leaving an opening in the centre of remaining side.

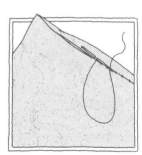

3 Trim seam allowance and cut across corners. Turn cover right side out. Insert cushion pad. Turn under edges of opening in line with remainder of the seam and slipstitch folded edges across the opening.

SEE ALSO:
. . . .
CONTEMPORARY STYLE   49
. . . .
FABRIC FILE   9
. . . .
SEWING GUIDE   200
. . . .

ROUND CUSHION COVER

For a round cover, you will need to make a circular pattern. You may be able to use a large plate as a template for a small cover.

Materials

- Paper for pattern
- String
- Pencil
- Drawing pin
- Round cushion pad
- Suitable fabric
- Matching sewing thread

Making up

1 Cut a square of paper 5 cm (2 in) larger than the required diameter of the cover, and include a seam allowance of 1.5 cm (⅝ in). Fold the square of paper into quarters. Cut a length of string 20 cm (8 in) longer than the radius of the cover so there is enough string to tie round the pencil and drawing pin.

2 Tie one end of string round the pointed end of the pencil. Anchor the drawing pin in the folded corner of the paper with the string the same length as the radius of the cover plus the seam allowance. Holding the drawing pin firmly in position and with the string taut, draw an arc from edge to edge. Cut along marked line and unfold paper.

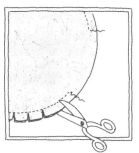

3 Using the paper pattern, cut out two pieces of fabric. Place fabric pieces with right sides together; pin and stitch two-thirds of the way round the cover, taking 1.5 cm (⅝ in) seam allowance. Snip notches in seam allowance at 4 cm (1½ in) intervals and turn cover right side out.

4 Insert cushion pad. Turn under seam allowance and slipstitch folded edges together.

*L*arge square cushions have been made to match the dramatic blue and white striped fabric covering the mattress on this wrought-iron day bed. Cushions in a contrasting blue and white floral print help to create a softer, more comfortable look. The cushions all have a wide flat border.

Zip fastenings

A zip can be added either to one of the seams on a cushion cover or across the back of a cover. There are also a number of other fastenings that can be used, such as press fasteners, press fastening tape and touch-and-close fasteners or tape.

ZIP IN SEAM

Make sure that the opening is large enough for the cushion pad to fit in the cover. Choose a zip that is 5 cm (2 in) shorter than the edge of the cushion which is to have the zip opening. If the fabric design dictates which way the cushion lies, position the opening along the lower edge of the cushion. On piped cushions, a zip can be inserted to one side of the piping.

Making up

1 Cut out the two square cover pieces (*see* Square Cushion Cover). Pin and stitch three sides of cover and stitch 5 cm (2 in) in at either end of the fourth side which will hold the zip. Turn cover right side out. Turn in opening edges and tack.

2 Open zip. Tack right-hand side of zip under right-hand side of opening and stitch in place.

3 Position left-hand side of opening over second half of zip, covering the teeth. Pin in place, open zip, then tack and stitch in position.

4 Remove tacking stitches. Insert cushion pad and close zip.

ZIP ACROSS BACK COVER

A zip can be inserted across the centre of the back cover or be set just above the seam, if preferred. Choose a zip that is 12 cm (5 in) shorter than the width of the cover. You will need to add 1.5 cm (⅝ in) allowance round both pieces of fabric, plus an extra 3 cm (1¼ in) to the back cover piece for the zip seam allowance.

Making up

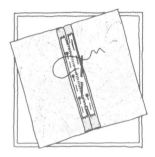

1 Cut out one square front cover piece to size (*see* Square Cushion Cover) plus 1.5 cm (⅝ in) seam allowance. Cut out one square back cover piece 3 cm (1¼ in) larger than front piece. Fold back cover piece in half and cut along fold.

2 Pin and tuck back pieces together with right sides facing. Stitch in from each end for 6 cm (2½ in), leaving a central opening. Trim and neaten seam allowances. Press seam open.

3 Place zip right side down over tacked section of seam. Pin and tack. Turn zip over and stitch in place all round from right side.

4 Remove tacking stitches and open zip. Join front and back covers round outer edge with right sides facing. Turn to right side through zip. Insert cushion pad and close zip.

SEE ALSO:

CONTEMPORARY STYLE 49

FABRIC FILE 9

SEWING GUIDE 200

SQUARE CUSHION COVER 146

e dgings

Decorative edgings for cushions of all shapes include covered piping and single or double frills in matching or contrasting fabric. Square cushions can also be finished with a flat single or double border. For simple trimmings, edge cushions in lace or broderie anglaise.

PIPING

One of the quickest ways of creating an attractive cushion cover is to add piping all round the outer edge. Piping cord is available in a variety of thicknesses and can be covered with matching or contrasting fabric, plain or gathered. Measure each side of the cushion to be piped and add 5 cm (2 in) for joining.

Materials

- Covered piping cord
- Suitable fabric
- Matching sewing thread

*R*eady-made edgings include cording and tassels.

Making up

1 For a square cover, pin and tack the covered piping round the right side of first cover piece with cord facing inwards and raw edges level with raw edge of cover. Snip piping fabric from each corner point up to stitching to turn piping neatly.

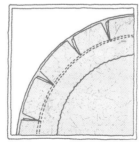

2 For a round cover, pin and tack the covered piping round one cover piece in the same way, but snip the piping fabric at 4 cm (1½ in) intervals all round.

3 To join piping, trim cord ends so they butt firmly together. Bind over the join firmly with sewing thread. Trim fabric so one end is 2 cm (¾ in) longer than the other. Turn under 1 cm (⅜ in) and overlap opposite raw edge. On square covers place the join centrally in one edge (this should be the base edge on patterned covers).

4 Join cover front and back as before (*see* Square Cushion Cover and Round Cushion Cover), using a piping attachment on the sewing machine.

SEE ALSO:

CONTEMPORARY STYLE   49

FABRIC FILE   9

SEWING GUIDE   200

For gathered piping, allow 1½ to 2 times more piping strip than cord. Cut out enough strips on the bias of the fabric and join together with plain flat seams to make one long strip.

Materials

- Suitable fabric
- Piping cord
- Matching sewing thread

Making up

1 Wrap the fabric strip evenly round the cord with wrong sides together. Stitch cord to one end of fabric strip. Using a piping attachment on the sewing machine, stitch alongside cord for 20 cm (8 in). Be careful not to stitch tightly against cord.

machine foot. Gently pull the cord through the fabric tube to gather it up. Continue stitching and gathering the cord in this way until you reach the end of the strip.

2 Leaving the needle in the fabric, raise the

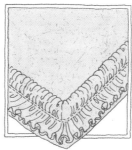

3 Add gathered piping to cover in the same way as before, joining ends together to fit.

SINGLE FRILL

A single frill is a strip of fabric with a double hem along its base edge and its top edge gathered into the cushion cover. Single frills are usually cut on the straight of the grain, but they can be cut on the bias of the fabric if a soft effect is desired.

Materials

- Suitable fabric
- Matching sewing thread
- Tailor's chalk

Measuring up

- Single frills vary between 3 cm (1¼ in) and 10 cm (4 in) wide. When measuring round the cushion cover, allow 1½ to 2 times the circumference for the frill length. On the frill width, allow an extra 3.5 cm (1⅜ in) allowance for seams and double hem.

Making up

1 Cut out on the straight of grain (across the fabric width) enough strips of the correct depth to make the required frill length. Pin and stitch the strips together with French seams into a ring of fabric.

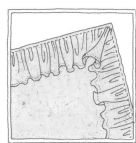

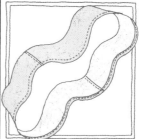

2 Turn under a double 1 cm (⅜ in) hem along base edge of frill. Pin and stitch all round.

3 Run two rows of gathering stitches round the frill on either side of the 1.5 cm (⅝ in) seamline. If the cover is large and the frill therefore long, divide both the frill edge and the outer edge of the cover into four equal sections and mark with tailor's chalk. Work two rows of gathering stitches in each section in turn, beginning and ending stitches at the marked sections.

4 Place the frill on the cover with right sides together, frill facing inwards and raw edges together. On long frills, match the marked sections together as necessary. Space the gathers evenly round the cover; on square covers, allow for slightly more fabric round each corner. Pin and stitch frill in place.

5 Join cover front and back as before, stitching just inside the previous stitching.

DOUBLE FRILL

A double frill is a strip of fabric folded in half before being gathered and inserted into a seam. As the fabric is folded, there is no right or wrong side to the finished cushion. Double frills are usually cut on the bias to help them to lie well round the corners, but they can be cut on the straight of grain if preferred.

Materials

- Suitable fabric
- Matching sewing thread

Measuring up

- Finished double frills are generally between 3 cm (1¼ in) and 10 cm (4 in) wide. Measure the cushion and frill as described before (*see* Single Frill), allowing twice the frill depth plus 3 cm (1¼ in) for seams.

Making up

1 Cut out bias strips for the frill. Cut out sufficient strips to make up the required length and join together into a ring with plain flat seams. Trim and press seams open.

2 Fold frill strip evenly in half lengthways with raw edges matching. Gather up frill and stitch round cover in the same way as for a single frill (*see* Single Frill).

SINGLE BORDER

A single border is stitched all round the cover holding the square cushion pad firmly in place. The border width can range from 5 cm (2 in) to 15 cm (6 in).

*D*ensely patterned fabrics made into cushions look striking when the same fabric is used for the frilled edging.

Materials

- Suitable fabric
- Matching sewing thread

Measuring up

- Decide on the size of the cover and the size of the border. You will need two pieces of fabric, each one to the finished size of the cushion cover plus the border width and 1.5 cm (⅝ in) seam allowance all round.

Making up

1 Cut out two pieces of fabric for front and back. Place right sides together; pin and stitch round four corners and three sides, leaving central opening in fourth side. Trim seams and across corners. Turn right side out.

2 Press with seam to outer edge. Pin and stitch round cover at border width, leaving an opening in the same side as previous opening.

3 Insert cushion pad through both openings. Turn in outer opening edges and slipstitch to close. Complete stitching across inner opening.

Soften the edges of lace-covered cushions with the addition of a gathered frill.

Sewing Skills

*T*est your sewing-machine skills by using a decorative stitch round the border of your cushions. Use one of the machine's embroidery stitches in a contrasting or toning thread. If the machine only has zigzag stitch, set this to a wide measure and work over a narrow ribbon or braid trim.

DOUBLE BORDER

A double border provides an opportunity to mix and match fabrics, as the border is made up in two halves before being joined together.

Materials

- Suitable fabric
- Matching sewing thread

Measuring up

- To measure up, decide on the size of the cover and the border. You will need two pieces of fabric, each one to the finished size of the cushion cover plus twice the border width and 1.5 cm (⅝ in) seam allowance all round.

Making up

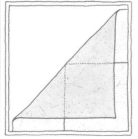

1 Cut out two cover pieces to required size. Lay first cover piece wrong side up. Turn in the border to the required width plus 1.5 cm (⅝ in); press. Unfold and turn in each

corner until pressed lines on corners match lines along each side; press.

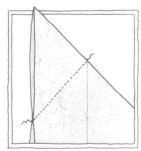

2 Open out a corner again. Turn cover over then, with right sides

facing, fold corner diagonally in half matching all fold lines. Press. Stitch across the corner along centre fold line, which is at right angles to the folded edge.

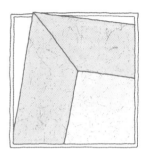

3 Trim down to within 6 mm (¼ in) beyond stitching; press seam open. Turn corner through to right side and press. Repeat at each corner.

4 Make up the second cover piece in the same way. Place cover pieces with wrong sides together. Pin and stitch all round the required border width, leaving one side open. Insert cushion pad and complete stitching.

Cushions with welts

· ·

To add depth to cushions, a narrow gusset or welt can be inserted between the front and back cushion pieces. This strip can be used to provide a contrasting band of colour or pattern, and can also be gathered. The cushions can be filled with a pad or with a piece of foam the same thickness as the welt. Welts are usually between 2 cm (¾ in) and 8 cm (3 in).

SQUARE CUSHION WITH A WELT
· ·

For welts on square and rectangular covers, cut out as many pieces as there are sides, with the seams matching the corners of the cover pieces.

Materials

- Suitable fabric
- Cushion pad
- Matching sewing thread

Measuring up

- Add 3 cm (1¼ in) seam allowance to the front and back cushion pieces.

- Each welt piece should be the length of each side of cushion plus 3 cm (1¼) seam allowance by the chosen depth plus 3 cm (1¼ in) seam allowance.

SEE ALSO:
· ·
CONTEMPORARY STYLE   49
· ·
FABRIC FILE   9
· ·
ROUND CUSHION COVER   147
· ·
SEWING GUIDE   200
· ·

Making up

 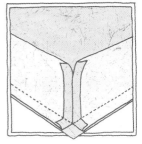

1 Cut out one front and one back cushion piece and four welt pieces as required. Pin the short edge of welt pieces together into a ring, with right sides facing. Stitch, leaving 1.5 cm (⅝ in) free at each end of each seam.

2 With right sides together, place welt round outer edge of one cover piece. At each corner the welt seam allowance will separate to provide neat corners. Pin and stitch all round. Pin and stitch second cover piece to opposite edge of welt, leaving central opening in one side. Trim and turn cover right side out.

3 Insert cushion pad; turn under edges of opening and slipstitch folded edges together across the opening.

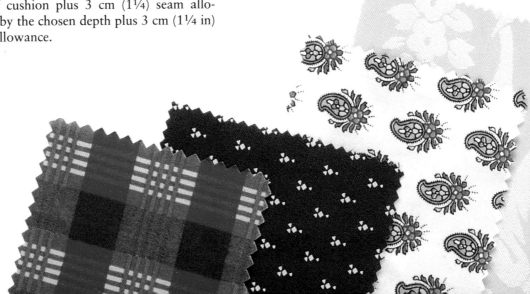

ROUND CUSHION WITH A WELT

For round covers, the welt goes round the cover with just one seam.

Materials

- Suitable fabric
- Cushion pad
- Paper for pattern
- Matching sewing thread

Measuring up

- Add 3 cm (1¼ in) seam allowance to the front and back cushion pieces.

- The welt piece should be the circumference of the cover plus 3 cm (1¼ in) seam allowance in length by the chosen depth plus 3 cm (1¼ in) seam allowance.

*T*o give a finished look to a round cushion with a welt, add covered piping to both the front and back cushion pieces.

Making up

1 Cut out front and back cushion pieces using a paper pattern as described before (*see* Round Cushion Cover), plus one welt piece to the required dimensions.

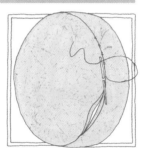

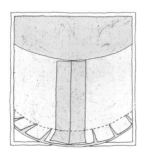

3 Trim and turn cover right side out. Insert cushion pad; turn in opening edges and slipstitch to close as before.

2 Pin and stitch the welt into a ring. Trim and press seam open. Snip into seams all round welt edges at 4 cm (1½ in) intervals. With right sides together place welt round outer edge of one cover piece. Pin and stitch; the snipped edge will help welt to curve round cover piece. Repeat on opposite side, leaving opening for cushion pad.

VARIATION: CUSHION WITH A GATHERED WELT

Allow for 1½ to 2 times the finished welt length for a gathered welt.

Materials

- Suitable fabric
- Cushion pad
- Matching sewing thread

Making up

1 For a square cover, make up the welt with seams at each corner in the same way as before. Either run two gathering threads all round the whole welt or gather up each section of the welt in turn.

seams to corners and pulling up gathers evenly to fit. Pin and stitch in place. Pin and stitch remaining edge of welt to second cover piece in the same way, leaving a central opening in one side. Complete as before.

3 For a round cover, join the welt into a ring and gather in the same way. Stitch to front and back covers in the same way, spacing out gathers evenly to fit.

2 Place welt to first cover piece with right sides together, matching

CORNER TREATMENTS

*A*nother interesting way to treat corners on plain piped cushions is to gather just round the corners. Work a row of gathering stitches for approximately 6 cm (2¼ in) on either side of each corner on both cover pieces. Pull up the gathers, add the covered piping and complete the cover.

VARIATION: CUSHION WITH A MOCK GUSSET

A narrow mock gusset can be achieved by stitch-ing across each corner of a plain square cushion cover. For the cushion cover, you will need two pieces of fabric, each one to the finished size of the square cushion cover plus the depth of the gusset or welt and adding a 1.5 cm (⅝ in) seam allowance all round.

Materials

- Suitable fabric
- Cushion pad
- Matching sewing thread

Making up

1 Cut out two pieces of fabric for the front and back of the cushion. Place the cover pieces with right sides together; pin and stitch together all round all four corners and three sides, leaving the remaining side open.

2 Pull the cover pieces apart at each corner and centre the seams flat, one on top of the other. Pin in place.

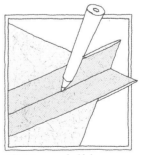

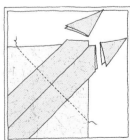

3 Measure half the finished welt depth from corner point up the seam and mark.

4 Stitch diagonally across the corner through marked point, at right angles to the seam. Repeat for each corner. Trim and turn cover right side out.

$b$olster

These cylindrical shaped cushions are a good way of providing arms or a back for a plain divan. Small bolsters also look good on a bed, as they can make comfortable neck pillows. Bolsters can be made with either plain flat or gathered ends. The simplest form of bolster can be made by stitching a long tube of fabric and tying it at each end on either side of the cushion pad. A zip opening is quickly added to a fitted bolster cover.

Materials

- Bolster cushion pad
- Paper for pattern
- Suitable fabric
- Matching sewing thread
- Zip

Measuring up

- Measure the end of the bolster cushion pad and make a circular pattern to this size as described before (*see* Round Cushion Cover), adding 1.5 cm (⅝ in) seam allowance.

- Measure round the pad and add 3 cm (1¼ in) seam allowance. Measure the length of the pad and add 3 cm (1¼ in) seam allowance.

Making up

1 Cut out one piece of fabric for the main centre section. Using the paper pattern, cut out two end pieces.

2 Fold centre section lengthways with right sides together; pin and tack into a tube. Stitch in from each end for at least 4 cm (1½ in), leaving the central section tacked. Press seam open.

SEE ALSO:

CONTEMPORARY STYLE 49

FABRIC FILE 9

ROUND CUSHION COVER 147

SEWING GUIDE 200

VARIATION: BOLSTER WITH GATHERED ENDS

To make a bolster with gathered ends, measure both the length of the pad and across the end. Add these two measurements together and add 3 cm (1¼ in) seam allowance. Measure round the pad and add 3 cm (1¼ in) seam allowance.

Materials

- Bolster cushion pad
- Suitable fabric
- Matching sewing thread
- Zip (optional)
- Two self-covering buttons

Making up

1 Cut out one piece of fabric to required measurements.

2 With right sides together, fold fabric into a tube; stitch across seam or insert a zip in the same way as before. Trim and turn right side out.

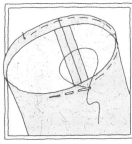

3 Turn in seam allowance at one end of tube. Gather round the end, taking large stitches, close to the folded edge.

4 Pull up firmly and fasten off. If not adding a zip, slide the cushion pad inside the cover before the second end is gathered up.

5 Gather up the second end in the same way as before. Cover each button with fabric, following the manufacturer's instructions, and sew to the centre of each gathered end to finish.

M ake a bolster to fit across the width of a bed to provide a comfortable headrest. For a co-ordinated look, pick a fabric that has already been used somewhere else on the bed, such as on the headboard or valance.

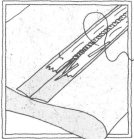

3 Tack a zip right side down over the central tacked section. Turn right side out and stitch zip in place all round zip edge.

4 Snip notches at 4 cm (1½ in) intervals round each centre section end, taking care not to cut beyond seam allowance. Snip round the end circles in the same way. Open zip. With right sides together, pin and stitch circle to each end of tube. Turn right side out through zip. Insert cushion pad and close zip.

Shaped squab cushion

This cushion is ideal for traditional kitchen chairs. It is cut to the shape of the chair seat and ties in place. The narrow gusset (welt) is normally between 2.5 cm (1 in) and 4 cm (1½ in) deep. If the cushion is very shaped, the curves can be reinforced before joining together with a row of stitching round the corners. The cover pieces can then be snipped safely. The finished cushion can be buttoned either at the centre or in a pattern. The ties can be replaced by a fabric loop and button, large decorative bows, long ballerina ties or an elasticated strap.

Materials

- Paper or tracing paper for pattern
- Suitable fabric
- Covered piping cord
- Matching sewing thread
- Foam of the same thickness as gusset

Measuring up

- Place the paper over the chair seat. Draw round the outside of the seat. Mark the position of the ties, the centre back and centre front. Fold pattern along marked centre and cut round the marked outline. Unfold pattern and check against the chair seat. Check tie positions on the pattern. Allow 1.5 cm (⅝ in) seam allowance for all edges.

- For gusset, measure round edge of cover pattern. Add 3 cm (1¼ in) for seams. Decide on depth and add 3 cm (1¼ in) for seams.

- Measure round the cover pattern and allow two lengths of covered piping to this measurement plus 5 cm (2 in).

- For the two ties, you will need two strips of fabric of 60 × 5 cm (24 × 2 in).

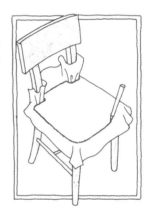

A shaped squab cushion for a kitchen chair with ties and piped edging (above).

Make a paper pattern of the chair seat (left).

FABRIC CHOICES

*U*se squab cushions to make a bold design statement in the kitchen. Make them up in a fabric that co-ordinates with the tablecloth and curtains or one that totally contrasts with the rest of the room. Mix and match the ties, picking out a different colour from the cushion fabric for each chair. To complete the effect, button through the centre of each cushion in a colour to match the ties.

SEE ALSO:

CONTEMPORARY STYLE   49

FABRIC FILE   9

SEWING GUIDE   200

Making up

1 Using the pattern, cut out one front and one back cover piece, adding 1.5 cm (⅝ in) seam allowance to all edges. Cut out gusset to the required size.

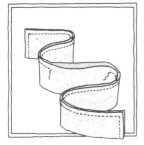

2 Cut out two strips of fabric 60 × 5 cm (24 × 2 in) for the ties. Fold one tie in half lengthways with right sides together; pin and stitch ends and sides together, leaving a central opening in one side. Trim seams and turn right side out. Turn in opening edges and slipstitch together to close. Make up second tie in the same way. Topstitch round tie as desired.

A squab cushion provides a comfortable seat on this simple bedroom chair. The addition of a symmetrical pattern of buttons on the top adds a subtle decorative touch.

3 Pin covered piping cord to right side of first cover piece with cord facing inwards and raw edges level with raw edge of cover. Join ends together centrally in back edge to fit, snipping into piping fabric at curves. Pin and stitch piping round second cover piece in the same way.

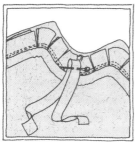

4 Fold one tie piece in half and pin over piping at marked position. Pin second tie piece to opposite side over piping in the same way.

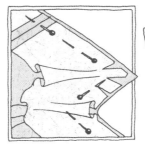

5 Pin and stitch gusset strip together into a ring. With seam at centre back, pin gusset round one cover piece over piping and ties. Snip into gusset seam allowance to help it lie smoothly round the curves and corners. Stitch in place. Stitch the remaining edge of gusset to second cover piece in the same way, but leaving a central opening in the back. Turn.

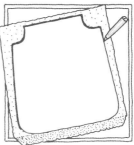

6 Place pattern on foam and mark round. Cut out with large scissors. Insert into cover; turn in opening edges and slipstitch folded edges together. Place cushion on chair and fasten ties round back struts to hold in position.

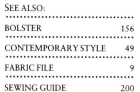

$d$eep gusset cushion

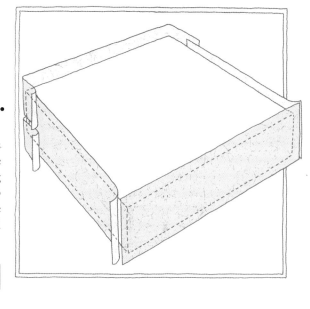

Gusset cushions are box shaped to fit into sofas and large easy chairs. Different fabrics can be combined in one cushion. The zip fastening should be long enough to enable the deep cushion pad to be easily inserted, so on square and rectangular cushions the zip extends round into the side edges.

Materials

- Gusset cushion pad
- Suitable fabric
- Covered piping cord
- Matching sewing thread

Measuring up

- Measure the cushion pad and add 3 cm (1¼ in) to both the length and width measurements for front and back pieces.

- The gusset is subdivided into four sections: one front, one back and two side pieces. For the front gusset, measure the length and depth of the cushion front, adding 3 cm (1¼ in) all round for seams. For the back gusset, measure across the back and add 19 cm (7½ in). Measure the depth and add 6 cm (2½ in) for seam allowance. For the side gusset pieces, measure the length and depth of the cover side. Deduct 5 cm (2 in) from the length and add 3 cm (1¼ in) to the depth.

- Allow sufficient covered piping cord to fit round front and back cover pieces plus 5 cm (2 in) for each length.

SEE ALSO:

BOLSTER 156

CONTEMPORARY STYLE 49

FABRIC FILE 9

SEWING GUIDE 200

Making up

1 Fold the back gusset piece in half lengthways; cut down the fold. Pin, tack and partially stitch the two back gusset pieces together.

2 Add central zip in the same way as before (*see* Bolster). Pin and stitch short edges of gusset pieces together in the correct order – back, side, front, side – leaving 1.5 cm (⅝ in) unstitched at each end of front seams. Trim and press seams open.

3 Pin and stitch piping cord round right side of each cover piece with cord facing inwards and raw edges together. Join piping together at centre of back to fit.

piece, right sides together, over piping and with front gusset seams to front corners of cover. Snip into seam allowance at back corners of gusset to help to form sharp back corners.

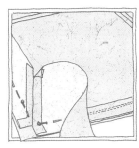

5 Open zip. Pin and stitch remaining side of gusset to remaining cover piece in the same way. Turn right side out. Insert cushion pad and close zip.

4 Pin and stitch one side of gusset to cover

CUTTING THE FOAM

Thick foam can be awkward to cut at home. It may be easier to take the template of the cushion pad to the foam dealer and ask him to cut it to size. When working at home, place the template on the foam with one or more edges touching the foam edges (this will save cutting out all the sides) and mark round the outline. Use a bread or electric carving knife to cut the shape out. Take great care to keep fingers well away from the blade.

A beautiful velvet has been used for the fitted cover and deep gusset cushions on this large comfortable sofa. To create a fairly neutral, easy-to-live-with look, the sofa and cushions have been edged with a pale-coloured braid to contrast.

loose covers

· ·

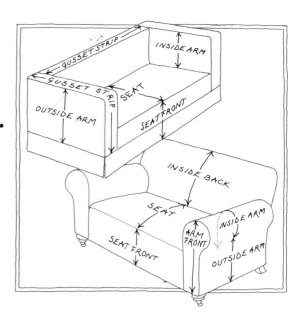

Loose covers are made by cutting out rectangles of fabric for each section of the seating to be covered and pin-fitting these in place over the furniture before stitching them together. The cover is held in position by a tuck-in of fabric all round the seat edges and this extra fabric needs to be added to the inside back, seat and inside arm pieces. Big patterns will have to be matched across the furniture with any large motifs centred on the main sections. Choose a good quality fabric that is suitable for loose covers. Make sure that it can either be washed or dry cleaned, is colour-fast and pre-shrunk. A loose cover for an armchair is measured and made up in exactly the same way as for this loose-covered sofa.

Materials

- Suitable fabric
- Matching sewing thread
- Hook and eye fastenings
- Piping cord
- Paper for pattern and graph paper
- Tailor's chalk

Measuring up

- Each section of the sofa is measured lengthways across the widest point and widthways. Measure the outside back, inside back, seat, seat front, inside arm, outside arm and arm front. On modern box-shaped sofas, the arm front is replaced by a gusset strip which runs along the top of the back and arms.

- Make a rough drawing of the sofa and as each piece of the sofa is measured, write down the relevant measurements. At the same time mark in the direction of the fabric grain. Add 4 cm (1½ in) to each measurement for seam allowance and a further 15 cm (6 in) to the measurement of the base and side edges of the inside back, back and side edges of the seat

and the back and base edges of the inside arms for the tuck-in allowance.

- Decide on the type of sofa skirt; this runs round the base of the loose cover to give a neat finish. Choose from a plain tie-on cover, a tailored straight skirt with side pleats, or a gathered or pleated skirt. For a tailored skirt, measure across the back, front and sides of the sofa, adding an extra 18 cm (7 in) to each length for inverted corner pleats and for seams. The depth of the skirt should be between 10 cm (4 in) and 15 cm (6 in) plus 4 cm (1½ in) for seams. Each corner pleat should be 18 cm (7 in) by the skirt depth plus 4 cm (1½ in) for seams.

- Measure and make up each seat cushion in the same way as for deep gusset cushions (see Deep Gusset Cushion).

- To work out how much fabric is needed for the loose cover, draw each fabric piece to scale and place the pieces on a scale drawing of the fabric. Check the direction of the grain and any pattern repeats and motifs.

- Remember to allow for extra fabric to cover the piping cord (unless using a contrast); allow about 14 m (15½ yd) of piping for a three-seater sofa, using 4 cm (1½ in) wide strips from across the fabric bias.

SEE ALSO:
· ·
CONTEMPORARY STYLE   49
· ·
DEEP GUSSET CUSHION   160
· ·
FABRIC FILE   9
· ·
SEWING GUIDE   200
· ·

- Lay the fabric out right side up. Using the scale layout as a guide, measure and mark the rectangles for each piece. Check any pattern matching across the relevant pieces. Mark each piece with its name, the top and base edges and sew a row of tacking stitches along the centre of each piece.

Making up

1 Cut out each piece. If it is necessary to stitch two fabric widths together to gain the width needed for the larger pieces, such as the outside back, position the seams centrally and match any pattern across the join. Cut out sufficient strips from across the fabric bias to cover the piping cord.

2 Mark the centre of the back, inside back and seat of the sofa with tailor's chalk or use a row of pins.

3 First pin the outside back fabric on sofa, right side out, matching centres. Pin along the 2 cm (¾ in) seam allowance all round the outside edge. Then pin on the inside

back, pinning it to the outside back fabric along the top edge. Trim off any excess fabric to within 2 cm (¾ in) of the pinned seamline.

4 On modern box-shaped sofas, pin the gusset strip across the top of the back before pinning the inside back in place.

5 Place the seat fabric centrally in position on the sofa with a 2 cm (¾ in) seam allowance at the front and the tuck-in allowance at the back and sides. Pin the seat to inside back fabric, along tuck-in.

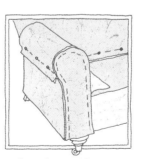

6 Pin the outside arms and the inside arms together to fit round the arm. Pin the inside arms to the inside back and seat allowing for the tuck-in. Pin the outside back to the outside arms. Pin the front arms in place, pinning them to inside and outside arms.

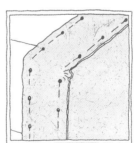

7 On modern box-shaped sofas, the arm will have a gusset strip instead of a front arm piece.

8 Pin the front seat fabric centrally to the seat, pinning to seat and front arm pieces.

*L*arge patterns can look striking on a loose cover. For a professional look, the motifs must be centred on the main sections of the sofa or chair.

9 When the cover has been pinned on the sofa, check for fit and smooth the fabric pieces out from the centre points. Then check that all the seam allowances have been trimmed to within 2 cm (¾ in) of the pinned seamline and remove cover from the sofa. Do not trim tuck-in allowance.

10 Tack all the pieces together in the right order, with right sides facing and adding covered piping cord between the seams. Turn right side out and check for fit over the sofa before stitching.

On a modern, high-sided sofa, use bow ties to attach a loose cover at the front to give it the appearance of a well-wrapped gift.

11 Stitch the cover together between outside back and inside back, inserting back gusset strips as necessary. Add the arms, leaving the left-hand seam between the outside back and outside arm open for fastenings. Stitch the inside arms to inside back and then stitch the tuck-ins

all round the seat, before adding the seat front. Trim seam allowance and neaten raw edges. Turn cover right side out and check for fit over the sofa.

12 Cut a strip of fabric twice the length of the back opening plus 3 cm (1¼ in) hem allowance and 7.5 cm (3 in) wide. Pin and stitch one long edge of strip all round opening at side of sofa. Turn strip to the inside, turn under seam allowance on remaining long edge and slipstitch over previous stitching, enclosing the seam allowance. Press. Turn up hem edges of strip and stitch in place.

13 Fit the cover on the sofa and mark round skirt line with a row of pins. Trim edge of cover to within 1.5 cm (⅝ in) of marked line. Taking 1.5 cm (⅝ in) seams, pin and stitch skirt pieces together in the following order: outside back, pleat, outside arm, pleat, front, pleat, outside arm and pleat. Turn under a double 1 cm (⅜ in) hem and stitch; turn-in side seams, tucking under raw edges and slipstitch in position.

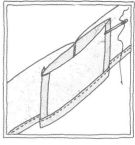

14 Form an inverted pleat at each corner by folding in seam lines for 7.5 cm (3 in); tack across top and base edges to hold in position. At skirt ends, fold back 7.5 cm (3 in) to wrong side of shorter end and make or pleat as before at remaining end. With right sides together and matching pleats to the corners, pin and stitch the skirt all round the lower edge of cover, leaving opening edge free.

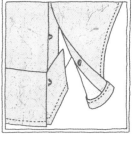

15 Fit cover over sofa and mark position of hooks and eyes down the back opening. Tuck opening pleat behind skirt end and mark position of fastenings. Handsew fastenings in place.

Cushion with skirt

This simple padded cushion for a chair seat has the addition of a skirt all round to cover the legs. To allow for the back struts, the skirt is made in two sections: a front piece that covers the front and sides, and a separate piece for the back. The cushion is fastened in place with large bows tied round each back strut.

Materials

- Paper for pattern
- Furnishing fabric
- Heavyweight wadding
- Covered piping cord
- Matching sewing thread

Measuring up

- Measure the chair seat and make a pattern as described before (*see* Shaped Squab Cushion), adding 1.5 cm (⅝ in) all round for seam allowance.

- For the front skirt length, measure from the seat down the chair legs to the chosen length. Allow 3 cm (1¼ in) for hem and seam.

- For the front skirt width, measure round the seat from one back strut, round the side, across the front and round the side to the opposite back strut. Double the measurement to allow for gathers and add 1.5 cm (⅝ in) for seam allowance.

- The back skirt length is the same as for the front skirt. For the width, measure across the back of the chair from one end strut to the other. Double the measurement to allow for gathers, and add 1.5 cm (⅝ in) for hems.

- For the wadding, you will need two pieces to the finished chair seat size.

- For the two ties, you will need four strips of fabric of 88 x 18 cm (34 x 7 in).

- For the covered piping, measure round the chair seat and allow one length of piping to this measurement plus 5 cm (2 in).

Making up

1 Using the pattern, cut out one front and one back cover piece, adding 1.5 cm (⅝ in) seam allowance to all edges. Mark the position of the back struts. Cut out two pieces of wadding to the finished chair seat size.

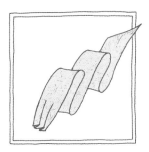

2 Cut out front and back skirts to required sizes. Turn under a 6 mm (¼ in) then 1 cm (⅜ in) hem along side and base edges of both skirt pieces. Pin and stitch in place.

3 Pin and stitch piping round cushion top. Join ends to fit (*see* Shaped Squab Cushion).

4 Fold one tie piece in half lengthways with right sides facing. Pin and stitch together along long edge and one end, stitching diagonally across the end. Trim and turn right side out. Pleat raw short edge into three pleats. Make up other ties in the same way.

SEE ALSO:

CONTEMPORARY STYLE   49

FABRIC FILE   9

SEWING GUIDE   200

SHAPED SQUAB CUSHION   158

5 With raw edges facing outwards, position ties over piping on cushion top, one either side of each marked strut.

6 Divide the outer edge of the front of the chair seat into equal sections and mark. Do the same for the back of the chair. Divide the front and back skirts in the same way and mark. Run two rows of gathering stitches round the front and back skirts either side of the 1.5 cm (⅝ in) seamline, beginning and ending stitches at marks.

Chair seat cushions with skirts are easy to make, and will transform even the plainest of chairs.

7 With right sides together, place front skirt to cushion top over ties and piping. Pull up gathers evenly in each section in turn. Pin and tack. Position back skirt to cushion top in same way.

8 Place cushion base to cushion top with right sides together over skirt. Pin and stitch, leaving an opening centrally across the back. Trim and turn cover right side out. Insert wadding. Turn in opening edges and slipstitch together. Place cushion on chair and fasten ties.

VARIATION: CUSHION WITH A BOX-PLEAT SKIRT

To make a chair seat cushion with a box-pleated skirt, measure the width of the skirt pieces in the same way as before, but multiply by 3 instead of 2 to allow for the pleats. Measure for front and back cover pieces, wadding, covered piping cord and ties as before.

Materials

- Furnishing fabric
- Heavyweight wadding
- Covered piping cord
- Matching sewing thread

Making up

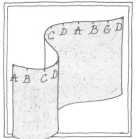
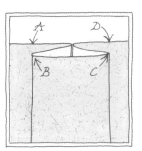

1 Hem the base and sides of the skirt pieces as before. Decide on width of pleat, then measure and mark out each pleat size across top edge of each skirt piece. Adjust pleat size, if necessary, to fit skirt width exactly. Label each mark in order – A, B, C, D – and repeat until end of skirt width.

2 To form pleats, fold along line B and place to A. Fold along line C and fold over to D. Pleat up rest of skirt in the same way.

3 Join skirt to cushion top and complete cushion as before.

VARIATION: CUSHION WITH A STRAIGHT SKIRT

To make a chair seat cushion with a straight skirt, measure the length and width of the skirt pieces in the same way as before. Do not double the measurements, but allow for 1.5 cm (⅝ in) seam allowances. Measure for cushion cover pieces, wadding, covered piping cord and ties as before. Hem the side and base edges of the skirt pieces, then join to the cushion top and complete the cushion in the same way as before.

UPRIGHT CHAIR COVER

Disguise a plain upright chair with a smart fabric cover. The cover is made up of a back panel which falls from the top of the chair to the floor, a front skirt which drapes from the seat top to the floor with a pleat set into each front corner, and two side skirts. If the chair back is shaped or curved, a zip or back vent may have to be added to achieve a good fit.

Materials

- Paper for pattern
- Furnishing fabric
- Iron-on interfacing
- Covered piping cord

Measuring up

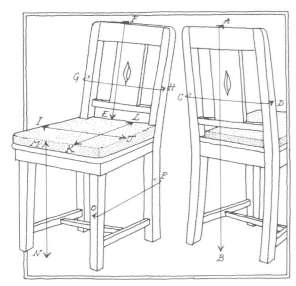

- Before measuring the chair, pad the seat with foam. Make a pattern of the seat (*see* Shaped Squab Cushion). Place the pattern on the foam and mark round with a felt tip pen. Cut out. Secure the foam to the seat with adhesive.

- Measure each chair section across its largest area. For the chair back, measure the length from the top of the chair to the floor, AB. Take away 1.3 cm (½ in) for clearing the floor, then add 4 cm (1½ in) for hem and seam. For the outside back width, measure

across the back from the edge of one back strut to the edge of the opposite strut at the widest point, CD. Add 3 cm (1¼ in) for seams. For the inside back length, measure from the chair top to the seat, EF. Allow 3 cm (1¼ in) for seams. Measure the width in the same way as for the outside back width, GH, and add 3 cm (1¼ in) for seams.

- Measure the width, IJ, and length, KL, of the chair seat, and add 3 cm (1¼ in) for seams.

- For the front skirt, measure the length from the seat to the floor, MN. Take away 1.3 cm (½ in) for clearing the floor, then add 4 cm (1½ in) for hem and seams. The width of the skirt should be the same as the width of the chair seat, IJ. Allow 3 cm (1¼ in) for seams.

- Make each side skirt the same length as the front skirt, MN. Measure the width from the corner of the back strut to the corner of the front leg, OP. Add 3 cm (1¼ in) for seams.

- For the front pleats, you will need two pieces of fabric each 34 cm (13½ in) wide by the front skirt length.

- For the interfacing, you will need sufficient to cover all the chair cover pieces.

- For the covered piping, you will need a length measuring KL × 2 + IJ, plus 5 cm (2 in) for neatening ends.

Making up

1 Cut out all the cover pieces to the required sizes. Cut out and iron interfacing to the wrong side of each fabric piece.

2 Pin and stitch back piece to inside back piece. Trim and neaten raw edges together.

3 Pin and stitch covered piping cord round side and front edges of chair seat piece.

4 Neaten base edges of skirt and pleat pieces by turning up a 2.5 cm (1 in) hem. Pin and stitch hems in place.

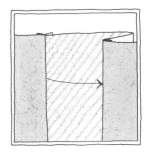

5 Mark the centre of each front pleat. Pin, tack and stitch a pleat in between skirt front and skirt side pieces. Fold skirt pieces along side seamlines and match them, right sides together, over centre of pleat. Pin and tack along top edges.

6 Pin skirt to seat section, matching front pleats to front corners of seat, then stitch all round. Pin and stitch back to inside back and skirt sides.

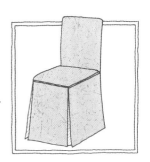

7 Check cover fits neatly over chair. Remove cover and trim all seams to neaten. Fit cover over chair.

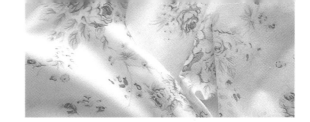

Beds

• •

Why not choose a bold floral pattern for a duvet cover (right)? Add a decorative scalloped edge, and make some cushions to match to scatter on top of the bed.

If you have space, a pair of single four-poster beds (below) can look very pretty in a bedroom. The curved canopies of these American-style beds are emphasized by placing frilled drapes at the head and across the tops of the beds.

The bed is likely to be the largest piece of furniture in the bedroom, and will naturally form a focal point, so it's important that you treat it not only in a style that creates the atmosphere you want, but also in one that suits the proportions of the room and the size and shape of the bed itself. Most important of all, remember that the bed is for sleeping in: whatever you choose, it should be comfortable as well as stylish.

If you want to create a crisp, tailored look, opt for simple duvets or choose rectangular covers made from fabrics like ticking or white linen, which mould themselves to the form of the bed and hang in neat folds to the floor. Using patterned or textured fabrics, and adding contrasting piping or borders, can dress up this look without making it too fussy. Most beds are better

Bed valances are designed to hide the bed base (left) and can be straight, gathered or pleated. Here, box pleats are made in a fabric that complements the blue and white checked bedcover.

Crisp geometric patterns (above) on a patchwork quilt will prove eye-catching in any setting.

To create a simpler, American-style look (far right), try hanging a sheer fabric or lace across the frame of a four-poster canopy. This kind of treatment requires minimum sewing and gives a charming effect.

fitted with a valance, which adds a decorative touch and will hide an ugly divan base. An attractive wooden or metal bedstead, on the other hand, can have the bedclothes tucked round the mattress to show off the lines of the frame. Shaped and padded headboards add a decorative focal point to a bed and provide somewhere comfortable to rest your head. You can even dress up a plain wooden headboard by slipping over a simple loose cover in a fabric to match the bedspread.

Hanging curtains at the head of the bed creates a striking visual impact in a room. For an understated look, hang simple curtains against the wall on a metal or wooden curtain pole, and for something a little more grand consider a half-tester or corona. Half-testers frame the head of the bed with drapes that extend across the back and jut out slightly along the sides of the bed as far as the pillows. The curtains can be lined with a contrasting fabric, and frilled or braided edgings help to define their outline. Coronas also frame the head of the bed, but with a circular arrangement of drapes that may be topped with a dome.

CHEAP CHIC

A four-poster effect can be achieved without using metres of filmy lace or chintz. Invest in inexpensive wide-width muslin. Fit a simple track to the ceiling, then run the muslin round the track attached to curtain heading tape and hooks. The extra fabric can be gathered up into swathes at each corner of the bed and bound round with lengths of plain white piping cord. To complete the look, sew on a few pale-coloured silk flowers and leaves.

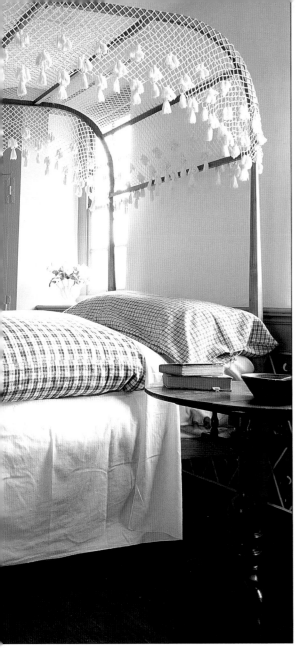

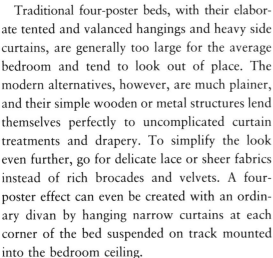

*T*his unusual treatment (left) would be a good choice for a bedsitter or studio flat. The partition wall built across the entire width of the room provides not only a niche for the bed but also a separate adjacent walk-in wardrobe. Tailored curtains topped with a French-pleated and deeply fringed valance frame the bed and can be let down to hide it from view when required.

*D*uvet covers are easy to make and often double as the bedcover (above). The headboard and valance have been made in a similar striped fabric to that of the cover to keep the look clean and modern.

Traditional four-poster beds, with their elaborate tented and valanced hangings and heavy side curtains, are generally too large for the average bedroom and tend to look out of place. The modern alternatives, however, are much plainer, and their simple wooden or metal structures lend themselves perfectly to uncomplicated curtain treatments and drapery. To simplify the look even further, go for delicate lace or sheer fabrics instead of rich brocades and velvets. A four-poster effect can even be created with an ordinary divan by hanging narrow curtains at each corner of the bed suspended on track mounted into the bedroom ceiling.

Bed linen should blend with the style of any coverings and drapery, and matching or co-ordinating fabrics work best. Sometimes the design of the bed itself might suggest a suitable treatment. A decorative iron or wooden bed, for example, could easily take on the country cottage look, and calls for a patchwork quilt, appliquéd or embroidered bedcover. If in doubt, however, there's nothing to beat a crisp white cover. Left plain, it will fit in with almost any decor, or add lace-edged pillows for a softer, more feminine touch. Any large expanse of bedcover can be made more interesting by using cushions, throws or blankets to break up the surface.

Sheets

Sheets are sold in standard sizes, but making your own can be cheaper and you can also cater for unusual bed-sizes.

Sheeting is available in a good range of plain and printed cotton and cotton-mix fabrics. It generally comes in two widths – 228 cm (90 in) and 280 cm (110 in) – to match standard bed-sizes, so each sheet can be cut from one width, eliminating the need for uncomfortable seams.

Measuring up

- Remove all the bedclothes except for the underblanket or mattress cover.

- For the length, measure the centre of the mattress, from the top edge to the bottom edge, AB. Measure the mattress depth from the top edge to the base edge, EF. The total length measures AB plus 2 × EF + tuck-under + hem.

- For the width, measure across the centre of the mattress from one side to the other, CD. The total width measures CD plus 2 × EF + tuck-under + hem.

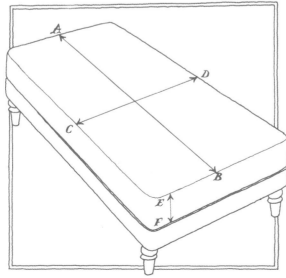

SEE ALSO:

CONTEMPORARY STYLE   49

FABRIC FILE   9

SEWING GUIDE   200

FLAT SHEETS

Flat sheets are quick and easy to make. Measure the mattress as described, adding a tuck-under allowance of 50 cm (20 in) to both the length and the width, plus 12 cm (5 in) for top and bottom hems. If possible, use the selvedge edges of the sheeting as the side edges. Otherwise, add 4 cm (1½ in) to the final width measurement.

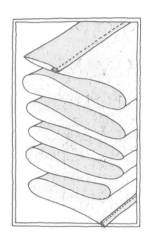

A flat sheet has a double hem along the base edge and, if needed, a double hem along both sides. The top edge is then turned under to form a plain hem.

Materials

- Sheeting fabric
- Matching sewing thread

Making up

1 Cut out one piece of fabric to required size. If side hems are needed, turn under a double 1 cm (⅜ in) hem to the wrong side; pin and stitch across hem close to fold.

2 Along base edge, turn under a double 2.5 cm (1 in) hem to the wrong side; pin and stitch across hem close to fold.

3 Along top edge, turn under a 7.5 cm (3 in) hem to the wrong side; tuck under 1 cm (⅜ in), pin and stitch across hem close to fold.

4 For a corded top edge, stitch across hem again 1 cm (⅜ in) above previous stitching, to form a channel. Thread a length of cord or cotton knitting yarn through the channel with a bodkin. Stitch across ends to hold cord in place.

FITTED SHEETS

Fitted sheets are ideal for any bed. The fabric can either match or tone with the duvet or quilt cover, or top sheet.

Measure the mattress as described, adding a tuck-under allowance of 26 cm (10¼ in) to both the length and the width, plus 3 cm (1¼ in) all round outside edge for hem.

Materials

- Sheeting fabric
- Tailor's chalk or marking pencil
- Matching sewing thread
- Elastic
- Safety pin

Making up

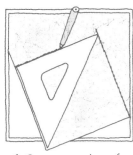
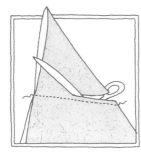
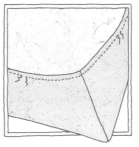
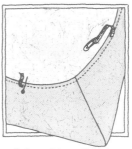

*B*ed treatments don't need to be lavish or expensive to work well. Simple striped bed linen in blue and white and a co-ordinating checked blanket creates a look reminiscent of the Scandinavian style.

1 Cut out one piece of fabric to required size. Lay fabric out flat. Mark each corner in the same way: measure mattress depth plus half the tuck-in, 13 cm (5⅛ in), along the outer edge on either side of the corner point and mark. Use a steel rule or set square to draw a line with tailor's chalk in at right angles from each mark, and mark where the two lines meet.

2 At each corner, fold fabric with wrong sides together, matching lines and marks, and pin dart formed. Stitch 1 cm (⅜ in) outside pinned line. Trim down to within 6 mm (¼ in) of stitching. Refold with right sides together; pin and stitch 1 cm (⅜ in) from folded edge to complete dart.

3 Fold under and pin a double 1.5 cm (⅝ in) hem all round outside edge of fabric. For elastic corner casings on fitted sheet, measure 22 cm (8½ in) on either side of each corner point and mark a space 1.5 cm (⅝ in) wide for threading through the elastic. Stitch all round close to folded edge, making sure that marked openings are left free for the elastic.

4 Cut a 30 cm (12 in) length of elastic for each corner. Fasten a safety pin to one end of elastic and thread round the corner from one opening to the next. Pin elastic at each opening and remove safety pin. Stitch across casing to hold elastic firmly in place, then join up stitching across each opening to finish.

duvet cover

Duvets are a popular alternative to sheets and blankets. The covers are usually made from sheeting fabric so they can be easily laundered. Dress cottons are a good option, even if they are less hard-wearing, but make sure that the fabric can be washed in the same way as sheeting. Different colours or patterns can be combined to make the cover reversible. The edges can be trimmed with a frill or lace border. Duvet covers are normally fastened with ready-made press-fastening or stud tape. They can also be closed using a touch-and-close strip or discs, buttons and buttonholes, ribbon ties or zips.

Materials

- Suitable fabric such as sheeting
- Press-fastening tape
- Matching sewing thread

Measuring up

- Duvets generally come in the following standard sizes: single, 140 × 200 cm (55 × 80 in); double, 200 × 200 cm (80 × 80 in); and king size, 230 × 230 cm (90 × 90 in). Add 6.5 cm (2⅝ in) to the length for hems and seam, and 3 cm (1¼ in) to the width for side seams.

Making up

1 Cut out two pieces of fabric to required size. Turn under a double 2.5 cm (1 in) hem along the base edge of each piece. Pin and stitch across hems. Mark the centre of each hem edge.

2 Cut a 100 cm (40 in) length of press-fastening tape for a single cover and 140 cm (55 in) for a double or king-size cover. Separate the fastening tape into two halves. Place one half centrally to right side of hemmed edge of one piece. Tuck under raw ends; pin and stitch in place. Pin and stitch the other half of tape centrally to hemmed edge of second piece.

SEE ALSO:

CONTEMPORARY STYLE   49

FABRIC FILE   9

SEWING GUIDE   200

VARIATION: DUVET WITH A DOUBLE FRILL

The frill should be added to the side and base edges only on a duvet cover so that it will not irritate the sleeper. Make the frill double so that the cover can be turned over on the bed. Decide on a frill depth between 6 and 18 cm (2½ and 7 in). Measure the side and base edges and double for frill length. Cut out enough strips from across the fabric, twice the frill depth plus 3 cm (1¼ in) for seams.

A scheme that mixes several different patterned fabrics can be very effective (left). Here, a simple checked bedhead and valance are strikingly contrasted with bold spots and checks on the bed linen.

Materials

- Suitable fabric such as sheeting
- Press-fastening tape
- Matching sewing thread

Making up

1 Pin and stitch the frill strips together into one length with plain flat seams. Trim seam and press open. Fold frill in half lengthways, with right sides together; pin and stitch across ends. Trim and turn frill right side out. Tack top raw edges together.

2 Turn under a double 2.5 cm (1 in) hem along base edge of each duvet piece; pin and stitch. Mark the sides and base edge of one cover piece into four equal sections. Divide raw edges of frill into four equal sections. Work two rows of gathering stitches along raw edges of each frill section, beginning and ending at marks.

3 With right sides together, matching marks and raw edges, place frill to cover with side edges of frill 1.5 cm (⅝ in) down from top raw edge of cover. Pull up gathers evenly in each section in turn to fit cover. Pin and tack frill to cover.

4 Pin and stitch a length of press-fastening tape to hemmed edges of cover as before, covering raw edges of frill. Stitch base edges together as before. With right sides together, pin and stitch side and top edges of cover, being careful not to catch frill ends into corner seams. Trim seams and zigzag stitch together to neaten. Turn duvet cover right side out.

3 Place the pieces with right sides together. Fasten the tapes together. Pin and stitch alongside hem line from outer edge to just beyond end of tapes. Then continue at right angles towards base edge, stitching across the hem and catching down the end of the fastening tape. Repeat on opposite side of cover.

4 Fold cover with wrong sides together; pin and stitch side edges, taking 6 mm (¼ in) seam allowance. Turn inside out with right sides together and seams to edges; pin and stitch 1 cm (⅜ in) from folded edges. Repeat to stitch the top edges together with a French seam in the same way. Turn cover right side out.

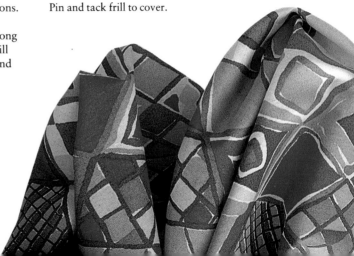

Pillowcases

∙∙

Pillowcases can be made from sheeting or similar cotton and cotton-mix fabrics. You will find more original print designs amongst the dress fabrics and these can be chosen to tone with plain sheets. Use different types of trimmings to add interest and detail depending on the decor of the bedroom. A mass of white cotton lace pillowcases looks very feminine; plain pillowcases with scalloped edges look clean and crisp.

A standard pillow measures 75 × 50 cm (30 × 20 in) and pillowcases are usually made to this size for a comfortable fit.

PLAIN PILLOWCASE
∙∙

Also known as a housewife pillowcase, a plain pillowcase is made from one piece of fabric folded over. Add twice the pillow length plus 24 cm (9½ in) for flap and seams. Add 3 cm (1¼ in) to pillow width for seams.

Materials

- Suitable fabric such as sheeting
- Matching sewing thread

PILLOWS

Check whether a pillow needs re-stuffing by hanging it over your arm. If it droops on each side it needs extra filling. To make a new pillow, choose a filling from down, feathers or a mixture of both. For the cover, you will need down-proof cambric or feather-proof ticking, depending on the filling used. Synthetic fillings need only a firm cotton cover. Cut out the fabric to a standard pillow size and double stitch all round, leaving a gap through which to push the filling, then handsew closed.

SEE ALSO:
∙∙∙∙∙∙∙∙∙∙∙∙∙∙∙∙∙∙∙∙∙∙∙∙∙∙∙∙∙∙∙∙∙∙
CONTEMPORARY STYLE   49
∙∙∙∙∙∙∙∙∙∙∙∙∙∙∙∙∙∙∙∙∙∙∙∙∙∙∙∙∙∙∙∙∙∙
FABRIC FILE   9
∙∙∙∙∙∙∙∙∙∙∙∙∙∙∙∙∙∙∙∙∙∙∙∙∙∙∙∙∙∙∙∙∙∙
SEWING GUIDE   200
∙∙∙∙∙∙∙∙∙∙∙∙∙∙∙∙∙∙∙∙∙∙∙∙∙∙∙∙∙∙∙∙∙∙

Making up

1 Cut out one piece of fabric to required size. Turn under a double 6 mm (¼ in) hem on one short edge; pin and stitch across hem. At opposite end, turn under 1 cm (⅜ in), then 4 cm (1½ in); pin and stitch across hem close to folded edge.

2 Place the fabric flat, wrong side up. Turn in the narrow hemmed end for 18 cm (7 in) to form the flap; press and pin in place. Fold the remaining fabric in half with wrong sides together over flap, so the wide hem is aligned with folded edge; pin.

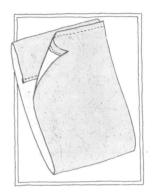

3 Pin and stitch side edges of pillowcase, taking 6 mm (¼ in) seam allowance. Refold pillowcase with right sides together and seams to edges. Pin and stitch sides taking 1 cm (⅜ in) seam allowance.

4 Turn pocket and pillowcase right side out and press.

VARIATION: PILLOWCASE WITH A FRILL
∙∙

When adding a frill, the pillowcase must be made up in three separate pieces: front, back and flap. The frill can either be single, with a hem, or double so that the pillowcase can be turned over.

For the back, add 6.5 cm (2⅝ in) to the length and 3 cm (1¼ in) to the width of the pillow for seams and hems. For the front, add 3 cm (1¼ in) to the length and 3 cm (1¼ in) to the width of the pillow for seams. The flap is 18 cm (7 in) deep plus 2.5 cm (1 in) for seams and the same width as the back.

For the frill length, allow twice the outside measurement of the pillowcase. Decide on the frill depth between 2 cm (¾ in) and 8 cm (3½ in). For a single frill, add 2.5 cm (1 in) for hem and seam. For a double frill, double the width and add 3 cm (1¼ in) for seams. Cut out sufficient strips from across the fabric width to give the correct length when stitched together.

Materials

- Suitable fabric such as sheeting
- Matching sewing thread

Making up

1 Cut out one back, one front and one flap to required sizes.

2 To make the frill, cut out from across the fabric as many strips of the correct depth as necessary. Pin and stitch frill strips together into a ring with plain flat seams (for a double frill) or French seams (for a single frill).

3 For a single frill, turn under a double 6 mm (¼ in) hem along lower edge of frill; pin and stitch. For a double frill, fold in half lengthways, then pin and tack raw edges of frill together.

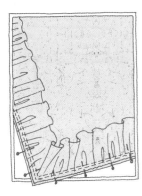

4 Work two rows of gathering stitches round frill on either side of seamline. Pin frill to right side of front piece of pillowcase, raw edges matching. Pull up gathers evenly to fit round front piece; pin and stitch frill in place.

5 Turn under a double 6 mm (¼ in) hem on one long edge of flap; pin and stitch. On back piece turn under a double 2.5 cm (1 in) hem on one short edge; pin and stitch.

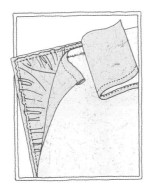

6 With right sides together, place back piece to front over frill, with hemmed edge of back against seamline of front. Place flap right side down over back, with hemmed edge facing inwards and matching raw edge to raw edge of front. Pin and stitch all round pillowcase.

7 To finish, trim allowances and zigzag stitch together to neaten.

VARIATION: PILLOWCASE WITH A BORDER

This pillowcase is made up of three pieces: front, back and flap. The front edges are turned in to form a wide flat border all round the case. Decide on a border width between 4 cm (1½ in) and 12 cm (5 in) wide.

For the back, add 6.5 cm (2⅝ in) to the length and 3 cm (1¼ in) on the width of the pillow for seams and hems. For the front, add twice the border width plus 1.5 cm (⅝ in) seam allowance all round. The flap is 18 cm (7 in) deep plus 2.5 cm (1 in) for seams and the same width as the back.

Materials

- Suitable fabric such as sheeting
- Matching sewing thread

Making up

1 Cut out one back, one front and one flap to required sizes. Turn under a double 2.5 cm (1 in) hem on one short edge of back; pin and stitch. Turn under a double 6 mm (¼ in) hem on one long edge of flap; pin and stitch.

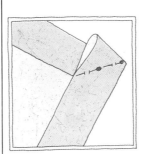

2 Lay front piece wrong side up. Turn under border width plus 1.5 cm (⅝ in) on each side and press in position. At each corner, pin excess fabric into a dart, graduating to a point in the corner. Trim off excess fabric to within 1.5 cm (⅝ in) of pins.

3 Refold corner darts with right sides together; pin and stitch to within 1.5 cm (⅝ in) of inner edge. Press darts open. Turn front case right side out.

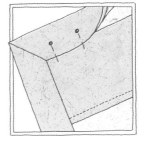

4 Turn under 1.5 cm (⅝ in) all round raw border and press edges. Lay front piece wrong side up and place flap on top, wrong sides together. Tuck seam allowance on long edge and both short edges of flap under border edge; pin and stitch across border, catching down long end of flap.

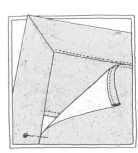

5 Place back piece on front over flap, with wrong sides together and hemmed edge of back matched to stitched end of pillowcase. Tuck raw edges of back under border edges on remaining sides and pin. Stitch all round border to meet up with stitching holding flap in place. Topstitch all round pillowcase again, 6 mm (¼ in) outside previous line of stitching.

bed valance

To complete the bed linen set, make a valance to cover the unsightly bed base and feet. It can be straight with kick-pleats or gathered or box-pleated onto a piece of fabric covering the top of the bed. The valance skirt can also be bound along the base edge.

Materials

- Suitable fabric such as sheeting
- Small plate or saucer
- Tailor's chalk or marker pencil
- Matching sewing thread

Measuring up

- Remove the bedclothes and the mattress.

- For the base top, measure the length of the bed base from top to bottom. Measure the width of the bed base top from side to side, and add 1.5 cm (⅝ in) all round for seams.

- For the skirt depth, measure from the top of the bed base to the floor, and add 6 cm (2½ in) for seam and hem. For the skirt length, add together the mattress length multiplied by 4 and the width multiplied by 2.

SEE ALSO:

CONTEMPORARY STYLE   49

DUVET COVER   174

FABRIC FILE   9

SEWING GUIDE   200

Making up

1 Cut out a piece of fabric to size for bed base top. For the skirt cut out from across the fabric as many strips of the correct depth as necessary to make up the required length.

2 Lay the top piece flat, right side up. Place a small plate or saucer on one of the bottom corners with its edges touching fabric edges; mark round the edge of the plate with tailor's chalk. Remove plate and cut round the marked line. Fold the fabric in half lengthways and use the cut corner as a template to mark and cut round the remaining bottom corner.

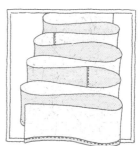

3 Make up the valance skirt. Pin and stitch the skirt pieces together into one long length with French seams. Turn up a double 2.5 cm (1 in) hem along lower edge of skirt; pin and stitch. Run two rows of gathering stitches along top edge of skirt.

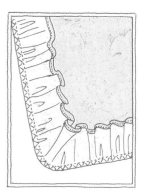

4 Divide the side and base edges of top piece into four equal sections and mark with tailor's chalk. Divide the skirt into four equal sections and mark. Gather up each section as for duvet frill (*see* Duvet Cover). Position skirt to top piece, with right sides together matching marks. Pull up gathers evenly in each section in turn to fit top piece; pin and stitch skirt to top. Trim allowance and zigzag stitch the raw edges together.

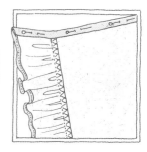

5 Turn under a double 1 cm (⅜ in) hem along raw edges of top piece and skirt ends. Pin and stitch.

*b*edcovers

. . . .

Bedspreads range from a simple throw-over cover, which is often quilted, to a more formal fitted cover. Suitable fabrics include linen and heavy-weight or textured cotton. To ensure that they hang properly and for extra warmth, bedspreads should be lined and preferably interlined. A quilted cover also provides extra warmth.

THROW-OVER BEDSPREAD

The simplest of bedcovers, the finished result can be an elegant lined bedspread or a simple hemmed throw-over. The former can also be quilted in diamond shapes or squares by adding a layer of wadding between the fabric and lining and topstitching from side to side. The whole bedspread can then be bound all round the outer edge to finish.

Materials

- Suitable fabric, such as furnishing cotton
- Lining fabric
- Matching sewing thread

Measuring up

- Measure the bed when made with the usual bedclothes.

- For the length, measure from the top of the pillow along the centre of the bed to the floor at the foot of the bed, AB, and add 10 cm (4 in) allowance for seams.

- For the width, measure from the floor on one side of the bed over the centre of the bed to the floor on the opposite side, CD, and add 10 cm (4 in) allowance for seams.

- The lining should measure AB for the length and CD for the width plus 3 cm (1¼ in) seam allowance all round.

SEE ALSO:
....
BED VALANCE   178
....
CONTEMPORARY STYLE   49
....
FABRIC FILE   9
....
QUILTING   184
....
SEWING GUIDE   200
....

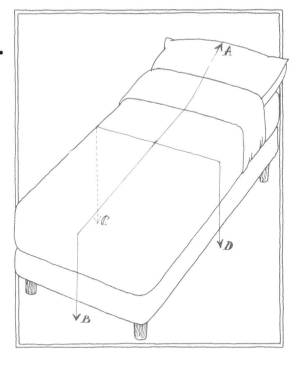

Making up

1 Cut one piece of fabric to the finished size plus 5 cm (2 in) all round for hems. Cut out the lining to the same size.

stitch hem in place all round bedspread.

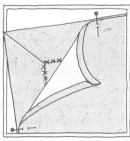

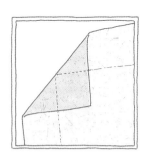

2 Turn under a 5 cm (2 in) hem all round fabric and press. Mitre edges at each corner by unfolding hem and pressing in corner point so pressed edges match. Refold hem over pressed-in corner and slipstitch across corner folds. Herringbone

3 Lay fabric flat, wrong side up. Place lining on top, with wrong sides together. Turn back lining and lockstitch to fabric down centre and 30 cm (12 in) from sides. Trim off excess lining level with folded edges of bedspread. Turn under lining for 3 cm (1¼ in); pin and slipstitch to fabric all round.

Co-ordination is so often the key to successful interiors. Here, the same fabric has been used for the bed hangings and padded bedhead, and the linear part of the design has been cleverly appliquéd in squares onto the plain cream bedcover to add visual interest.

VARIATION: UNLINED THROW-OVER

If you prefer to use a heavyweight fabric, which does not need a lining, add a braid trim or fringing all round the edge. The hem allowance need only be 1.5 cm (⅝ in) all round.

Materials

- Suitable fabric
- Matching sewing thread

Making up

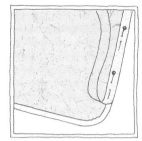

1 Measure and cut out the fabric in the same way as for the lined throw-over, but adding only 1.5 cm (⅝ in) all round for the hem.

2 If necessary, seam fabric widths together with plain flat seams. Round off the base corners using a small plate, as for valance (*see* Bed Valance). Turn the hem edge up onto the right side of the fabric.

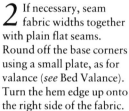

3 Position the braid or trimming on the right side, covering the raw fabric edges; pin and top-stitch in place, catching down hem at the same time.

BEDSPREAD WITH PLEATED CORNERS

A more formal look is achieved with a fitted bedspread. Outline the bed top section with piping, then attach a plain skirt with inverted pleats at each base corner. Add a gusset on either side of the bedspread top so the cover will be curved round the pillows. The easiest way to do this is to make a paper pattern for the gusset.

This bedspread will hang better if it is lined. The bed top section can also be quilted with the addition of a layer of wadding.

A BEDSPREAD MADE FROM MORE THAN ONE FABRIC WIDTH

*I*t may be necessary to seam two fabric widths together to achieve the required size. If so, avoid an unsightly centre seam and make two seams, one on either side of the bed top. Cut two fabric widths to the correct size. Fold one in half lengthways, matching selvedge edges. Carefully cut down fold. Pin and stitch each half to the central piece with plain flat seams, matching any fabric design across each seam. Trim off any excess fabric equally from both side edges. Cut and seam lining pieces, if using, together in the same way.

Materials

- Suitable fabric
- Lining fabric
- Covered piping
- Paper for pattern
- Steel rule
- Matching sewing thread
- Tailor's chalk or marking pencil

Measuring up

- Measure the bed when made with the usual bedclothes.

- For the bed top length, measure from the top edge of the pillow to the foot of the bed, and add 3 cm (1¼ in) for seams.

- For the bed width, measure the bed top across the centre from side to side, and add 3 cm (1¼ in) for seams.

- For the skirt depth, measure from the edge of the bed top to the floor, and add 3 cm (1¼ in) for seams. For the skirt length, you will need twice the bed length plus one width. Add 40 cm (16 in) for each corner pleat plus 3 cm (1¼ in) for seams.

- For the covered piping, you will need twice the bed length plus one width plus 10 cm (4 in). If including gussets, measure round curved edge of gusset and make up two pieces of covered piping to this length plus 5 cm (2 in).

Making up

1 Cut out one bed top (plus seam allowance) from both fabric and lining. For the skirt, cut out from across the fabric as many strips of the correct width as necessary. Cut out matching strips of lining.

2 If you want side gussets, you will need to make a paper pattern. On paper, rule a line the width of the pillow, 50 cm (20 in). At bed top end, rule a line at right angles, to height of pillow – approximately 15 cm (6 in) for one pillow, 30 cm (12 in) for two. Graduate this point down to opposite end in a gentle curve. Add 1.5 cm (⅝ in) all round pattern; cut out two pieces from both fabric and lining.

3 Pin and tack covered piping round curved top edge of each gusset piece, with cord facing inwards and raw edges and right sides together; stitch in place. Matching top straight edges, pin and stitch curved edge of gussets to either side of bedcover top, over piping.

4 Pin and stitch covered piping to sides and base edges of bedcover top, including base edge of each gusset. Neaten ends of piping.

5 Make up the pleated skirt. Pin and stitch skirt pieces together into one length with plain flat seams; trim and press seams open. Make up lining skirt in the same way. Place fabric skirt to lining with right sides together. Pin and stitch side and base edges. Trim and turn skirt right side out. Press seam to edge and tack top raw edges of skirt together.

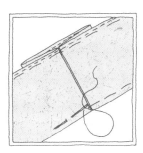

6 From one edge of skirt, measure the bed length and mark with tailor's chalk. Then measure 10 cm (4 in), 20 cm (8 in) and 10 cm (4 in) for the inverted pleat. Match the two outer marks together and press to form the pleat. Tack across the top and base edges of pleat. Repeat on opposite side.

7 Place skirt to bed top, with right side 1.5 cm (⅝ in) below top edge and matching pleats to centre of base corners. Pin and stitch skirt in place.

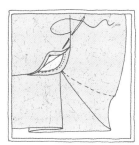

8 Place lining top on bedspread top with right sides together; pin and stitch across top edge of bedcover. Trim seam and turn lining back over wrong side of fabric top. Tuck under seam allowance on remaining three sides and slipstitch over previous stitches round side and base edges, covering raw fabric edges.

$p$leated divan cover

. . . .

Cover a spare bed or transform a bed into an attractive seating unit with a smart practical cover with a box-pleated skirt. The cover fits neatly over the mattress and the skirt pleats out from the level of the mattress base. This cover can be made in linen, although furnishing cotton or a cotton-mix fabric will not crease so easily.

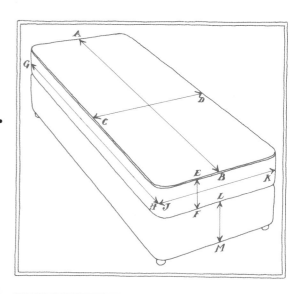

Materials

- Suitable fabric
- Covered piping cord
- Matching sewing thread
- Card for template

Measuring up

- Either measure the bed without bedclothes or measure over any bedding you want to store on the bed.

- For the bed top, measure from top of bed to base, AB, and from side to side, CD, and add 1.5 cm (⅝ in) all round for seams.

- For mattress sides, measure from mattress top to mattress base, EF. Measure one long side, GH, and one short side, JK. You will need two pieces each EF × GH plus 1.5 cm (⅝ in) seam allowance all round and two pieces each EF × JK plus 1.5 cm (⅝ in) for seams.

- For the skirt depth, measure from base of mattress to floor, LM, and add 5.5 cm (2¼ in) for seam and hem. For the length, add GH × 2 to JK × 2 and multiply by 3, plus 3 cm (1¼ in) for seams.

- For the piping, you will need two lengths each measuring the length of the outer edge of bed top, N, plus 5 cm (2 in) for joins.

SEE ALSO:
. . . .
BEDCOVERS   179
. . . .
CONTEMPORARY STYLE   49
. . . .
FABRIC FILE   9
. . . .
SEWING GUIDE   200
. . . .

Making up

1 Cut out one piece of fabric to size for bed top and the four pieces of fabric to size for mattress sides (two pieces GH × EF, and two pieces JK × EF). For the skirt, cut out from across the fabric as many strips of the correct depth as necessary.

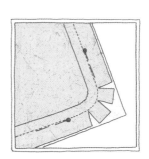

2 Pin and tack covered piping all round outer edge of top piece. Position piping with cord facing inwards and raw edges together; stitch piping ends together to fit. Stitch piping in place.

3 Pin and stitch side pieces together in this order: long, short, long and short. Stitch with plain flat seams, beginning and ending stitching 1.5 cm

(⅝ in) from each end of seam. Trim; neaten and press seams open. Pin and stitch covered piping cord round base edge of side piece in the same way as before (*see* Bedspread with Pleated Corners).

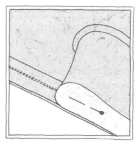

4 Place top edge of side piece to bed top piece, matching seams to corners of top piece. Pin and stitch in place just inside previous stitching line. Trim and neaten edges.

5 Pleat up the skirt. Pin and stitch short ends of skirt pieces into a ring with French seams. Turn up a 4 cm (1½ in) hem along base edge of skirt, tuck under 1 cm (⅜ in); pin and stitch.

6 The pleats are usually 10 cm (4 in) wide, but the size will depend on the finished measurement. Divide N by the pleat size; adjust if necessary. There should be an inverted pleat at each corner, so begin and end the pleat markings at each corner.

7 To help to mark the pleats accurately on the fabric skirt, cut out a piece of card the same size as a finished pleat.

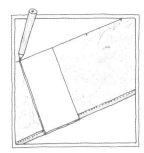

8 Lay the skirt out, wrong side up, and place the card template on the fabric. Mark the top and bottom of the skirt and repeat along the whole length. Make sure that each pleat line is at right angles to the hem edge and along the straight of the grain. Try to position any seams so they will be hidden at the back of a pleat.

9 Form the pleats by folding along the second marked line and placing the fold on the first line; press. Then fold up the third line and place it

on the fourth line; press. Continue in this way round the skirt. Tack across the skirt top and hem edge to hold the pleats firmly in place. Press.

10 Place skirt on base edge of side, over piping, with right sides together; pin and stitch in place. Remove tacking stitches and press again.

QUICK CHANGE

*I*f the divan is used as a spare bed, the pillows can be stored on the divan top inside smart cushion covers. In this way they will be disguised as scatter cushions during the day, but be quickly at hand when the divan changes into a bed for the night.

*B*eds or divans can easily be turned into sofas during the day with the help of neat, tailored covers and lots of cushions. A bolster at either end of the bed adds definition as well as extra comfort.

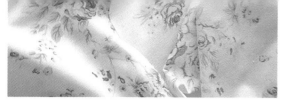

bed corona

• •

A bed corona consists of a semicircular bracket fixed to the wall about 220 cm (7 ft) above the bed from which lined curtains are hung to drape softly either side of the bed. The lining can be plain and blend in or contrast with the main fabric, or choose a patterned fabric for the lining – this looks particularly effective when the main fabric is plain. Curtaining is also pleated to provide a backing for the corona. Ready-made coronas can be found in some department stores, but it is not difficult to make your own out of blockboard – if you do not have the equipment to cut wood in a curve at home, your local wood merchant will do this for you.

Materials

- Furnishing fabric
- Furnishing lining fabric
- Pencil-pleat curtain heading tape and tapes
- Specialist touch-and-close pencil-pleat curtain heading tape
- Piece of 2 cm (¾ in) thick blockboard 50 × 30 cm (20 × 12 in) and angle brackets plus fixing screws for support
- Paint to match lining fabric (optional)
- Matching sewing thread
- Staple gun with 6 mm (¼ in) staples
- Two tiebacks and two wall hooks

Measuring up

- Decide on the height of the corona above the bed, approximately 220 cm (7 ft), and mark the position on the wall.

- For the back curtain, measure from the marked position to the floor to find the length and add 5 cm (2 in) hem allowance. You will need one standard fabric width (approximately 122 cm/48 in) to the required length.

SEE ALSO:
CONTEMPORARY STYLE   49
CURTAINS   72
FABRIC FILE   9
SEWING GUIDE   200

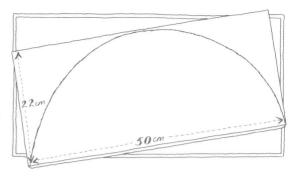

- For the side curtains, measure from the corona to the floor, allowing extra for the fabric to drape over each side of the bed, and add 4.5 cm (1¾ in) for heading and hems. As each curtain is made from one-and-half standard fabric widths, you will need three lengths each of fabric and lining to the required length.

- The valance should be about 30 cm (12 in) long. Measure round the front edge of the semicircle and double this to give the width of the valance. Add 4.5 cm (1¾ in) for heading and hem. The lining for the valance should measure the same.

- For the curtain heading tape, allow for the width of each side curtain plus 8 cm (3½ in).

- For the touch-and-close heading tape, allow for the width of the valance.

Making up

1 Following the diagram at the top of the page, mark and cut out a semicircle from the blockboard. Fix the angle brackets equally spaced across the straight edge on the top of the shaped blockboard. Either paint underside of blockboard or cover with fabric.

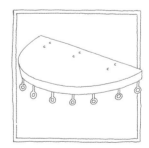

2 To cover with fabric, use blockboard as a pattern to cut a piece of fabric large enough to be stapled to the underside of the board – allow an extra 1.3 cm (½ in) to turn raw edges under before fixing.

3 Insert screw eyes into underside of blockboard round curved edge, spacing them about 6 cm (2½ in) apart. These will hold the two side curtains.

4 Cut out one fabric width for back curtain to the required length. Turn in a double 1.3 cm (½ in) hem down each side edge; pin and stitch. Turn up a double 2.5 cm (1 in) hem along lower edge of fabric. Pin and stitch, forming neat corners. Zigzag stitch across raw top edge.

5 Pleat up top edge by hand to fit across straight edge of corona and tack pleats in place. Staple pleated curtain along back edge of corona, with right side of fabric facing.

To give a more decorative edge to a valance on a bed corona, trim it with fringing or braid.

6 Fix angle brackets to top of corona as marked. Fix corona and back curtain on to wall at marked position above bed. Fix the 'grip' half of the touch-and-close tape round front edge of corona.

7 Cut out three fabric widths for side curtains, each to the required length. Cut one piece in half lengthways. Pin and stitch one half width to outside edge of each full width with plain flat seams.

8 Repeat with lining to make two lining curtains. Place fabric to lining, right sides together; pin and stitch all round, taking 1.5 cm (⅝ in) seam allowance and leaving top edges free. Trim corners and turn curtains right side out.

9 Turn down top edge by width of curtain heading tape. Cut length of curtain heading tape to curtain width plus 8 cm (3½ in). Place heading tape to wrong side of curtain top at required position, and covering raw edge of curtain.

10 At leading centre edge of curtain, pull out cords on wrong side of tape for 4 cm (1½ in) and knot. Turn under tape end in line with edge of curtain. At outside edge, pull out cords from right sides of tape. Turn under tape end, avoiding cords, in line with curtain edge. Pin, tack and stitch heading tape in place, catching down cords at inner edge but leaving them free on outer edge.

11 Cut out two fabric widths and two lining widths for the valance, each to the required length. Make up the valance in the same way as the side curtains, but stitch a length of the 'press' half of the touch-and-close heading tape along top edge.

12 Pull up heading tape across top of each side curtain evenly to fit half way round corona. Fasten off. Attach curtain hooks, spaced 6 cm (2½ in) apart. Hang curtains from screw eyes round front of corona so curtains meet together in the centre. Pull up heading tape on valance and press in place over tape round edge of corona.

13 Hold back each side curtain and mark position of tiebacks. Fix a hook into the wall at each position. Fasten tiebacks round side curtains, allowing curtains to drape softly back to frame bed.

Child's room

··

There are a number of items you can make for a child's room. Here are two projects – one for a snug quilt to cover a child's cot or bed, and the other for a handy shoe bag.

QUILT
··

A simple but effective quilt can be made from fabric and wadding stitched into squares. A double border of co-ordinating fabric is then stitched all round the outside edge. The quilt can be made to different sizes by increasing the number of squares or expanding or reducing the width of the border. Alternative patterns can be created by stitching round the design on a patterned fabric or by stitching diamonds across the central section.

Materials

- Suitable fabric
- Suitable fabric for backing if different from top fabric
- Contrast fabric for border
- Wadding
- Matching sewing thread

Measuring up

- The finished quilt should be the same size as the top of the child's bed or it can be slightly larger. Measure the bed as before, then deduct the border measurement. Make sure that the remaining area – the central section – divides into equal squares, approximately 10 cm (4 in) across, adjusting the measurements slightly up or down accordingly. Add 1.5 cm (⅝ in) seam allowance on all sides. You will need two pieces of fabric to these measurements, a top and back piece.

- Decide on the border width – it will look best if it is not less than 5 cm (2 in) – and double this measurement. Add 1.5 cm (⅝ in) seam allowance all round. To make the border with mitred corners you will need four strips: two measuring the length of the central section plus a double border width plus 3 cm (1¼ in), and two measuring the width of the central section plus a double border width plus 3 cm (1¼ in) for seam allowance.

- For the wadding, you will need one piece to the finished size of the quilt.

Making up

1 Cut out two pieces of fabric, front and back, each to the required size. Cut out wadding to finished size of quilt.

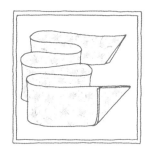

2 Measure and mark the square quilting pattern across the top fabric. Position top fabric right side up over centre of wadding. Place backing fabric with wrong side to wadding, matching top fabric. Pin and tack the three layers together, working from the centre.

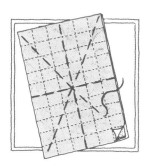

3 Set the sewing machine to larger-than-average stitch. Stitch across then along quilt, following marked lines, to form squares. Work each row in opposite direction from previous one to even out stitching.

4 Cut out border strips to required sizes. Press each border strip in half lengthways, wrong sides facing. Form mitred corners at each end by folding up raw edges diagonally across to meet folded edge and press. Unfold and cut diagonally across marked fold line. Make sure short ends of each strip are facing in towards the centre.

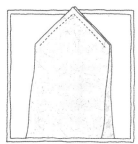

5 Unfold border strips. Pin and stitch pointed ends of strips together to

SEE ALSO:
··
CONTEMPORARY STYLE   49
··
FABRIC FILE   9
··
SEWING GUIDE   200
··

form a ring in following order: short, long, short, long, taking 1.5 cm (⅝ in) seam allowance and ending 1.5 cm (⅝ in) from ends.

6 Matching corners, place one right side edge of border to right side edge of quilt. Turn under 1.5 cm (⅝ in) seam allowance. Pin and stitch 1.5 cm (⅝ in) from edge of central section. The border corners will ease open to help stitch border neatly round quilt. Turn border over edge of wadding. Turn under seam allowance on remaining border edge, pin and slipstitch to quilt over previous stitching. Topstitch all round quilt in the ditch of the border seam.

SHOE BAG

This shoe bag measures approximately 46 × 34 cm (18½ × 13½ in) when it is finished, but this size can always be adjusted according to your child's needs.

Materials

- Suitable fabric such as medium-weight cotton fabric
- Matching sewing thread
- Cord or ribbon for drawstring
- Safety pin

Measuring up

- For the fabric, you will need two pieces, each measuring 53.5 × 37 cm (21 × 14½ in).

- For the cord, you will need a length 180 cm (72 in) long.

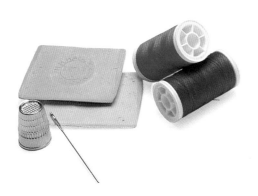

*W*hen making shoe bags, choose strong medium-weight cotton that will stand up well to wear and tear.

Making up

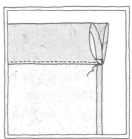

1 Place fabric pieces with right sides together. Pin, tack and stitch together down sides and along lower edge, taking in 1.5 cm (⅝ in) seam allowance. Begin and end stitching 11 cm (4⅜ in) down from top edges. Work a few stitches in reverse at the end of the stitching on each side.

2 Turn down top edge on each side to wrong side of fabric for 6 cm (2½ in) and turn under hem for 1 cm (⅜ in). To form casings, pin and stitch across each side of bag, catching in hem. Stitch second row of stitching, 1.5 cm (⅝ in) above first row on both sides. Turn bag right side out. Slipstitch edges closed above casings.

3 Cut cord in half to give two lengths, each approximately 90 cm (36 in). Fasten end of first length to safety pin and thread through both casings, starting from one left side opening. Knot ends together. Thread second length round casing from opposite side opening and knot together in the same way. Pull up each cord from opposite sides to close bag.

4 On larger bags the corners can be stitched in the same way as mock gusset cushions (*see* A Mock Gusset) to form a base for the bag.

Tables

- -

Pretty floral prints (left) are always a good choice for outside tables, echoing the natural surroundings. And they can turn even the plainest piece of furniture into something special.

Strong checks (below) are particularly effective in modern settings, especially in clear primary colours.

A plain circular tablecloth (opposite) can take centre stage when it is made in a bold, vibrant colour. Use any inexpensive fabric in a colour that co-ordinates or contrasts with the rest of the scheme and simply hem the lower edge for a very stylish tablecloth.

Cloths can be used to transform the cheapest piece of furniture into interesting and eye-catching items in a room. If the budget doesn't stretch to an expensive mahogany table for instance, a simple deal table can be transformed by covering it with a beautiful floor-length cloth. A worn-out dressing table can be given a new lease of life by laying over a specially made cloth, and you can ring the changes in a dining room simply by covering the table with cloths in different styles and fabrics according to the occasion, the season, or simply the time of day.

Plain cloths and covers can create striking visual effects, but with a little imagination you can make the most basic cloth into something

*F*or a distinctly feminine look (right) use delicate white voile to drape over a dressing table mirror and add a deep frill along the top edge of the table. If there are drawers underneath, put the front of the skirt on a track that allows the drapes to be pulled back out of the way.

*A*dding a lining to a floor length circular tablecloth (below) helps to give a fabric shape and body. A smaller cloth draped over (here, matching the cushions) with a bound and frilled edge makes more of a feature of the table.

really special. Embellishing it with embroidery, appliqué or cutwork adds a truly individual touch, as does edging the hems with braid, lace or fringing. For a less busy look, arrange the skirt of the cloth into soft sculptured drapes, or drape circular tables with two or more layers of fabric, one over the other in contrasting colours or textures. Lace over a plain cloth will work on any table shape.

The length of a tablecloth is very important, particularly when you are trying to hide a less-than-perfect piece of furniture underneath, so make sure that the cloth reaches right down to the floor, rather than leaving the fabric hanging at half mast.

You should always line and interline floor-length cloths like this to give them enough weight so that they hang properly. Short cloths can be used, but they are best restricted to tables which have elegant or shaped legs.

Table covers and cloths can be made in fabrics that match other furnishings in a room so that everything co-ordinates, or you could go for something in a stark contrast to make a bold statement on its own. Whatever the colour and

PATCHWORK TABLECLOTH

*T*he craft of patchwork has a long and rich history, and is still extremely popular today in Europe and the United States. To make a patchwork tablecloth, use the American method, which is particularly suited for block patterns and can be sewn relatively quickly. Choose any firmly woven fabric scraps and make sure they are washable, pre-shrunk and colour fast. Ready-made templates are available or make your own from stiff card (triangles, squares and oblongs are all traditional shapes). On the back of the fabric trace round the design with a pencil. Cut out, adding a 6 mm (¼ in) seam allowance. Pin patches together, then hand stitch using running stitches or machine stitch. Press seams open. Finish by adding a lining.

style of fabric, remember to consider practicalities when making your choice. A pretty occasional table in the sitting room, for instance, is not likely to get dirty very often, so can be covered in a more ornate or decorative fabric. But the table in a busy family kitchen is likely to come in for a considerable amount of wear and tear, and the cloth should be made in washable cotton or synthetic fabric. Protect the top of hand-embroidered or appliquéd cloths by covering them with a sheet of glass cut to size; scorch marks on a precious dining table can be prevented by using a thick quilted tablecloth or by placing a layer of thick felt cut to the size of the table top underneath the decorative cloth. If your dressing table has drawers or shelves underneath the top, fit a curtain track to the underside of the table and attach the skirt so that it can be drawn back when necessary to allow you access.

*P*lastic coated cotton fabrics (above) are tough and wipeable, making them ideal for kitchen tables. They come in a wide range of attractive designs and colours to suit all tastes.

A patchwork tablecloth (left) is easy to sew, and economical too when it is made up from fabric scraps. If you don't want the end result to look too busy, choose a colour theme and make sure all the patches blend together.

$t$ablecloths

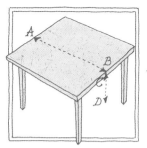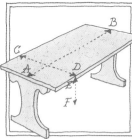

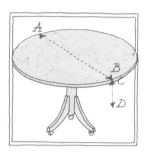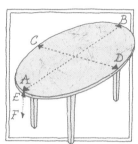

Although the primary purpose of table linen is to cover and protect a table while eating, it can be decorative as well as functional. The simplest cloth is one made from PVC, which needs no stitching and is just wiped clean after a meal, but most fabric cloths need to be hemmed.

Tablecloths can be made up in plain or printed fabrics and even follow the theme for special occasions such as Christmas. Choose practical easy-care fabrics such as cotton-mix that are quick to wash and require little or no ironing. For extra large tables use double-width sheeting to eliminate the need for seams.

The overhang for dining tables should be between 20 cm (8 in) and 30 cm (12 in). Do not make it any longer, as the fabric would become entangled in the legs of the diners. Most dining-room tables need protection from hot plates, so cut a length of heat-resistant material to fit the table top before covering with a tablecloth.

Floor-length cloths covering small round tables can be a feature of a room's decor. Another decorative effect, more suitable for a bedroom, can be achieved by layering cloths over small tables. The undercloths can be matched to the other fabrics, while the top cloth can be made in a plain fabric of a different texture, or a lace or pretty sprig print and finished in a variety of different ways. The hem can be left plain or trimmed with lace, appliqué, binding or piping. Alternatively, shape the hem into scallops or stitch it with a decorative machine stitch.

How to measure tables

Use a retractable steel ruler rather than a cloth tape for accurate measurements.

SEE ALSO:

CONTEMPORARY STYLE   49

FABRIC FILE   9

SEWING GUIDE   200

SQUARE TABLE

Measure across the table top through the centre from one edge to the opposite edge, AB. Then measure from the table edge to the bottom of the required overhang plus hem allowance, CD. The finished size of the tablecloth is CD + AB + CD for the length and CD + AB + CD for the width.

RECTANGULAR TABLE

Measure the length across the table top through the centre, AB, then the width, CD. Measure from the table edge to the bottom of the required overhang plus hem allowance, EF. The finished size of the tablecloth is EF + AB + EF for the length and EF + CD + EF for the width.

ROUND TABLE

Measure the diameter of the table top from one edge through the centre to the opposite edge, AB. Then measure from the table edge to the bottom of the required overhang plus hem allowance, CD. The diameter of the finished tablecloth should be CD + AB + CD.

OVAL TABLE

Measure the length across the table top through the centre, AB, then the width, CD. Measure from the table top to the bottom of the required overhang plus hem allowance, EF. The finished size of the tablecloth is EF + AB + EF for the length and EF + CD + EF for the width.

SQUARE TABLECLOTH

This simple square tablecloth has neat, mitred corners and machine-stitched hems.

Materials

- Fabric
- Matching sewing thread

Measuring up

- Measure across the centre of the table top as described and add twice the required overhang measurement to the table top measurement, plus 6 cm (2½ in) allowance for hems.

Making up

1 Cut out a square of fabric to required size. On each edge press in 1.5 cm (⅝ in) to wrong side. Fold over another 1.5 cm (⅝ in) on each edge to form a double hem and then press.

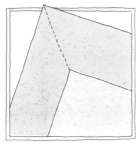

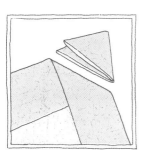

2 Open out second hem. Cut diagonally across a corner, 6 mm (¼ in) from the point, through all thicknesses. Fold back edges with right sides together. Pin and stitch across corner point, 6 mm (¼ in) from raw edges. Press seam open. Repeat at each corner.

3 Turn corners through to right side. Refold the double hem, forming a mitre at each corner. Pin and stitch all round cloth, close to folded hem edge.

VARIATION: TABLECLOTH WITH A TRIM

To add a decorative ribbon or braid trimming to a square cloth, measure the tablecloth in the same way as before, but with only 3 cm (1¼ in) allowance for hems. You will need enough ribbon or braid to cover all four edges.

Materials

- Fabric
- Ribbon or braid
- Matching sewing thread

Making up

1 Cut out fabric to required size. Fold over 1 cm (⅜ in) to right side on all four edges and then press.

2 Position trimming on right side of fabric along outer edge of cloth, covering raw fabric edges. Stitch ends of trimming together and check fit.

3 At each corner tuck under the excess trimming into a neat mitre and position trimming join at the centre of one side. Pin and stitch trimming in place, along both edges.

*T*o successfully mix different patterns in one scheme, choose designs that are balanced in scale and proportion and that can be linked in some way through colour. Here, designs from the same collection of Provençal-style fabrics have been used in blue and yellow for the main tablecloth, napkins and smaller round tablecloth in the background.

RECTANGULAR TABLECLOTH

This tablecloth is made in the same way as a square cloth. When seaming two fabric pieces together for a large cloth, position the seams so they fall across the side of the table top.

Materials

- Fabric
- Matching sewing thread

Measuring up

- Measure across and along the table top as described, adding twice the required overhang measurement, plus a 6 cm (2½ in) allowance for hems.

Making up

1 Cut out a rectangle of fabric to required size. If the total width measurement is greater than the chosen fabric, two pieces of fabric will have to be seamed together. Cut one centre panel and stitch two similar-sized widths on either side, with flat fell seams. Position the seams so they fall across the side of the table top. Match any fabric design across the seam lines.

2 Turn under and hem the outside edges in the same way as for the square cloth.

CIRCULAR TABLECLOTH

A circular tablecloth is easy to make, and always looks best if it reaches the floor. This cloth has a decorative double frill round the base edge, and covered piping inserted into the frill seam. For a more substantial circular tablecloth, a lining can be added.

Materials

- Fabric
- Covered piping cord to match
- Paper for pattern
- Drawing pin, pencil and string
- Matching sewing thread
- Tailor's chalk

Measuring up

- Measure the table top as described, then measure the overhang to the floor. Add twice the overhang measurement to the table top measurement. Decide on the frill depth and deduct this from both overhang measurements; then add a 3 cm (1¼ in) allowance for seams to give diameter of cloth.

- For the base frill, you will need a length twice the measurement round the tablecloth hem. For the depth, double the frill depth and add 3 cm (1¼ in) for seams.

- For the covered piping cord, you will need a length equal to the measurement of the tablecloth hem.

Making up

1 Cut out a square of fabric, each side measuring the same as the diameter of the table top. Fold the fabric in half, exactly matching the raw edges. Fold in half again, matching the raw edges.

2 To make a pattern, cut a piece of paper slightly larger than the folded fabric. Cut a length of string 20 cm (8 in) longer than the radius of the cloth. Tie one end of the string round the pointed end of the pencil.

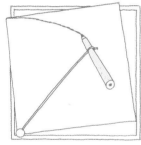

3 Push the drawing pin through the string and into one corner of the paper, with the string the exact length of the folded cloth. Holding pin firmly, and keeping string taut, draw an arc from one side of the paper to the other. Cut along the marked line. This is the pattern for one quarter of the cloth.

4 Position the pattern on the folded fabric, exactly matching centre

points; pin in place. Cut round the pattern. Unfold the fabric.

5 To emphasize the frill seam, pin and tack the covered piping round the outer edge of the cloth, with cord facing inwards and raw edges together. Stitch piping to fit the outer edge.

6 To make the base frill, cut out from across the fabric as many strips of the correct depth as necessary. Pin and stitch frill strips together into a ring, using plain flat seams. Trim and press seams open.

7 With wrong sides facing, fold the frill in half lengthways and press; pin and tack raw edges together. Divide the outer edge of the cloth into four equal sections and mark. Divide the frill into four equal sections and mark. Work two rows of gathering stitches on either side of the seamline in each

section of frill in turn, beginning and ending stitches at marks.

8 Position frill to cloth over piping, pinning at marks. Pull up the gathers evenly in each section in turn and pin. Tack and stitch round cloth, catching in piping and frill together. Trim down piping edges. Match frill and tablecloth edges together over raw edges of piping; zigzag stitch together to neaten.

*S*et off a special piece of fabric (above) by laying it over a plain circular tablecloth.

COPING WITH LARGE CIRCULAR TABLES

*I*f the tablecloth diameter is larger than the fabric width, cut two half-widths of fabric and stitch one on either side of a full fabric width to gain the correct size. Join the side pieces with flat fell seams. Position the seams so they fall across the edges of the table top and make sure that any fabric design matches across the seam line.

VARIATION: TABLECLOTH WITH A BOUND FRILL

As an alternative, a bound frill can be added to the right side of a tablecloth. Both edges of the frill must be neatened with binding. Bind the edges with ready-made bias binding in your chosen width and colour or make your own from contrasting fabric.

When measuring the table, remember to deduct twice your chosen frill depth from the cloth length and add 2 cm (¾ in) allowance for hems. The frill length should measure 1½ to 2 times the outer edge of the tablecloth measurement.

Materials

- Fabric
- Matching sewing thread
- Bias binding
- Tailor's chalk

Making up

1 Make the circular cloth in the same way as before, steps 1–4. Use a zigzag stitch round the outer edge to neaten.

2 To make the frill, cut out from across the fabric as many strips of the correct depth as necessary. Pin and stitch the frill strips together into a ring with flat fell seams. Bind over both the top and lower edges of the frill with bias binding.

3 Divide the frill edge into four equal sections and mark. Divide the cloth edge in the same way. Work two rows of gathering stitches, 2 cm (¾ in) and 3 cm (1¼ in) down from top edge, in each section of frill in turn, beginning and ending stitches at marks.

4 Pin frill to right side of cloth, 2.5 cm (1 in) down from frill top edge and 1 cm (⅜ in) over edge of right side of cloth, matching marks and pulling up gathers evenly to fit as before. Pin and stitch frill in place, 2.5 cm (1 in) from top edge of frill.

VARIATION: TABLECLOTH WITH A PIPED SKIRT

Edge the tablecloth top with covered piping cord and add a gathered skirt.

Measure the table top as described and add 3 cm (1¼ in) for seams. Following the previous instructions, cut out a paper pattern to this size. The length of the tablecloth skirt should measure 1½ to 2 times the outer edge of the table top. The skirt depth should measure from the table edge down to the floor, adding 3 cm (1¼ in) for seam and hem. The covered piping cord should measure the circumference of the table top, plus 5 cm (2 in) to neaten ends.

Materials

- Fabric
- Covered piping cord
- Matching sewing thread
- Tailor's chalk

Making up

1 Use the paper pattern to cut out one piece of fabric to fit the table top.

2 Pin and tack the covered piping cord round the outer edge of the tablecloth top, with cord facing inwards and raw edges matching. Stitch piping ends together to fit.

3 Cut out enough skirt strips from across the fabric width to give the required length. Pin and stitch the skirt strips together into a ring with flat fell seams. Turn under a double 1 cm (⅜ in) hem all round lower edge; pin and stitch.

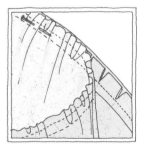

4 Divide the skirt top into four equal sections and mark. Divide the outer edge of the tablecloth top into four equal sections and mark in the same way. Gather and stitch skirt to cloth top as before, taking 1.5 cm (⅝ in) seam allowance. Trim and neaten raw edges of tablecloth and skirt by zigzag stitching together.

place mats

Individual place mats are a good alternative to a tablecloth for protecting the dining table. Place mats can be rectangular, oval, square or circular. They should be large enough to hold a plate; some also hold the cutlery. Rectangular and oval place mats are generally 45 × 30 cm (18 × 12 in) or 40 × 35 cm (16 × 14 in); square mats are 25 cm (10 in) and circular mats between 20 cm (8 in) and 25 cm (10 in) in diameter.

Choose strong firm cottons for plain or quilted place mats and add a central layer of either wadding, interlining or a thermal curtain lining to protect the table.

QUILTED OVAL PLACE MATS

Quilted mats will give some protection to a table from heated plates. Rounding off the corners will make the mats easier to bind.

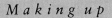

Materials

- Fabric
- Lightweight wadding or curtain interlining
- Matching sewing thread
- Tailor's chalk
- Small plate or saucer for template
- Bias binding

SEE ALSO:

CONTEMPORARY STYLE   49

FABRIC FILE   9

SEWING GUIDE   200

Making up

1 Cut out two pieces of fabric and one piece of wadding to the chosen size. Place the fabric pieces with wrong sides together, matching outer edges. Slide the wadding between the fabric pieces; pin and tack across the place mat both ways to hold the three fabrics firmly together.

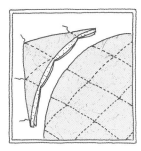

2 Stitch diagonally across the mat from one corner to the opposite corner. Decide on the spacing between quilting lines and set the space bar on the sewing machine to this width. Place the machine with the space bar over the first stitched line and stitch the next row. Repeat, using the space bar so that each row will be equally spaced. Alternatively, use tailor's chalk and a ruler to draw diagonal lines, evenly spaced across the mat. Stitch over the marked lines.

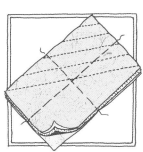

3 Stitch across the place mat in the opposite direction in the same way, forming quilted squares.

4 For an oval mat, the corners have to be rounded. Place a small plate or saucer upside down on one corner with the edges touching the edges of the mat on either side of the corner. Mark round the outer edge of the plate with tailor's chalk. Remove the plate and cut round the curve. Fold the mat, matching all edges, and use the cut corner as a template for the remaining corners, so they will all be identical.

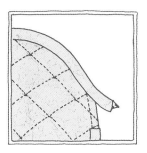

5 Stitch round the mat, 6 mm (¼ in) from outer edges. Bind round the outer edge of the mat with shop-bought or home-made bias binding.

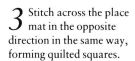

PLACE MATS WITH MITRED BORDER

The outer edges of this unlined place mat are finished with a mitred border of contrasting fabric or ribbon or braid. Depending on the size of the place mats, make the border between 6 cm (2½ in) and 10 cm (4 in) wide.

Materials

- Fabric
- Strip of border fabric or ribbon or braid
- Matching sewing thread

Measuring up

- Decide on the required size of each place mat and add 2 cm (¾ in) to the width and 2 cm (¾ in) to the length.

- For the border strip length, add the length and width of the finished mat together and double this measurement. Add an extra 4 cm (1½ in) for joining. For border width, add 2 cm (¾ in) to the chosen width (this is not necessary if using braid or ribbon).

PLACE MATS

Unlined place mats are used purely for decorating the formal table. Choose fabrics in linen or damask and trim with ribbons or braids to match. For heat resistance, a layer of metallic-coated curtain lining can be added to the back of the mat. This will conduct the heat and help to safeguard the table. Place the lining on the wrong side of the fabric and make up in the same way. Alternatively, for total protection, lay the place mats over shop bought coasters or cut cork mats from do-it-yourself cork tiles. The cork mats should be slightly smaller than the fabric place mats so that the cork can be slipped underneath.

Making up

1 Cut out one piece of fabric to required size. Fold 1 cm (⅜ in) to right side on all edges and then press.

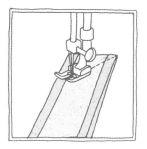

2 Cut one complete length of fabric for border to required size. Fold in 1 cm (⅜ in) on side edges of border strip and press. (If using a braid or ribbon, this is not necessary.) Lay border strip, right side up, over place mat with short edge protruding by 2 cm (¾ in) over edge of mat.

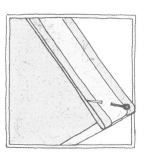

3 Pin border strip along sides of mat. At each corner, fold back border strip so it is level with edge of mat. Form a right angle and pin across diagonal fold. Fold end of border strip diagonally where it joins at the last corner.

4 Remove border strip from mat and stitch across each diagonal fold line. Trim seams and then press open.

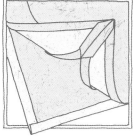

5 Replace border frame on right side of mat, covering raw hem edges and matching outer edges together. Pin and stitch border in place along inner and outer edges.

NAPKINS

Napkins can be made in a range of washable fabrics from plain cotton to damask and can co-ordinate or contrast with the tablecloth or place mats. They come in a variety of sizes from small tea napkins of 20 cm (8 in) square to large dinner napkins of 50 cm (20 in) square. It is sensible to choose a size that makes the best use of the fabric width.

Napkins are generally finished with a double 6 mm (¼ in) hem and topstitched all round. The corners can be mitred or folded straight.

EDGING VARIATIONS:

Fringed Topstitch all round the napkin, 1 cm (⅜ in) from outer edges. Pull out threads up to the stitching line.

 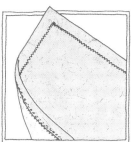

Decorative machine-stitched Turn under a single 1 cm (⅜ in) hem and straight stitch, then work a decorative machine stitch of your choice over the raw hem edges and previous stitching.

Appliquéd Cut out appliqué shapes and tack round the raw edge of napkin. Work a tight zigzag stitch round the appliqué shapes and trim.

Scalloped Fold the mat into four. Use an upturned tumbler or cup to mark the scallops evenly round the outer edge, placing a scallop over the corner. Cut round the outer edge. Unfold and neaten the edge with bias binding.

*U*se a thread (left) that complements or contrasts with napkin fabric when embroidering edges.

*A*ny even-weave fabric (far left) can be used for fringing napkins.

*N*apkins (above) can be decorated in a number of ways, from a simple machine-stitched edging to hand-embroidered or appliquéd details.

Sewing guide

. . . .

This guide covers all the basic stitches and techniques you need to know in order to produce successful results every time.

HAND STITCHES
. . . .

Backstitch
Backstitch is the strongest hand stitch and is the one used to imitate machine stitch.

Work backstitch from right to left. Begin with a couple of stitches worked on the spot, then take a stitch and a space. Take the needle back over the space and bring it out again the same distance in front of the needle. Continue to the end of the seam. Fasten off with a couple of stitches on the spot.

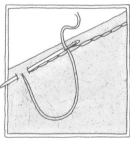

Backstitch   *Running stitch*

Running stitch
Running stitch is a basic hand stitch used for seams and for gathering.

Fasten the thread with a few backstitches (*see* Backstitch) worked on the spot. Work small stitches by passing the needle over and under a few fabric threads and pulling through the fabric. Keep the stitches and spaces the same size and evenly spaced.

Tacking
Tacking stitches are used to hold the fabric in position while it is being permanently stitched.

Work with a single or double thread. Tie a knot in the end of the thread, then take evenly spaced stitches in and out of the fabric. The spaces in between the stitches should be the same size as the stitches. End a line of tacking with one backstitch. To release tacking stitches, cut off the knot and pull out the stitches.
Diagonal tacking Diagonal tacking holds pleats in position. Work with a single thread and begin with a knot. With the needle pointing horizontally, take horizontal stitches from right to left, working parallel to each other to form slanting stitches on the right side of the fabric.

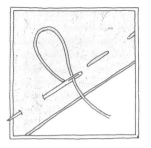

Tacking   *Hemming*

Hemming
Work from right to left with a single thread. Fasten the thread with a knot inside the hem. Bring the needle out of the hem and pick up a few threads of flat fabric just below the edge of the folded fabric. Take the same stitch through the folded fabric. Continue in this way, making the stitches as invisible as possible.

Catchstitch
Catchstitch is a hemming stitch. It is often used for hemming thick or bulky fabrics or for curved areas.

Work from right to left. Fasten the thread on the edge of the folded fabric. Take a diagonal stitch from right to left, then, with the needle pointing to the left, take a small stitch in the fabric from right to left. Bring the needle out and take a diagonal stitch from right to left. Do not pull the thread too tight.

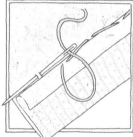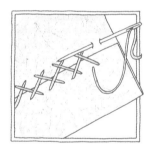

Catchstitch   *Herringbone stitch*

Herringbone stitch
Use this stitch to catch down single hems on curtains.

Work from left to right. Secure the thread with a few backstitches (*see* Backstitch) worked on the spot in the hem. Take a long diagonal stitch from left to right across the folded edge and back through the flat fabric, about 6 mm (¼ in) from the hem edge. With the needle pointing to the left, take a small stitch in the fabric from right to left. Bring the needle out and take another long diagonal stitch from left to right so that the threads cross. Keep the stitches evenly spaced and the same size.

Ladder stitch
Ladder stitch, also known as slip tacking, is the best way to join two heavily patterned fabrics so that the designs match exactly across the seamline.

Press under the seam allowance down one fabric length and place it over the seam allowance of the second piece, exactly matching the fabric. Pin firmly. Work the stitching from the right side of the fabric and from right to left.

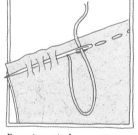

Work with a single thread, secured with a knot. Take the needle 6 mm (¼ in) along the back of the folded edge, then pull the needle through and take a small stitch to join together the folded edge and the flat fabric. Continue in this way, forming small straight ladder stitches over the join. When the stitching is complete, fold the fabric with right sides together and stitch the seam, following the tacking stitches.

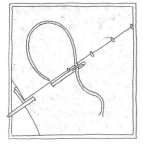

Ladder stitch

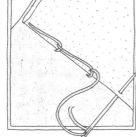

Lockstitch

Lockstitch

Use lockstitch to hold interlining to the back of the fabric on curtains and pelmets where there is a certain amount of 'give' in the fabric.

Lay the top fabric right side down on a flat surface. Position the lining, right side up, over the top fabric. Pin the two fabrics together down the centre. Work with a thread that matches the top fabric. Fold the lining back over the pins. Secure the thread with a knot in the lining. Take a small stitch, picking up one or two fabric threads, and pull out with the thread under the needle. Take the needle 5 cm (2 in) to the right for the next stitch, thus forming a looped stitch.

Oversewing

Oversewing, or overcasting, is the best way to neaten a raw fabric edge by hand and prevent the fabric from fraying. Relate the length of the stitch to the fabric and how badly it will fray.

Begin with a few backstitches (*see* Backstitch) worked on the spot. Take diagonal stitches over the raw edge, spacing them equally apart and the same length. Work against the fabric grain, being careful not to pull the stitches too tight.

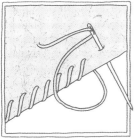

Oversewing

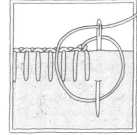

Buttonhole stitch

Buttonhole stitch

This stitch gives a strong finish to the edge. It is used for such things as buttonholes or for sewing on fasteners. The stitch length can be short or long.

Work from left to right, with the needle pointing inwards towards the fabric. Fasten the thread with a few backstitches (*see* Backstitch) worked on the spot. Insert the needle into the fabric behind the edge. Take the working thread and twist it round the point and pull the needle through. Pull the thread so that a knot forms on the edge of the fabric.

Blanket stitch

Blanket stitch can be used to neaten the fabric edge or as a decorative stitch when worked in a contrasting colour.

Begin with a few running stitches (*see* Running stitch). Insert the needle into the fabric 6 mm (¼ in) from the edge with the needle pointing away from the fabric. Hold the thread under the needle point and pull the needle through, forming a loop along the fabric edge.

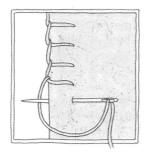

Blanket stitch

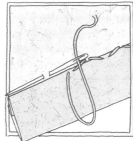

Slipstitch

Slipstitch

This stitch is used for holding a folded edge to a flat piece of fabric or for joining two folded edges together.

Work from right to left with a single thread. Fasten the thread with a knot, hidden inside the hem. Bring the needle out through the top of the folded edge. Pick up a few threads of fabric, then work through the fold of the fabric. Slide the needle along, then come out of the fold to make the next stitch.

SEAMS

Plain seam

Place the fabric pieces with right sides together, matching raw edges. Pin, tack, then stitch together 1.5 cm (⅝ in) from the raw edges. Work a few stitches in reverse at either end of the seam to secure the stitches firmly.

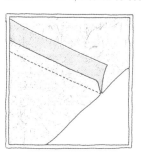

Flat fell seam: trim one seam to 6 mm (1¼ in).

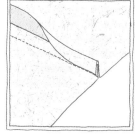

Fold over wider seam.

Press folded edge.

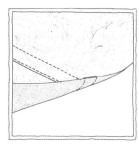

Stitch close to fold.

Flat fell seam

This is a strong, self-neatening seam which is often used in soft furnishings.

With right sides together, edges matching, pin, tack and stitch the fabric, taking a 1.5 cm (⅝ in) seam allowance. Trim down one seam allowance to 6 mm (¼ in). Fold the wider seam allowance in half to enclose the trimmed seam allowance. Press the folded edge against the fabric. Pin, tack and stitch down the seam, close to the fold.

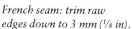

French seam: trim raw edges down to 3 mm (⅛ in).

Stitch second seam with right sides together.

French seam

This is another self-neatening seam.

With wrong sides together, edges matching, tack and stitch the fabric, taking a 6 mm (¼ in) seam allowance. Press the seam flat, then trim the raw edges down to 3 mm (⅛ in). Refold the fabric with right sides together. Pin and stitch a second seam, taking a 1 cm (⅜ in) seam allowance, enclosing the raw edges.

GATHERING

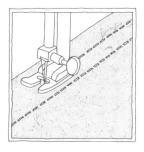

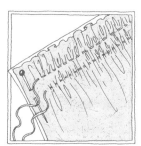

Gathering: work stitches across fabric.

Place a pin at each side of the gathering.

Gathering is the method of disposing of excess fabric into a seam, such as with frills.

A frill before it is gathered usually needs to be twice the finished length to give a fully gathered effect. Join fabric widths together to gain the correct length, either with plain seams (*see* Plain seam) on a double frill or flat fell seams (*see* Flat fell seam) on a single frill. A single frill will also need to be hemmed.

When gathering on a sewing machine, use a heavy-duty thread on the bobbin for extra strength. Loosen the upper tension slightly. Set the stitch length to the largest setting. Place the fabric right side up on the machine bed. Stitch across the fabric just inside the seamline. Work a second row of stitches 6 mm (¼ in) above the first.

Place the frill strip to the flat fabric and insert a pin vertically at each side of the gathering. Gently pull up the bobbin threads from one end only of the fabric, feeding the fabric evenly down the gathers. Wind the threads in a figure of eight round the pin at the side. Pull up the other half of the fabric in the same way. Space out the gathers evenly and stitch over with a plain stitch between the two lines of gathering.

Alternatively, lay a length of cord across the fabric. Set the sewing machine to a large zigzag stitch and work over the cord. Pull up the cord to gather the fabric.

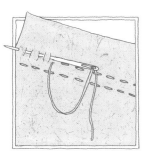

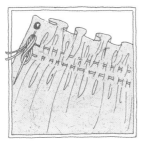

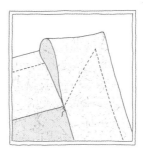

Gathering by hand: make rows of running stitches.

Wind threads in a figure of eight round pin.

Mitring bound edge: stitch in place along one edge.

Stitch diagonally across corner.

Gathering by hand To gather by hand, use running stitches (*see* Running stitch) for gathering

MITRING

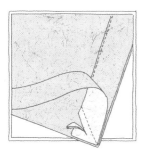

Mitring flat braid: stitch diagonally across corner.

Refold trimming to right side.

At the last corner, leave 10 cm (4 in) unstitched.

Mitring flat braid or ribbon

The following method is suitable when mitring a flat braid or ribbon trimming which is overlaid on a fabric.

Pin and tack the trimming in position down the first side. Stitch in place along the inner edge only up to the first corner, then fold the trimming back on itself. Stitch diagonally between the inner and outer corners through the trimming and the fabric. Trim down the trimming along the diagonal seam to 6 mm (¼ in). Press the seam. Refold the trimming to the right side and continue stitching the inner edge only to the next corner. At the last corner, mitre as before, but leave 10 cm (4 in) unstitched. Turn back the trimming over the first strip with right sides together. Stitch diagonally across the corner in the crease line. Trim as before. Complete the stitching along the inner edge and then stitch all round the outer edge.

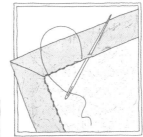

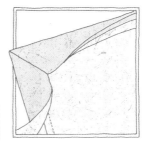

Press the seam.

On wrong side, fold binding into neat diagonal.

Mitring on a bound edge

The following technique is suitable for mitring a binding on a corner when binding a raw edge.

Stitch the binding in place along one edge, ending the stitching at the point where the stitching line begins on the next side. Fold the binding back over the stitched length, forming a 45-degree angle; press. Stitch diagonally across the corner. Continue stitching along the stitching line on the next side. When the binding has been stitched all round, fold it over the raw edge to the wrong side. On the wrong side, fold the excess binding into a neat diagonal fold over each corner. Hem the binding edge in place.

BIAS BINDING

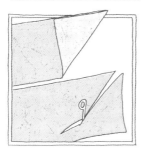

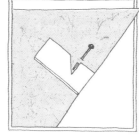

Find the crosswise grain.   *Make a marker.*

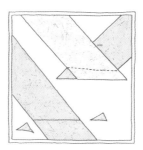

Join strips if required.

Bias binding strips are cut on the cross, that is diagonally across the fabric. Fold the fabric diagonally so that the selvedge edge lies exactly parallel to the weft (horizontal) threads. Press along the fold, then unfold and cut along the creased line.

Make a cardboard marker to mark the strips. Cut a piece of card 10 × 4 cm (4 × 1½ in). Mark the required depth of the bias strips at one end and cut a notch with a straight top edge. Place the marker to the cut line and pin at the notch. Continue the length of the fabric and mark the second and subsequent rows in the same way, aligning the marker against the pinned line. Carefully cut along the marked lines.

Bias strips may need to be joined together to gain the required length. Make sure that all the joins slant in the same direction. Place two strips right side up with ends parallel to each other. Turn the left-hand strip over and place it on the right-hand strip to form a right angle. Slide the top strip up for 3 mm (⅛ in). Pin and stitch across the join, taking a 6 mm (¼ in) seam allowance. Press the seam open. Cut off the projecting points.

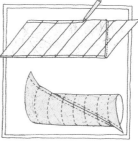

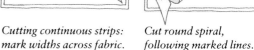

Cutting continuous strips: *Cut round spiral,*
mark widths across fabric.   *following marked lines.*

Cutting a continuous bias strip
This is a quick way of cutting a long length of bias strip.

Cut a rectangle of fabric with the length more than twice the width. Fold up the left-hand corner until the crossways edge is parallel with the selvedge. Press and cut along the fold. Pin and stitch this corner to the opposite edge, right sides together, taking a 6 mm (¼ in) seam allowance. Measure and mark the bias strip widths across the fabric, parallel to the ends. Measure and mark a 6 mm (¼ in) seam allowance on each side edge. Fold the fabric in half, matching points as shown. Pin and stitch, making sure that the marked lines match across the seamline. Press the seam open. Cut round the spiral, following the marked lines.

PIPING

Piping: stitch strip close to   *Snip into seam to ease*
cord.   *piping round corners.*

Piping cord is covered by bias strip fabric to give a smooth finish. To gauge the width of the bias strip, measure round the chosen cord and add an extra 3 cm (1¼ in) to the measurement for seam allowance. Measure the length of the cord you need, allowing an extra 4 cm (1½ in) for joining cords.

Cut out and make up a bias strip to the required length (*see* Bias binding). Fold the bias strip evenly in half round the piping cord, wrong side inside. Pin and stitch close to the cord. If machine stitching, use a piping or zip foot.

To attach the covered piping to the edge of a piece of fabric, lay the covered cord on the right side of the fabric with the cord facing inwards and raw edges matching the raw fabric edge. Pin, tack and stitch in place, positioning the stitches just inside the previous stitching line. To ease

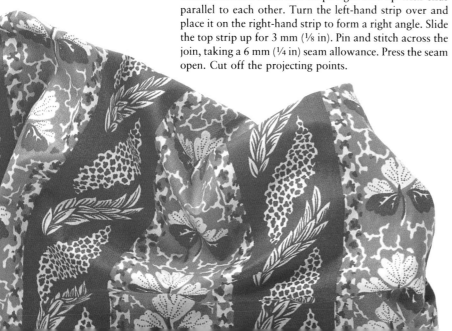

the covered cord round a corner, snip into the seam allowance up to the stitching line.

To neaten a piping cord end, complete the stitching 5 cm (2 in) from the end. Trim off the cord 6 mm (¼ in) from the end. Trim down the fabric to within 1 cm (⅜ in) of the end. Turn under the fabric in line with the end. Complete stitching the cord to the fabric. If necessary, slipstitch (*see* Slipstitch) across the end of the piping tube by hand.

Double piping cord: stitch alongside first cord.

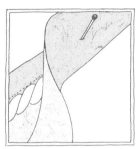

Lay second cord over strip alongside first strip.

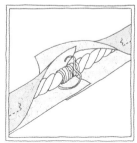

Joining piping: bind join with thread.

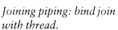

Stitch over join, matching previous stitching lines.

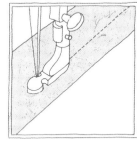

Stitch between cords.

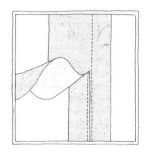

Trim off excess fabric.

Joining piping

To join piping together, leave 5 cm (2 in) unstitched at each end of the cord. Pin across the cord at the meeting point, unstitch the covering strip and trim cord so the edges butt together well. Bind over the join with sewing thread. Trim the covering strip so one end is 2 cm (¾ in) longer than the other. Turn under one raw end for 1 cm (⅜ in) and cover the opposite raw edge for 1 cm (⅜ in). Pin and stitch over the join, matching the stitches on both sides with the previous stitching line.

Gathered piping

Gathered piping makes a good alternative round a plain cushion cover.

Measure and cut the cord as before. Measure and cut the bias fabric strips (*see* Bias binding), allowing an extra ½–1 times the cord length.

Fold the strip round the cord in the usual way. Stitch alongside the piping cord for approximately 15 cm (6 in). Leaving the needle in the fabric, gently pull the cord through the fabric tube, gathering up the fabric evenly. Work like this along the whole length, forming a neatly gathered tube. If machine stitching, fit a piping or zip foot attachment. Simply raise the presser foot at each gathering stage, leaving the needle in the fabric, then lower the foot and continue. Attach the gathered piping to the fabric in the same way as for covered piping cord.

Double piping cord

Double piping cord makes a neat trim for upholstered pieces of furniture. It is easiest to sew using a sewing machine, but for hand sewing follow the instructions using backstitch. This trimming is stuck in position over the seamlines with fabric adhesive.

Measure the cord as before, allowing two lengths to the required measurement. Measure and cut the bias fabric strips (*see* Bias binding), allowing twice the width of the cord measurement plus 2 cm (¾ in). Place the strip right side down. Place the piping to the wrong side. Fold one edge over the cord and extend for 1 cm (⅜ in). Fit a piping or zip foot attachment. Stitch alongside the cord. Lay the second piece of piping over the strip alongside the first length. Wrap the free end of the strip over the second length of piping and pin together between the cords. Loosen the tension on the sewing machine and sit the presser foot on top of the piping. Stitch in place between the piping cords. Trim off excess fabric. Place the double piping in position with the raw edge on the inside.

index

• •

Accessories, 25
American country style,
  50–1
American Independence,
  44
Art Deco, 46
Art Nouveau, 46
Arts and Crafts
  Movement, 45
Austrian blind, 120–2
  frilled edges, 123, 131
  making up, 130–1
  materials, 129
  measuring up, 129
  track, 130
  trimming, 123
  Victorian style, 122

Backstitch, 200
Bauhaus, 46
Bed valances
  making up, 178
  materials, 178
  measuring up, 178
  pleated, 169
  use of, 170
Beds
  choosing, 169
  corona, 184–5
  curtains at head of, 170
  duvet covers. *See* Duvet
    covers
  four-poster effect, 170
  four-posters, 171
  headboard, 170
  linen, style of, 171
  pillowcases. *See*
    Pillowcases
  pleated divan cover,
    182–3
  quilt, child's, 186
  sheets. *See* Sheets
  valances. *See* Bed
    valances
Bedspread
  pleated corners, with,
    180–1
  pleated divan cover,
    182–3
  throw-over, 179–80
Blanket stitch, 201

Blinds
  Austrian. *See* Austrian
    blind
  bay window, for, 118
  fabrics, 30–1
  festoon. *See* Festoon
    blind
  finishing touches, 123
  lambrequin, 123
  London. *See* London
    blind
  roller. *See* Roller blind
  Roman. *See* Roman
    blind
  screen, as, 120
  Sloping glass, for, 120
  small windows, for, 121
  styles, 116
Blood
  stain removal, 34
Bolster, 145
  gathered ends, with, 157
  making up, 156
  materials, 156
  measuring up, 156
Braid, 25
  mitring, 203
Bullion fringe, 25
Buttonhole stitch, 201

Café curtains
  making up, 99
  materials, 99
  measuring up, 99
  tabs, with, 100
Calico, use of, 36
Candlewax
  stain removal, 34
Catchstitch, 200
Chair tieback, 25
Chairs
  cushion with skirt for,
    165–7
  dining room, loose
    covers for, 138, 141
  upright chair cover, 167
  uprights, loose covers
    for, 143
Chewing gum
  stain removal, 34
Child's room, projects for,

186–7
Chinese motifs, 49
Chintz, use of, 36
Chocolate
  stain removal, 34
Coffee
  stain removal, 34
Colonial style, 60–1
Cord trimming, 25
Corona, bed, 184–5
Cotton
  furnishing, use of, 36
  sateen, use of, 36
  types of, 16–17
Covers, fabrics for, 18–19
Cretonne, use of, 36
Cross-over curtains, 105
Curry
  stain removal, 35
Curtain heading tape
  box-pleat, 91
  cartridge-pleat, 91
  goblet-pleat, 91
  pencil-pleat, 86, 90–1
  range of, 90
  smocked, 91
  standard, 90
  tiebacks with, 108
  triple-pleat, 90
  Tudor ruff, 91
Curtain headings,
  handmade lace, 97
  making up, 97
  materials, 97
  measuring up, 97
  triple-pleat, 97
Curtain linings, 28–9, 83
  detachable, 94
  making up, 95–6
  materials, 95
  recycled, 96
Curtain poles
  accessories, 88
  finials, 84, 88
  fixing, 88
  materials for, 88
  steel, 84
  straight runs, for, 88
  traditional or modern,
    83–4
  wood finishes, 84, 88

Curtain rods
  fixing, 88
  portière, 88
  tension, 88
Curtain tiebacks, 25
  corded and tasselled, 79
  heading tape, 108
  plaited, 107
  rosettes, 108
  traditional shape, 79,
    106
Curtain tracks
  accessories, 88
  cording set, 88
  fixing, 86, 88
  materials for, 86
  multi-layered, 89
  overlapping arms, 90
  range of, 86
Curtain valances
  making, 82
  making up, 111
  materials, 111
  measuring up, 111
  pencil-pleated, 82
  pleated, 81
  self-bordered fabrics, 82
  use of, 81
Curtains
  arched window, for, 102
  bed, at head of, 170
  bedroom, in, 73
  café, 99–101
  care and cleaning, 32
  colourful linings,
    adding, 81, 83
  cross-over, 105
  decorative borders, 76
  draped, 115
  draw rods, 88, 90
  electronic opening sets,
    90
  ethnic designs, 75
  fabric, choosing, 91
  fabrics for, 78, 81
  fabrics, 30–1
  fitted window seat,
    round, 85
  floor, hung to, 73–4, 76
  formal window
    treatment, 80

interior design, in, 73
interlined, 28–9, 96
jardinière, 104
lambrequin, 112–13
lined, 95–6
lining. *See* Curtain
  linings
neutral-coloured, 73
pelmets, 109–10
room, suiting, 73–4
sheer, casings for, 101
shower, 103
shower screen, 73
swags and tails, 83–5,
  114–15
unlined, 92–4. *See also*
  Unlined curtains
unusually shaped
  windows, for, 76
view, framing, 83
wall, across, 89
window, dressing, 76
Cushions
  bed, for, 137
  bolsters, 145, 156–7
  box-pleat skirt, with,
    166
  corners, 155
  country-style, 139
  deep gusset, 160–1
  double border, 152
  double frill, 151
  edgings, 140, 149–52
  fabrics for, 18–19, 142
  foam, cutting, 161
  gathered piping, 150
  gathered welt, with, 154
  mock gusset, with, 155
  piping, 149
  range of, 142
  round with welt, 154
  scatter. *See* Scatter
    cushions
  shape of, 145
  shaped squab, 158–9
  single border, 151
  skirt, with, 165–6
  square with welt, 153
  straight skirt, with, 166
  use of, 138
  welts, with, 153–5

window seats, in, 139
Cutting equipment, 38

Darning, 33
Dressing tables
  covers, 189–90
Duvet covers
  making up, 174
  materials, 174
  measuring up, 174
  patterned, 169

Eclectic style, 70–1
Empire style, 44
English country cottage
  style, 66–7
English country house
  style, 58–9
English town house style,
  62–3

Fabrics
  American country style,
    50–1
  blinds, for, 30–1
  Colonial style, 60–1
  colours and patterns,
    12–13
  cottons, 16–17
  covers and cushions, for,
    18–19
  curtains, for, 30–1, 78,
    81, 91
  eclectic style, 70–1
  English country cottage
    style, 66–7
  English country house
    style, 58–9
  English town house
    style, 62–3
  ethnic designs, 75
  French provincial style,
    52–3
  guidelines on, 36–7
  handmade textiles, 41
  lace, 26–7
  linings and interlinings,
    28–9
  man-made, 24
  Mediterranean style,
    54–5
  Middle Ages, in, 49
  minimalist style, 68–9
  natural fibres, 14–15
  oriental style, 64–5
  Scandinavian style,
    56–7
  sheers, 26–7
  sheeting, 172
  silks, 22–3
  sixteenth century, 49

style, inspiration for, 41
  tablecloths, for, 190–2
  weaves and textures,
    10–11
  wools, 20–1
Festoon blind, 120–2
  fabric for, 135
  making up, 135
  materials, 134
  measuring up, 134
  trimming, 123
Flannel, use of, 36
French provincial style,
  52–3
Fruit and fruit juice
  stain removal, 35
Furnishing
  American country style,
    50–1
  Colonial style, 60–1
  eclectic style, 70–1
  English country cottage
    style, 66–7
  English country house
    style, 58–9
  English town house
    style, 62–3
  French provincial style,
    52–3
  Mediterranean style,
    54–5
  minimalist style, 68–9
  oriental style, 64–5
  Scandinavian style,
    56–7

Gathering, 202
Gravy
  stain removal, 35

Hand stitches, 200–1
Hemming, 200
Herringbone stitch, 200
High Tech, 47

Ink
  stain removal, 35

Japanese rooms, 64–5
Jardinière curtains, 104

Lace, 26–7
  curtain heading, 97
  use of, 36
Ladder stitch, 200
Lambrequin, 112–13, 117,
  123
Linen union, use of, 36
Lockstitch, 201
London blind, 121
  covering batten with
    fabric, 133

edges, binding, 133
  making up, 132–3
  materials, 132
  measuring up, 132
Loose covers, 138–9
  enlivening, 142
  keeping in place, 145
  making up, 163–4
  material for, 140
  materials, 162
  measuring up, 162
  skirt, cushions with,
    165–7
  upright chair cover, 167

Man-made fibres, 24
Measuring and marking
  equipment, 38
Mediterranean style, 54–5
Middle Ages
  style of, 49
Minimalist style, 68–9
Mitring, 203

Napkins, 199
Natural fibres, 14–15
Needles, 39
Net, use of, 36
Neo-classicism, 43, 49

Oriental style, 64–5
Oversewing, 201

Paint
  stain removal, 35
Palladian style, 43
Patchwork tablecloths,
  190–1
Pelmets, 81, 109–10
Period style, 41–7
  American Independence,
    44
  Art Deco, 46
  Art Nouveau, 46
  Arts and Crafts
    Movement, 45
  Bauhaus, 46
  eighteenth century,
    42–4
  Empire, 44
  High Tech, 47
  Neo-classic, 43
  nineteenth century,
    44–6
  Palladian, 43
  post-modernism, 47
  post-war modernism, 47
  Regency, 44
  Rococo, 43
  seventeenth century, 42
  traditionalism, 47

Victorian, 45
  1960s and 1970s, in, 47
Pillowcases
  border, with, 177
  frill, with, 176–7
  material for, 176
  plain, 176
Piping cord, 25
Place mats
  mitred border, with, 198
  quilted oval, 197
  shape of, 197
  unlined, 198
Post-modernism, 47
Post-war modernism, 47
Provençal prints, 53
PVC, use of, 36

Quilts, 51
  child's, 186

Regency style, 44
Repairs
  darning, 33
  small hole, patching, 32
Rococo style, 43
Roller blind, 117–18
  fabric, choice of, 125
  large windows, for, 125
  making up, 125–6
  materials, 124
  measuring up, 124
  shaped edges, 126
Roman blind, 117–18
  battening treatments,
    128
  making up, 128
  materials, 127
  measuring up, 127
  trimming, 123
Ruche, 25
Running stitch, 200

Scandinavian style, 56–7
Scatter cushions, 137, 140
  fastenings, 148
  round covers, 147
  square covers, 146
Scorch marks
  stain removal, 35
Seams
  flat fell seam, 202
  French seam, 202
  plain seam, 202
Sewing aids, 38
Sewing equipment
  aids, 38
  cutting, for, 38
  measuring and marking,
    for, 38
  needles, 39

threads, 39
Shaker look, 51
Sheers, 26–7
Sheeting, use of, 36, 172
Sheets
  fitted, 173
  flat, 172
  measuring up, 172
  sheeting, 172
  sizes, 172
Shoe bag, 187
Shower curtains, 103
Shower screen, 73
Silks
  types of, 22–3
  use of, 36
Slipstitch, 201
Stain removal
  first aid kit, 34
  materials for, 34
  preliminaries, 33
  safety checklist, 33
  specific stains, treating,
    34–5
Stitches
  backstitch, 200
  blanket stitch, 201
  buttonhole stitch, 201
  catchstitch, 200
  hand stitches, 200–1
  hemming, 200
  herringbone stitch, 200
  ladder stitch, 200
  lockstitch, 201
  oversewing, 201
  running stitch, 200
  slipstitch, 201
  tacking, 200

Tablecloths
  bound frill, with, 196
  checked, 189
  circular, 194–5
  decorative trim, 193
  embellishing, 190
  fabrics, 190–2
  floor-length, 192
  gathered and piped
    skirt, with, 196
  large circular table, for,
    195
  length of, 190
  lining, 190
  measuring tables, 192
  outside tables, for, 189
  oval table, for, 192
  overhang, 192
  patchwork, 190–1
  plain circular, 189
  plastic coated fabrics,
    191

rectangular, 194
rectangular table, for, 192
round table, for, 192
square, 193
square table, for, 192
use of, 189
Tacking, 200
Tapestry, use of, 36
Tasselled fringe, 25
Threads, types of, 39

Traditionalism, 47
Trimmings, 25
Unlined curtains
  cutting out, 93
  making up, 94
  materials, 92
  measuring up, 92
Upholstered covers
  style of, 137
Upholstery
  care and cleaning, 32

Urine
  stain removal, 35
Velvet, use of, 36
Victorian style, 45
White colour scheme, 79
Window seats, 139
Windows
  American country style, 50–1

bay, covering, 118
Colonial style, 60–1
curtains. *See* Curtains
eclectic style, 70–1
English country cottage style, 66–7
English country house style, 58–9
English town house style, 62–3
French provincial style,

52–3
Mediterranean style, 54–5
minimalist style, 68–9
oriental style, 64–5
Scandinavian style, 56–7
Windsor chair, 51
Wine
  stain removal, 35
Wools
  types of, 20–1

*A*cknowledgements

The publishers thank the following for their kind permission to reproduce the photographs in this book:

Boys Syndication pages 76 top, 78 bottom, 191 bottom; **Camera Press Ltd** pages 57 bottom, 120, 120–121 bottom, 146–7, 152, 173, 174–5; **Elle Decor** page 103; **Robert Harding Picture Library** pages 6, 48, 52–3, 56–7, 62–3, 67 bottom, 73 top, 74 right, 75, 82 left, 87, 89, 100–101 top, 106–107, 110, 111, 116, 117 bottom, 123 top, 126, 137 top, 139 top and bottom, 140, 143 top and bottom right, 145, 154–5, 166, 168, 169 top, 171 top, 189 bottom, 193, 199; **Ingrid Mason Pictures** page 53 bottom; **Osborne & Little plc** page 136; **Paul Ryan (J.B. Visual Press)** pages 137 bottom, 138–9 bottom, 160–1, 164, 170–1 right, 190–191 top; **Arthur Sanderson and Sons Ltd** page 122 bottom; **Fritz von Schulenburg** pages 2 (Richard Hudson), 50–1 (Ann Vincent), 51, 54–5 (Taco Munoz), 55 bottom (Mimmi O'Connell), 58–9 (W. Elphinstone), 63 bottom (S. Hoppen), 68–9 (Andrew Wadsworth), 70–1, 71 (Mimmi O'Connell), 72 (Lars Bolander), 73 bottom (Mimmi O'Connell), 74 left (C. Gollut), 76 bottom, 77 (Halkin Hotel), 78 top (Laura Ashley), 79 (Top Layer), 80, 81 top (Bea Tollmann) bottom (Vicky Rothcoe), 82 right (Joanna Wood), 83, 84–5 (Meltons), 85 top, 85 bottom (Pru Lane-Fox), 88 (Kelly Hoppen), 89 bottom, 93 (Mimmi O'Connell), 95 (George Cooper), 96 (Bingham Land), 109 (Leeds Castle) 112–13 (Marvic), 115 (Jim Sellars), 117 top (Conrad Jamieson), 118–119 top (Melanie Paine), 121 (Sally Metcalfe), 122 (Laura Ashley), 125 (Bingham Land), 140 top (Mimmi O'Connell), 141 (Bill Blass), 156–7 (Karl Lagerfeld), 163 (Bea Tollmann); 169 bottom, 170 left (Ann Vincent), 171 bottom (Laura Ashley), 180 (Karl Lagerfeld), 183 (Meltons), 185 (Jill Barnes-Dacey), 188 (Richard Hudson), 189 top (Chiquita Astor), 190 (Ann Vincent), 195 (Jill De Brand); **Elizabeth Whiting Associates** pages 49 (Michael Dunne), 60–61 (Tim Beddow), 64–5 (Debi Trelor/Habitat

France), 66–67, 79 top, 90–91 (Andreas V. Einsiedel/Erik Karson), 101 bottom (Clive Helm/Don Pallas), 119 top right (Graham Henderson/Sasha Waddell) and bottom, 118, 123 (Michael Dunne), 130, 133 (Michael Crockett/Neil Bradbury), 138 top (Di Lewis), 142–3 bottom (Spike Powell/Norma Bradbury), 144 (Graham Henderson/Sasha Waddell), 149 (Neil Lorimer), 151 (Spike Powell), 159, 187 (Michael Dunne), 191 top (Peter Aprahamian). Thanks also to the following for the photographs for Period Style: **National Trust Photographic Library** page 40; **The Bridgeman Art Library/Victoria & Albert Museum, London** page 41; **The Stapleton Collection** pages 42, 45, 46.

All photographs specially commissioned for this book by Paul Forrester.

The Publishers would also like to thank the following fabric houses for kindly supplying the fabric samples that appear in this book:

Anta, Laura Ashley, G.P. & J. Baker, Henry Bertrand, Nina Campbell, Manuel Canovas Ltd, Colefax and Fowler, Collier Campbell Ltd, Cooks Mills (Bradford) Ltd, Jane Churchill Ltd, Designers Guild and DG Distribution, Chanée Ducrocq, Pierre Frey, Fonthill Ltd, Anna French, Hammonds at Christian Fischbacher, Hesse & Co, JAB International Furnishings Ltd, John Lewis Partnership, Les Olivades, Liberty, MacCulloch & Wallis (London) Ltd, Ian Mankin Ltd, Andrew Martin International, Marvic Textiles, Monkwell Ltd, Mulberry at Home, Mrs Munro Ltd, Nice Irma's Ltd, Fernanda Niven Ltd, Nobilis-Fontan, Osborne & Little plc, Prelle at Guy Evans Ltd, Ramm Son & Crocker, S.A.T., Sanderson, Skopos Design Ltd, John Stefanidis & Associates Ltd, F.R. Street Ltd, Textiles Ltd, Titley & Marr, Warner Fabrics.